NOEL O'SULLIVAN is currently
Senior Lecturer in Politics at Hull
University. He is the author of
Conservatism (Dent, 1976), *Fascism*
(Dent, 1983) and *Revolutionary
Theory and Political Reality*
(Wheatsheaf Books, 1983).

Contents

The Contributors

Peter Calvert, Professor of Politics, University of Southampton. Author of *Revolution* (1970), *The Study of Revolution* (1970) and *The Concept of Class: An Historical Introduction* (1982); specializes in the politics of the Americas.

David Capitanchik, Senior Lecturer in Politics, University of Aberdeen. Author (with R. Eichenberg) of *Defence and Public Opinion* (1983). He writes and broadcasts regularly on the Middle East and has published a series of research reports on recent Israeli General Elections.

C. H. Dodd, Professor of Politics, University of Hull. Author of *Democracy and Development in Turkey* (1979), *Crisis of Democracy in Turkey* (1982) and other books and articles mainly on Middle Eastern subjects.

Richard Gillespie, Lecturer in the Politics of Mediterranean Europe at the University of Warwick and an authority on the Spanish and Latin American Left. He is the author of *Soldiers of Perón; Argentina's Montoneros* (1982) and of several articles on guerrilla warfare.

Norman Hampson, FBA, Professor of History, University of York. Author of various books on the Enlightenment and the French Revolution, including *A Concise History of the French Revolution* (1975) and *Danton* (1978).

Jeremy Noakes, Reader in European History, University of Exeter. Editor of *Government, Party and People in Nazi Germany* (1980) and other books and articles on German history and politics.

Noel O'Sullivan, Senior Lecturer in Politics, University of Hull, Author of *Conservatism* (1976) and *Fascism* (1983), and of articles on contemporary political thought. Editor of *Revolutionary Theory and Political Reality* (1983).

Bhikhu Parekh, Professor of Politics, Hull University. Former Vice Chancellor of the University of Baroda (1982–4). His recent publications include *Hannah Arendt and the Search for a New Political Philosophy* (1981), *Marx's Theory of Ideology* (1982) and *Contemporary Political Thinkers* (1982).

Charles Townshend, Senior Lecturer in History, University of Keele. Author of *The British Campaign in Ireland 1919–21* (1975) and *Political Violence in Ireland: Government and Resistance since 1848* (1983). Currently completing a study of the British experience of counter-insurgency in the twentieth century.

Paul Wilkinson, Professor of International Relations at the University of Aberdeen. His publications include *Social Movements* (1971), *Political Terrorism* (1974), *Terrorism and the Liberal State* (1977, new edition 1985) and *The New Fascists* (1981, new edition 1983). He is series editor of Key Concepts in International Relations, associate editor of *Terrorism: an International Journal* and editorial adviser of *Contemporary Review*.

Preface

These essays represent a concerted attempt to bring the resources of political theory, political science and history to bear on modern terrorism. For political theory, the point of interest lies in the general assumptions about man and society which inspire terrorist activity, and the relation of these assumptions to our moral and political values at large. For political science, on the other hand, the primary concern is with the empirical conditions which determine the success or failure of terrorism, together with its likely implications for the maintenance of international order. For the historian, finally, emphasis is characteristically placed upon the continuity of violence in human affairs, with the result that what may at first sight seem novel in modern terrorism appears to his eye merely as a long familiar beast which startled us for a moment only because the colour of its new spots was different. The danger with such an inter-disciplinary approach, of course, is that the different premises upon which the various contributors proceed may mean that their positions never meet but simply run parallel to one another. Fortunately, in the present case, broad agreement emerged about the way in which the study should be structured. This structure may be briefly indicated under three headings, although the real interest naturally lies in the essays themselves: the present remarks are no more than the sediment, so to speak, deposited in the course of the enterprise.

The first area of agreement was about the fact that terrorism in its modern form originated as a specifically European phenomenon. Whilst techniques such as assassination have been resorted to throughout history in order to influence governments or acquire power, what is distinctive about this modern form is the fact that it is only intelligible within the broader context of a new style of politics whose advent was symbolized by the French revolution in 1789. The main feature of the new style is its abstract, ideological character, although it must be stressed that subscription to the style does not necessarily mean the adoption of a conscious, highly articulate ideological position: it may instead be implicit in interpretations, purposes and actions themselves. The underlying assumptions about man and society which inspire the style, and the various intellectual modifications through which it has passed since it originally appeared, are explored in the first essay. This seeks to demonstrate that the intellectual roots of modern terrorism cut across conventional ideological divisions, with the result that terrorism cannot be understood by analysing it in terms of the 'left-right' dichotomy which is frequently used to interpret it. On the alternative view offered here, terrorism is far more closely related to the principal values of the liberal–democratic tradition than is commonly realized. More precisely, what is argued is that, ever since 1789, there has existed at the very heart of the Western political tradition a fundamental ambiguity which has not only left it—and continues to leave it—exposed to extremist interpretations of the terrorist sort, but has also ensured widespread sympathy in Western states for acts of violence perpetrated in the name of political causes. It is this ambiguity, and the consequent instability it has introduced into Western politics, upon which terrorism has been able to feed.

So far as the practical implications of this new style of politics for the European political world are concerned, there never was much room for doubt, since these were foreshadowed at an early stage in the use of terror by Robespierre and the Committee of Public Safety. Norman Hampson examines the early connection between ideology and terror established by this dramatic incident, whilst the changing part subsequently played by terror in the modern revolutionary tradition as a whole is explored by Peter Calvert.

The second area of agreement was about the fact that the recent study of terrorism has tended to concentrate heavily on oppositional groups, at the expense of neglecting its use by regimes. It is understandable that, in recent decades, attention should have been focused upon the former, in view of the striking upsurge in the use of violence by nationalist and separatist groups during post-war decades. One of the most intransigent of these, the IRA, is studied here by Charles Townshend, against the broader background of a long communal tradition validating the use of violence. The fact remains, however, that the most notorious use of terrorism in Western politics during the present century was by the Nazi regime. An opposition group, such as that led by Begin, which practises terrorism in order to found a state, or to acquire power, but then abandons it once its aim has been achieved, ceases to be a terrorist group; but when, after the acquisition of office, such a group sets out to destroy all legal forms whatsoever, the regime may properly be described as a terrorist one. In a penetrating study of Nazism both before and after 1933, Jeremy Noakes traces the shift from what he terms 'informal' to 'formal' terrorism.

Thirdly, there was agreement about the need to consider the implications for terrorist activity of the radicalizing impact of Western ideological politics upon the non-European world. In every case, the new style has been superimposed upon indigenous traditions, and it is therefore often difficult (as was remarked above) to distinguish what is merely a familiar feature of native tradition, although concealed now in Western guise, from what is solely attributable to the spread, in particular, of Western nationalist and Marxist ideas. In the case of the Middle East, for example, David Capitanchik argues that whilst the violence of a movement such as the PLO is inspired by ideas which are purely Western in inspiration, the violence of other extremist groups is more readily intelligible within the context of native Islamic fundamentalism. More generally, Clement Dodd draws upon Turkish experience in order to argue that a clear distinction must be made between violence which is due to anomie, on the one hand, and terrorism, on the other. In the former case, violence is the expression of the social and cultural dislocation caused in traditional societies by modernization, and therefore lacks the ideologically inspired political objectives which characterize terrorism. When this distinction is borne in mind, the observer will be far less ready to use the word terrorism to refer to incidents of the kind which occurred in Turkey during the 1960s and 1970s. In the case of Latin

America, Richard Gillespie's examination of urban guerilla tactics has a significance which extends beyond the immediate setting, revealing as it does how terrorism of this sort may suffer defeat partly through ideological confusion amongst the groups which resort to it, partly through its own counter-productive tendencies, and partly through the ability of the modern state (or rather, the Latin American military regime) to respond effectively. Casting the net still more widely, Bhikhu Parekh provides a timely analysis of one of the most fascinating debates of our century, that between Gandhi and the advocates of terrorism at the time of the Indian struggle for national independence. The two extreme positions of Gandhi and his opponents seen initially to be diametrically opposed, but, as Parekh shows, the ultimate gap between fellow extremists is not perhaps so great.

Of the three different academic approaches referred to above, it is the historical one that has received the greatest emphasis here. In a final essay, in which he examines the difficult legal, diplomatic, and military problems presented by the international control of terrorism, Paul Wilkinson emphasises the 'hydra-headed' character of the contemporary terrorist phenomenon. In order to do justice to it, Wilkinson rightly insists, it is first necessary to accept that 'Context is all in the analysis of political violence'. Although the demand for sensitivity to context can only be fully satisfied by an adequate historical perspective, it is precisely this perspective which has too often been absent from the literature on the subject. To attempt at least a partial rectification of this situation appears important, since it is primarily the historical dimension that distinguishes the academic study of terrorism from journalistic approaches which exaggerate the novelty of the phenomenon by ignoring the disparate traditions and contexts within which it occurs. The result is that the complexities of the hydra are oversimplified, and the practical problems of control themselves dangerously distorted, by a tendency to present all terrorist incidents as aspects of a single global conspiracy.* Even for scholars who rightly dismiss such purported explanations with a smile, the historical approach presents a salutary check upon the quest for political and socio-economic generalizations. There is little in the cautious studies contained here, for example, to support the kind of sweeping proposition recently advanced by Wolfgang Mommsen and Gerhard Hirschfeld in their otherwise valuable volume on *Social Protest, Violence and Terror in Nineteenth and Twentieth Century Europe*. In their view, 'the rise of terrorist groups or movements . . . must be seen as a by-product of a fundamental distortion in the socio-economic or constitutional development of the various European societies, or as the offspring of a widespread dissatisfaction with traditional systems of rule no longer in line with societies subjected to a process of modernisation.'[1] Unfortunately, there is no discernible preordained 'normal' course of development for modern European states, in relation to which we can distinguish a 'fundamental distortion' in their development; nor is there a 'process of modernization' which makes terrorism likely at certain points in its progress, and unlikely once it is complete. Indeed, one of the most remarkable features of terrorism since the Second World War is the fact that it has found notable exponents in Germany—in a state, that is, which is fully 'modernized', fully constitutional, and enjoys widespread support from its members.

It will be evident that, far from being exhaustive, the choice of topics offered here is highly selective. It will have served its purpose, however, if it is sufficiently comprehensive to illustrate the principal problems posed by the study of terrorism and helps, at the same time, to refine our sensitivity to the gradations by which the concept loses its distinctive connection with modern ideological politics and slides over into the ubiquitous phenomenon of violence.

NOTES

1. *Social Protest, Violence and Terror in Nineteenth and Twentieth Century Europe*, ed. W.J. Mommsen and G. Hirschfeld (London, 1982) p.x.

The Times recently provided a notable example of this kind of journalistic oversimplification. A leading article declared that terrorism, 'whatever its real or purported individual character and geographical origins, essentially knows only one frontier, that between totalitarian and liberal democracy. The totalitarian origins of terrorism are deeply rooted in Marxist-Leninism, whilst the liberal democracies are an affront to that philosophy and thus its perennial target'. From there it is only a small step to the conclusion that, 'however much on the surface the proliferation of terrorist groups seems to suggest a plurality and anarchy which would defy . . . supervision', Moscow is in fact the moving force behind it. (*The Times*, June 24th, 1985)

Acknowledgements

I am grateful to Dr Juliet Lodge for advice and assistance during the early stages of preparing this book, and to Professor Jack Hayward for some invaluable last minute help.

Professor Norman Hampson's comments vastly improved my own paper. I am solely responsible, of course, for the form it finally assumed.

The editor of *Conflict Quarterly* kindly gave permission for the inclusion of a revised version of a paper by Dr Richard Gillespie originally published there.

Part I
The Theory and Practice of Terrorism

1 Terrorism, Ideology and Democracy
Noel O'Sullivan

The contemporary study of terrorism is marked principally by continuing confusion about its general significance for modern political life, and in particular about its relationship to the democratic state. This confusion is nowhere more apparent than in the voluminous academic literature on the subject which has appeared during the post-war period. Briefly, two very different responses have characterized this literature. The initial response, as one study recently records, verged on incomprehension, mainly because 'the truth is that Europe had been taken by surprise when the hijackers, kidnappers and assassins first began to strike within its comfortable confines. Their acts were not expected in old established countries where the rule of law and constitutional practice made it possible to change governments and policies by the simple process of voting. In Europe,' it was assumed, 'there was no need for terrorism; that was the kind of unpleasantness to be expected in Latin American tyrannies rather than in London, Bonn and Paris.'[1]. Predictably, the result of such an attitude was a tendency to overreact to terrorism, in ways which made it appear both more novel and more dangerous than a more considered response might have suggested.

During the last few years, however, as terrorism has lost much of its novelty and works on the topic have proliferated, there has been a tendency for scholars to go to the opposite extreme and display a more blasé attitude in their assessment of its significance. In this vein, the study just quoted, for example, remarks at one point that 'The terrorists, like the poor, are always with us'.[2] In a similar vein, another scholar concluded, on the basis of reports in *The New York Times* during the decade 1961–70, that terrorist incidents had

3

occurred in sixty-three out of eighty-seven countries, with a total cost of approximately 4,600 lives. In his opinion, this loss of life was relatively minor compared with the three-quarters of a million people who lost their lives in all forms of civil strife during the same decade, or in the light of the city of Chicago's murder rate of nearly one thousand per annum.[3]

In the present essay, it will be suggested that neither the initial reaction of surprise nor the more blasé reaction which has superceded it has brought out the real significance of the terrorist phenomenon for an understanding of modern European political life. What both reactions have obscured, it will be argued, is the fact that the roots of terrorism lie concealed at the very heart of the modern democratic tradition itself. In the first part of the paper an attempt will be made to identify these roots, in a way which aims to build up a sort of identikit picture of the terrorist's ideological world. In the second part, the stages through which these extremist tendencies have passed will be sketched, in order to trace the evolution of the modern terrorist from the guerrilla fighter who dominated radical politics during the first half of the nineteenth century. Finally, the features of twentieth century life which are most relevant for understanding both the theory and practice of contemporary terrorism will be indicated, with a view to gauging its likely future significance for both Western and Third World politics. Before proceeding further, however, it is necessary to attempt a definition of terrorism, in order to distinguish terrorism in its modern form in particular from the long history of tyrannicide upon which the Western world has prided itself since at least the time when Brutus murdered Julius Caesar.

So far as definition is concerned, the problem is, of course, confined in the present context exclusively to political terrorism. Terrorism which is directed primarily towards criminal purposes or personal material gain, in other words, is not relevant. Excluded also is the terrorism which in various forms accompanies war, since the concept of terrorism is only intelligible in reasonably settled and stable social contexts within which it is possible to contrast the illegal practices of the terrorist with the constitutional procedures prescribed for established state representatives. Bearing these qualifications in mind, political terrorism may be said to occur when a group, whether holding governmental office or outside government, resolves to pursue a set of ideological objectives by methods which not only subvert or ignore the requirements of domestic and international law, but which rely for their success primarily upon the threat or use of violence.

It will be noted that this definition permits regimes as well as opposition groups to be described as terrorist, although the main concern of the present paper is with the latter. The definition also includes two important restrictions which require a word of explanation. The first restriction is legal, and is inserted because the frequent attempts to define terrorism in terms of threats of violence alone—that is, in psychological terms—would brand as 'terrorist' organizations like the German Social Democratic Party at the end of the last century, sinced this engaged in a lot of noisy rhetorical threats about violent revolution. The reference to legality, however, removes such a group from the terrorist fold by taking account of the fact that the party was in practice quite law-abiding, to the annoyance of a minority of its own genuinely radical members.

The second restriction in the definition lays stress on the ideological aspect of terrorism. It is this ideological aspect which is the key, in particular, to the vital distinction which must be made between 'terror' and 'terrorizing', on the one hand, and 'terrorism', on the other. Terror refers to a psychological state—the state, that is, of extreme fear and anxiety. The addition of an 'ism', however, lifts the concept out of the realm of psychology and relocates it in the sphere of beliefs and ideas. To that extent, Paul Wilkinson is perfectly correct when he observes that 'political' terrorism cannot be understood outside the context of the development of terroristic, or potentially terroristic, ideologies, beliefs and life-styles.[4] Terrorism as we know it, in a word, is essentially the creation of ideological politics.

The intimate connection between terrorism and ideological politics is vital for present purposes, since it is precisely this connection which distinguishes modern terrorism from earlier forms of political violence. In *The Prince*, for example,

Machiavelli expressed admiration for the success with which Cesare Borgia used terror in order to rule his subjects. Machiavelli admired the way, in particular, in which Borgia encouraged Remirro d'Orco to use ruthless techniques in order to tidy up Borgia's newly acquired province of Romagna, and then pacified his subjects, at the same time clearing himself of any responsibility for their sufferings, by having the wretched d'Orco laid out in a public square with stakes driven through him. This is terror, not terrorism. Even the long line of literature which defends tyrannicide by appeals to ideas like natural law and the social contract is not 'terrorist' in the modern sense, since it occurs outside the confines of ideological politics.

What must now be considered in some detail is the precise way in which ideological politics are related to the terrorist phenomenon. One familiar way consists of assuming that terrorism is a peculiarity of left or right wing fanatics, and then concentrating attention upon what are taken to be the relevant representatives of the wing in question. According to the present analysis, however, the intellectual and political assumptions which inspire terrorism completely cut across the left–right spectrum, and therefore prevent any such neat pigeon-holing of the phenomenon. A second way of proceeding appears to avoid the defects of the spectrum approach by selecting a variety of diverse figures, regardless of the political wing to which they might be conventionally assigned, and then holding them responsible for the atrocities of the contemporary period. Popular candidates for this treatment include, for example, nineteenth century thinkers like Max Stirner, Bakunin, Nechaev and Johann Most.[5] This way of proceeding is unsatisfactory, not because it is wrong, but because it disconnects terrorism from the mainstream of democratic thought and practice by confining attention too narrowly to a collection of more or less romantic and egotistical continental fanatics. The result is to encourage a sense of complacency, since the causes of terrorism are dismissively pushed to the eccentric fringe of the European intellectual and political world. What will be suggested here is that terrorism is far more intimately connected with the modern liberal–democratic tradition than such a view would imply. In order to understand this connection, and to appreciate why terrorism cannot be satisfactorily analysed within the 'left–right' spectrum approach, it is necessary to begin by returning to the precise point at which ideological politics emerged in Europe. By focusing attention on this point, it is possible, in particular, to identify the main sources of instability and extremism which the new ideological style injected into the modern political tradition.

The ideological style of politics with which we are now familiar is in fact a relatively recent development. The style emerged in Europe only at the end of the eighteenth century, acquiring practical significance in 1789, at the time of the French Revolution. It was originally generated, and has subsequently been sustained, by three crucial assumptions about the nature of man and society.

The first assumption appeared when the vast programme of destruction undertaken by the French Revolution led men to believe that it lay within the power of men's will to remake society from top to bottom, and even to refashion human nature itself. Previous history contained an abundance of Utopian visions, of course; but until 1789 no one had thought it was actually possible to do very much about them. Modern ideological politics, by contrast, arose precisely when it came to be assumed that it is perfectly possible to do a great deal about such visions. Without this belief in the possibility of radical change the more ambitious aspirations of modern terrorism would be inconceivable.

The second assumption was that man is naturally good. This optimistic view found expression in the form of a new theory of evil, which was first clearly stated by Rousseau but has since come to be almost universally accepted. According to the new theory, evil is not an eternal and ineliminable part of the human condition, but originates in the structure of society, and may therefore be removed from the world by making the appropriate social changes. This meant that, from being an activity in which men merely sought a stable framework of order within which to lead their lives, politics were now elevated to the status of a quasi-religious crusade, the aim of which was to awaken 'the people' from its long historical sleep, and inspire it to throw off its oppressors. To understand politics in this way assumed, of course, that the people really did want to be 'liberated', no matter how overtly reluctant they might seem to be. Finally, the new style meant that politics acquired a very simple and potentially lethal structure, since a vital part of the crusading mentality consists in endeavouring to identify an 'out group' which could be held responsible for everything amiss with the existing social order. Having identified the out group, it is but a small step to demanding its suppression, removal, or extermination. It is hardly necessary to mention what has happened in the two centuries since 1789, as a result of the acceptance of this way of thinking about politics. Originally, the out group was identified by Robespierre and the early French democrats as consisting of kings, aristocrats and priests, and as many of these as possible were accordingly sent to the guillotine. Subsequently, Marxism added capitalists to the out group. Thereafter, the Nazis redefined the out group to mean the Jews. Finally, in our own day, ideologists like Franz Fanon have identified the out groups as all imperialist powers. It is obvious, then, that the new style of politics readily lends itself to interpretations which make the use of terror for ideological ends appear as a natural and even admirable implication of the idealistic belief in man's natural goodness.

We must now turn, in the third place, to an element in the new ideological style which has done more than any other to facilitate the appearance of modern terrorism. This was the advent of a novel doctrine of political legitimacy which has since come to be accepted, not only in the West, but throughout the whole world. This is the doctrine of popular sovereignty proclaimed by the Declaration of the Rights of Man and the Citizen. According to this doctrine, power is legitimate only if it is conferred 'from below', by the people. In the words of the Declaration, 'The principle of sovereignty resides essentially in the Nation: no body of men, no individual, can exercise authority that does not emanate expressly from it'. It is not difficult to see how this doctrine, which was supposed to liberate the masses and inaugurate an era of world harmony, might instead produce the opposite result. It could do so because the concept of 'the people' can be defined in any way at all. This means not only that an appeal to popular sovereignty can be used to justify any government, no matter how appalling its policies may be, but that it can also be invoked by any one who wishes to defy the government, provided that he claims to be a truer representative of the popular will than the established authorities are. Needless to say, this way of legitimating their actions has been a great help to modern terrorists, all of whom claim to act in the name of the people.

The situation is made even worse in this respect by the fact that the new ideological style has deprived not only the word democracy, but also the word liberty, of any clear connection with the rule of law. Early in the nineteenth century the great French liberal thinker, Benjamin Constant, succinctly described the connection between law and liberty when he wrote that liberty is 'the right to be subject only to the laws, the assurance of being neither arrested, nor detained, not put to death, nor in any way restricted, by an arbitrary act of will of some one individual or of many'. At the very time Constant wrote, however, the idea of liberty had already become intimately connected (as it still is today) with ideals of 'personal autonomy' and 'self-realization' that refer purely to the *internal* spiritual state of the agent. It was in this way that it inevitably became detached from any necessary connection with the rule of law. As a result, ideological politics open the door to terrorism still further, since anyone at all may now perform any act he wishes, no matter how horrific, in the name of 'liberty'. Against this background it is possible to appreciate the significance, for example, of Franklin Ford's anecdote about the peculiar lady who, only a few years ago, fired several shots at the then President of the United States. Afterwards, Ford reports, he heard a noted psychologist say, with all professional solemnity, that '"Unfortunate as her action had been, it probably constituted the first clear statement she had ever been able to make"'.[6] More generally, Paul Wilkinson rightly notes that the purely subjective meaning of liberty sanctioned by ideological politics provides no barrier against its transformation into a formula for mere self-assertive egoism, according to which any action at all has value provided that it is deliberately willed and believed by the individual to give meaning to his life. As Wilkinson observes, liberty so understood can for example 'create a kind of politics of will and glorification of action for its own sake of the kind which Marinetti and the Futurists expounded . . . The fact is that for some, though by no means all terrorists, extreme violence is primarily undertaken as an act of self-assertion and self-expression'.[7]

So much, then, for the structure of the new ideological style of politics. The story of modern terrorism is the story of how this new political style has gradually destroyed all the old conventions which surrounded the use of violence in Western political life and created a world in which any political act at all can now be done with an easy conscience, since there is no conceivable act which our modern ideologies cannot present as morally defensible. The story passes through several stages, and the significance of contemporary terrorism can only be understood when related to the sequence which they display.

The first stage corresponds roughly to the century of European history between Napoleon's defeat at Waterloo and the end of the First World War. What principally marks this century is the spread of ideological politics, initially in the form of nationalist and republican doctrine, and subsequently in the form of socialist doctrine as well. Terrorism at this stage initially appeared as the mode of activity of the small conspiratorial groups, such as student bodies and secret societies, which grew up throughout Europe in the aftermath of the post-Napoleonic restoration. These early days were exciting, since Europe still abounded (as indeed it did until 1918) with kings, emperors and tsars to be eliminated. Their destruction by violent methods, moreover, could be contemplated with an especially good conscience since the advent of ideological politics meant that something quite extraordinary had now happened in the European intellectual world: for the first time in history, nearly all the leading thinkers of the age now regarded political violence as a respectable and even admirable phenomenon, in so far as it promoted what they chose to regard as the cause of progress.

Yet in spite of the abundance of suitable targets and the respectability of violence, there are very few incidents in this period which can be described as terrorism. In one well-known instance, it is true, one of the newly risen nationalist groups was responsible for carrying out an ideologically inspired murder that attracted such widespread attention throughout Europe, and seemed to have such disturbing implications for the future that it provoked Metternich into imposing the repressive Carlsbad Decrees. This was the murder, in 1819, of a minor German playwright called Kotzebue by a member of an intensely nationalistic student society whose members called themselves 'The Unconditionals'. But this incident, although significant, was nevertheless exceptional. For the most part, the figure who dominates radical politics in this early period is the guerrilla 'liberator'. It is true that the guerrilla undoubtedly deserves the name of terrorist to the extent that he consciously placed political and ideological commitments above military considerations. This is evident, for example, in Mazzini's *Rules for the Conduct of Guerrilla Bands*, which state that 'The political mission of the guerrilla bands is to contribute the armed apostolate of the insurrection'.[8] By comparison with the later emergence of a totally dedicated terrorist who lives only for the revolutionary cause and completely rejects the old military conventions about the use of violence against non-combatants, however, the early guerrilla appears in retrospect as a relatively civilized being. Having indulged his idealism to that extent, however, it is necessary to add straightaway that his ideological fanaticism was generally tempered by nothing more substantial than a naive romanticism which sought to blend an admiration for Jesus Christ, Robin Hood, and lyric poetry. Consider, for example, the portrait of the guerrilla given by Carlo Bianco (1795–1843), who was one of the organizers of Mazzini's disastrous attempt to invade Savoy, and an active member of the Italian nationalist opposition to Austria.

In 1830 Bianco drew on his experience of guerrilla war to publish a work entitled *A Handbook for Revolutionary Bands* (1833). Bianco's ideal man is 'the Italian citizen who, animated by a sacred enthusiasm, freely dedicates his life and possessions to his country and joins the patriot bands as a volunteer and takes up arms to serve Italy and play his part with all his strength in the sublime purpose of her regeneration'. The 'sacred enthusiasm' admired by Bianco enables ideological murder to masquerade as saintly, heroic, and self-sacrificing moral conduct. 'It is the attribute of the patriotic volunteer', Bianco writes, 'to be imbued with the pure joy that gladdens the life of one devoted to a good cause; with the ardent and clear-sighted valor of a man who feels a love for humanity and for what is just and true; and with the disinterestedness by which virtuous souls hold it a duty to sacrifice everything to the realization of a sublime idea for the good of mankind'. Warming to his theme, Bianco passes from the moral merits of the guerrilla into the realms of romantic fantasy as he describes his life. The guerrilla's life, Bianco writes, 'is all poetic ardor, continual emotions and transports of joy, fearful dangers, physical privations, and moral satisfactions. He moves from place to place in a group of loyal brothers; he finds that he belongs to an affectionate family, a gathering of fine and honorable young men all conspiring for the liberation of their country and the good of humanity. Strong as lions, swift as the mountain deer, they enjoy almost complete independence when charged with performing special operations'. Finally, we hear that, in the spirit of Christ and Robin Hood, the guerrilla 'aids the wretched, consoles the afflicted, and helps those who have been misled to find the right way. Thus are the powerful opposed and kings discomforted'.[9]

If we now turn from the first to the second half of the nineteenth century the situation changes as the figure of the guerrilla rapidly shades over into that of the terrorist. The explanation for this transformation lies in a decline of belief in the imminence of the spontaneous popular uprising upon which the guerrilla nationalist had pinned all his hopes. The point at which this decline became significant is easy to identify: it was in the year 1848. That year saw the complete failure of the revolutions which had occurred across the capital cities of Europe, and the consequent destruction of revolutionary hopes about a spontaneous uprising of the peoples. How then was the revolutionary to keep his idealism intact? Three answers emerged. One was that of Auguste Blanqui, for whom the setback merely confirmed his belief that mass spontaneity alone would never alter the course of history. What 1848 revealed, he thought, was that the people should be organized on military lines: 'It is essential', he wrote, 'to get organized (at whatever cost). No more tumultuous uprisings, with ten thousand isolated men acting at random, in disorder and with no thought or cohesion, each in his own little spot at his own fancy!' Just how a successful revolution was to be given military structure was naturally a little difficult to determine. Blanqui's solution was to insist that although this could not be done in advance, it could easily be done as the uprising began. With his eyes upon Paris, he explained that 'The people of Paris will provide the basic elements—old soldiers and former National Guards. Their scarcity will oblige us to reduce the number of officers and noncommissioned officers to a minimum. No matter, the zeal, ardor, and intelligence of the volunteers will make up the deficit'.[10] It was an optimistic view of the organizational problems involved; whether it was a realistic one is another matter.

A second response to the events of 1848 was that of two other ardent revolutionaries, Marx and Engels, who contemptuously dismissed those, like Blanqui, who identified revolution with a *coup d'état*. For them, the lesson to be learned was the need for further preparation of the proletariat for its revolutionary aim.

It is the third response, however, which marks the end of the old-type guerrilla and the beginning of the modern terrorist tradition. This response is represented by Karl Heinzen, who published in 1849 a little article, graphically entitled *Murder*, which has been described as 'the most important ideological statement of early terrorism'.[11] Reviewing the events of 1848, Heinzen concluded that the authorities were too powerful and bloodthirsty for a popular uprising ever to stand any chance of success. In this situation, the revolutionary must accept that 'murder is the chief instrument of historical progress', and is in fact 'an unavoidable instrument for the achievement of historical ends'.[12] Since murder is the means by which the reactionary authorities maintain themselves, it is entirely legitimate for the terrorist to repay them in kind. In practice, Heinzen continued, the need to use murder means that the terrorist will have to rely heavily on the development of new inventions in order to help him match the capacity for mass destruction which armies give to the established authorities. Failure to appreciate the facilities for murder created by modern science has been the great failure of revolutionaries so far: thus Kossuth, for example, 'was a man of great energy, but Kossuth did not show sufficient interest in inventions and overlooked the possibilities of fulminating silver'. Henceforth, Heinzen asserted, the true liberator of mankind will be a scientist, since 'The greatest benefactor of mankind will be one who makes it possible for a few men to wipe out thousands'.[13]

During the remainder of the period down to the First World War, Heinzen's brief portrait of the terrorist was fleshed out by a variety of individuals and groups—anarchist, socialist, and nationalist—whose detailed aims and purposes need not concern us in the present context. What is mainly of interest are the three different general lines of terrorist development which may be discerned during that time.

In the first place, the period saw what may be described as an increasing 'professionalization' of terrorist activity. This process was taken furthest in Russia, where Nechaev equipped the terrorist (with Bakunin's help) with what we may perhaps regard as his own code of professional ethics. This appeared in 1869, in the form of Nechaev's notorious *Catechism of the Revolutionary*. It was indeed a striking and prophetic code of conduct, since in it terrorism for the first time acquired that tendency towards pure nihilism which has been particularly noticeable in the period since the Second World War. Article 13, for example, declared that the principal rule of conduct is that the revolutionary 'is not a revolutionary if he feels pity for anything in this world. If he is able to, he must face the annihilation of a situation, of a relationship, or of any person who is a part of this world—everything and everyone must be equally odious to him. All the worse for him if he has family, friends and loved ones in this world; he is no revolutionary if they can stay his hand'. The final sections of the *Catechism* provided the terrorist with a useful division of people into categories, listed in the order in which they were to be annihilated. The guiding principle in compiling the list, Nechaev explained in section 16, had nothing to do with whether a particular individual had in fact injured anyone; the relevant consideration was whether his murder would help the revolutionary cause. It should be noted, finally, that Nechaev's professional terrorist would certainly not be guilty of the oversight of which Heinzen had accused earlier revolutionaries. The *Catechism*, that is to say, explicitly provides for the study of every aspect of modern science which relates to the technology of destruction: 'To this end, and this end alone,' article 3 stated, 'he will study mechanics, physics, chemistry, and perhaps medicine'.

The second major development reflects the rapid spread of urbanization and the new challenge and opportunities which it created for the terrorist. The development in question is the appearance of what is now euphemistically called the 'urban guerrilla'. In this case, the relevant publicist is Johann Most, who served for some time as a Social Democratic representative in the Reichstag but eventually left Germany after being disillusioned both by Bismarck's anti-socialist legislation and by his fellow socialists' reluctance to adopt the extreme techniques he advocated. After settling in America, Most published (in German) a book called *The Science of Revolutionary War* (1884), in which he combined tips on how to make and use everything from poison to letter-bombs with advice on how to behave if arrested with hand-grenades or nitroglycerine concealed under one's clothing ('it is vital . . . to remain calm and collected'[14]).

The third development during the period reflects the fact that terrorists were quickly adjusting, not only to the advance of technology and urbanization, but also to the increasing importance of the mass media as a device for promoting sympathy for their aims. The central concept in this connection was what came to be termed 'propaganda by deed.' The concept underwent a variety of formulations during the 1870s,[15] but the basic meaning was easy to grasp: in order to get publicity, as Kropotkin explained, anything goes—whether words, knives, rifles, or dynamite—provided that it is illegal. It was not until a century later that the development of television made possible the most spectacular example to date of propaganda by deed. On the 21st September, 1972, five hundred million people all over the world were able to watch the kidnapping and murder of eleven Israeli athletes by Black September Arab terrorists.

Such, in outline, is the story of terrorism down to the time of the First World War. Thereafter, the principal aspects of its development are to be found in three things. One, which is the increasingly barbaric conduct of terrorists, merely reflects a more general change in attitudes towards violence during the twentieth century. The second is the new significance given to terrorism by the spread of ideological politics from Europe to the world at large, with the result that acts of terrorism have become increasingly likely to exacerbate diplomatic conflicts and even to pose a direct threat to international order. The third consists in various social and technological changes which have affected both the means available to terrorists and the impact of their activities on public opinion.

So far as the change in general attitudes towards violence is concerned, the most important factor is undoubtedly the twentieth century phenomenon of total war. The Second World War, in particular, did much to eliminate any distinction between combatant and non-combatant by legitimating the deliberate massacre of civilians. To that extent, the horrific threats and actions by terrorists against innocent passengers which are now a familiar part of aircraft hijacks are symptomatic of attitudes towards violence which the West itself has sanctioned, in principle at least. To pinpoint when these attitudes first began to acquire respectability is obviously difficult, but a plausible case has recently been made by Franklin Ford for singling out the 1920s as the decade in which a new mood became clearly evident.[16]

In order to appreciate the change which occurred at that time, it is necessary to recall briefly the limited concept of violence which persisted throughout the nineteenth century, surviving down to the outbreak of the war itself. Even whilst they were outlawed as a party in Bismarck's Reich, Ford observes, the German Social Democrats repeatedly condemned terrorism; and afterwards, when they enjoyed legal status, they were especially emphatic in condemning such murders as that of the Empress Elizabeth in 1898.[17] In the same period, even extreme advocates of terrorism, like those to be found in the Russian Socialist Revolutionary Party, are well known for the limits within which they confined it. In the minds of the members of this small fanatical group, founded in 1903, the evils of terrorism were only justifiable when counterbalanced by a desire on the part of the perpetrator to atone for his actions by the sacrifice of his own life. It was in this spirit, for example, that Kaliayev, who was executed for terrorism in 1905, stated, during the course of preparation for the murder of Minister Plehva, his intention of killing himself under the horses' hoofs and perishing with the Minister.[18] Along with other members of the group, moreover, Kaliayev expressed deep concern about individual injury to parties who were not the direct target of the terrorists' attacks. In a well-known incident, for example, their first attempt on the Grand Duke Sergei failed because Kaliayev, with the full approval of his comrades, refused to kill the children who were riding in the Grand Duke's carriage. At the moment of escaping from a tsarist prison, another terrorist, Savinkov, decided to shoot any officers who might attempt to prevent his flight, but to kill himself rather than fire his revolver on an ordinary soldier.[19]

As evidence of the changed atmosphere in the post-war period, Ford points to an increase from an average of less than one assassination attempt per year in Europe at large during the half century before 1900, to an average of more than five per year throughout the decade beginning in 1919.[20] More suggestive (and less ambiguous) than this quantitative evidence, however, is the significant body of sentiment, even in supposedly responsible quarters, which looked approvingly upon the murder of Matthias Erzberger in 1921. It would have been virtually unthinkable, Ford remarks, 'for a pre-war reader to have opened his morning paper to any such editorial as appeared in Germany's nationalist *Oletzkoer Zeitung* on the day following Matthias Erzberger's murder at Bad Griesbach in 1921' and find words such as these: 'Erzberger . . . has suffered the fate which the vast majority of patriotic Germans have long desired for him. Erzberger, the man who is alone responsible for the humiliating armistice, etc.'. The new note was not peculiar to that paper; although more cautious, even a paper like the venerable *Kreuzzeitung* took a sympathetic view of the terrorist incident, declaring that 'Those who now praise Erzberger and attack his enemies seem to forget completely that the entire campaign against [him] has been essentially a defensive struggle'.[21]

The second novel feature of twentieth century terrorism is the new international significance it has acquired, more especially in the period since 1945. The new significance is partly explained by the spread of ideological politics from Europe to the world at large, in the form of an essentially hybrid dogma which combines nationalist doctrine, on the one hand, with the Marxist doctrine of class conflict, on the other. The resultant hotch-potch has become the most influential ideology in Asia, Africa, and Latin America. Its most notable contemporary proponent is Colonel Gaddafi, whose vision of international relations rests on a simple division of the world into wealthy 'Northern' exploiting nations and poor 'Southern' exploited ones. More will be said about his mentor, Franz Fanon, and about terrorism in the Third World generally, in a moment; before going further, however, it is necessary to complete the overall picture of the altered situation of terrorism in the twentieth century by noticing briefly the various cultural, technological and political changes which have occurred since the First World War.

Of these changes, the most significant is the extraordinary development of the mass media, of communications and transport techniques, and of industrial production at large. As a recent study notes, the skyjackings of the past decade or so pall into insignificance in comparison with the opportunities for terrorism created by the fact that the means of communication, of power supplies, of record storage, and of production and distribution are becoming increasingly small in number and increasingly vulnerable.[22] With the growing vulnerability caused by the centralizing impact of technology, the main cause for surprise is that contemporary terrorists seem to have been rather backward and unimaginative in the methods they employ.[23] Should terrorists in due course overcome the present limitations to their horizons, however, then the thoughtful pessimism of Wardlaw's conclusion seems unavoidable. This is that 'incremental changes in the nature of terrorism and terrorist organizations will eventually lead some group to attempt mass destruction terrorism'. The real danger, Wardlaw adds, 'lies not in this first event, but in the probability that once this inhibition has gone terrorism of this kind will be much more likely to be attempted more frequently'.[24]

Whilst technological change has strengthened the position of the terrorist, the spread of prosperity in the Western democracies, especially in the period since 1945, has meant that he has become more obviously isolated than ever before from the masses whom he claims to represent. This sense of isolation is reflected in the most influential restatements of radicalism which have appeared in the post-war era. It is evident, for example, in Marcuse's well-known portrait of *One Dimensional Man*, which presents modern society as now so plastic that there is no form of radicalism which it cannot absorb. This pessimistic mood does much to explain the most notable aspect of terrorism in the post-war period, which is the fact that its advocates have undoubtedly become more extreme. It is true that Russian terrorists like Nechaev had bordered upon nihilistic frenzy in their hatred of the world, but they had not gone so far as to elevate terror into the sole possible basis for social existence, and even into the very meaning of life itself. The theorists of our own age, however, have succeeded in doing precisely that. As has been seen, most nineteenth-century terrorists, no matter how extreme, accepted some idea of limits to how far they might ultimately go. By the time of the Second World War, however, this kind of vestigial moral restraint had been replaced by a theory which finally detached terrorism from all surviving humanist ideals and conventions, purporting instead to treat it in a wholly non-moral and supra-ideological way. This theory is most clearly presented in the writings of Carl Schmitt, who earned the title 'Crown Jurist of the Third Reich' by putting forward the one tolerably coherent defence of Nazism which that movement ever possessed.

Schmitt's philosophy, which made terror the foundation of social order at large, depended upon what may be called the theory of the existential encounter. The meaning of the existential encounter is best explained by considering the problem which gave rise to it. According to Schmitt, this was the problem of determining the nature of the political relationship itself. Every relationship, he maintained, is constituted by two opposed categories. Morality, for example, is constituted by the opposition of right and wrong; aesthetics by the opposition of beauty and ugliness; economics by the opposition of utility and waste; and so on. The problem, then, is to determine which opposites constitute the political relationship. Schmitt claims that it is those of Friend and Foe. In the political situation, he stressed, this opposition does not refer to an encounter of individuals, but of groups. Nor does the encounter involve personal animosity; it is simply that the existence of the Foe posits a total threat to the entire way of life of the Friends, and that the Foe must therefore be totally annihilated. This, then, is the existential encounter—an encounter, that is, in which life and death are at stake, and in which the whole personality of the combatants is engaged. Within the context of this encounter, terror performs two functions. On the one hand, the terror inspired by the Foe unites the Friends and enables them to form a society. On the other hand, the individual finds the meaning of life itself resolved for him within the context of the existential encounter. It must be added that the beauty of Schmitt's theory was that it did not require a specific historical Foe, such as the Nazis took the Jews to be; indeed, it did not even require that the Foe should be real. Provided that the mere thought of the Foe terrified the Friends, then a purely imaginary Foe (like the Jews) could in fact constitute an existential threat which could serve as the basis of social unity.

A recent study by Jillian Becker of the Baader–Meinhof Gang, *Hitler's Children*, provides an interesting sequel to Schmitt's work, describing as it does the post-war terrorist conversion of politics into a world of purely imaginary enemies. Reflecting on the fate of the group in her epilogue, Becker remarks that 'They did not, and never had, believed that they were struggling against real tyranny. They had no political or moral cause to fight for. They were', she notes, 'acting out perilous dreams at the cost of any number of other people'.[25] More generally, Schmitt's belief in the integral part played by terrorism in the maintenance of social order pointed to the thesis from which many of today's extremist groups derive their chief support, which is that the real terrorist is the state itself. A typical statement of this view is provided by the Italian radical Gianfranco Sanguinetti, whose recent book *On Terrorism and the State* is dramatically subtitled, 'The theory and practice of terrorism developed for the first time'.[26]

The theme of this book is that 'All states *have always been terrorist*', but that 'they have been so most violently at their birth and at the imminence of their death'.[27] The upsurge of terrorism in post-war Italy, Sanguinetti accordingly assumes, is evidence of the imminent death of the Italian state; yet he nevertheless opposes groups such as the Red Brigades. This is not because he is opposed to terrorism, but because terrorism of that kind is merely artificial, in the sense that it distracts from the 'real' terrorism of the state.[28] The fact is that 'the State needs terrorists', just to provide this distraction.[29] Since Sanguinetti's thesis illuminates the intellectual means by which Marxists endeavour to pull off the seemingly impossible feat of combining a wholesale indictment of the modern state with a critique of the terrorists who seek to destroy it, it deserves to be quoted in some detail. 'Those who today, either out of despair, or because they are victims of the propaganda the regime does in favour of terrorism as the *nec plus ultra* of subversion', Sanguinetti writes, 'contemplate artificial terrorism with a critical admiration, even attempting sometimes to practise it, . . . do not know that they are only *competing* with the State *on its own terrain*; and they do not know that, on its own terrain, not only is the State the strongest but that *it will always have the last word*'. The inevitable failure of 'artificial' terror, he concludes, serves only to strengthen the 'real' terrorism of the state, to the obvious disadvantage of the Marxist cause, since 'the unparalleled reinforcement of all the State powers of control, which has occurred these last few years under the pretext of spectacular terrorism, is already used against the entire proletarian movement, which is today the most advanced and the most radical in Europe.'[30] It is unfortunate, one may add, that this way of thinking is now so endemic that even a temperate socialist like Eric Hobsbawm slips into a version of Sanguinetti's distinction between 'real' and 'artificial' terrorism, when he insists that 'we have to distinguish two things, the violence of marginal groups and the violence which is built into state, class struggle, or if you prefer, social relations in general'.[31] In fact, the only basis for such a distinction is the purely personal prejudice of the writer. Serious thought therefore becomes impossible, since on this view anything goes, provided it happens to have one's personal approval. The door is therefore involuntarily opened to any sort of terrorism, instead of closed against it.

And yet, there is a salutary lesson to be derived from thinkers like Sanguinetti, for it is true—although not for the reasons he himself gives—that far from being weakened by terrorism, the modern state is more likely to be strengthened by it. It would be a mistake, however, to derive much consolation from this fact, since any growth of state power brought about in this way is likely to undermine the rule of law and the security of civil liberties. It means, in particular, the appearance of 'emergency laws' and 'emergency powers' whose dangerous implications rapidly became evident in West Germany, for example, in the aftermath of the Baader–Meinhof trials. As one commentator observed, the new powers which were conferred on the state meant that 'a defence lawyer can be excluded from the trial if he is suspected of being involved in the activities of the accused; the trial can take place in the absence of the defendants; correspondence between defendants and lawyers can be monitored; people suspected of belonging to a terrorist group or supporting it can be detained without the usual legal restrictions.'[32] Outside the courtroom, the Special Branch has not only been empowered to use bugging and other devices in its enquiries, but also to put its findings at the disposal of private persons, thereby possibly threatening (for example) the credit, business and employment opportunities open to the individual.[33] No less disturbing is the vague provision that anyone hearing of 'unconstitutional' activities or 'sympathy for terrorists' is legally obliged to notify the police.[34] This list of restrictive powers could be extended, but the point is already sufficiently clear.

It is now necessary to return for a moment to Schmitt's reduction of politics to the relationship between Friend and Foe. It is this simplistic kind of theory, as has just been seen, which opened the way to the concept of the state itself as the archetypal terrorist organization which has featured so widely in radical thought during the post-World War Two decades. These same decades, however, have also witnessed an extension of the same theory beyond the state to the international order, and more especially to the justification of terrorism in the cause of emancipation of the Third World. The key figure in this extension of the theory is Franz Fanon. Fanon did not derive his own theory directly from Schmitt, but its logical structure is fundamentally the same. Like Schmitt, his starting point is the existential encounter of Friend and Foe, transposed in Fanon's case into the encounter between Native and Settler. Within this schema, the task of the terrorist is to unite the Friends—that is, the Natives—by provoking them into an existential encounter with their oppressors, the Settlers. The result of this encounter is an orgy of violence which might seem to sane men to be purely destructive, but which Fanon and his admirers endeavour to present as a redemptive apocalypse. Consider, for example, the enthusiastic summary of Fanon's position given by Sartre, in an introduction he wrote to Fanon's book *The Wretched of the Earth*. Fanon, he asserted, 'shows clearly [that the outbreak] of irrepressible violence is neither sound and fury, nor the resurrection of savage instincts, nor even the effect of resentment: it is man re-creating himself. I think we understood this truth at one time, but we have forgotten it—that no gentleness can efface the marks of violence; only violence itself can destroy them. The native cures himself of colonial neurosis by thrusting out the settler through force of arms. When his rage boils over, he rediscovers his lost innocence and he comes to know himself in that he himself creates his self. Far removed from his war, we consider it as a triumph of barbarism; but of its own volition it achieves, slowly but surely, the emancipation of the rebel, for bit by bit it destroys in him and around him the colonial gloom'.[35]

But it may perhaps be said that there are far more relevant theorists than Fanon for understanding the role of terrorism in the Third World; the names of Che Guevara, Régis Debray and Marighela are those most likely to be mentioned. Since Che is the crucial figure here, being the source of the urban guerrilla cult which spread from Latin America to Europe, North America and the Middle East during the 1960s and 1970s, attention may be confined to him. Che's influence rested on the lesson to which the successful Cuban invasion seemed to point. This lesson, as spelt out by Régis Debray,[36] was that Mao Tse Tung's stress upon the need for organizing the peasant masses was superfluous. What Che's success had shown, according to Debray, was that the people were waiting to rise spontaneously, and that all that the guerrilla had to do was to put in an appearance in order to trigger off the uprising. The Cuban incident, in other words, marked a return to the kind of revolutionary optimism about an imminent spontaneous rising of the masses which had chracterized guerrilla activity in the period before 1848. In fact, this revived faith in the masses was based upon a complex misunderstanding of events in Cuba, where Castro's success had depended far more upon the ricketiness of the regime than upon the revolutionary zeal of the rural masses. Consequently, the endeavour to export the Cuban revolution to other rural countries immediately came to grief, when the masses proved to be inert. Che himself was a notable victim of this misunderstanding: he died in Bolivia in October, 1967. The subsequent spread of the urban guerrilla cult relied upon rectifying this disastrous piece of revolutionary logic by turning away from the passive rural masses to the intellectuals and proletariat of the towns for support.[37] Needless to say, the urban population has been no more enthusiastic than the rural one. This lack of enthusiasm is best illustrated by the fact that the urban guerrillas invariably have to rely for their funds on bank robberies and arson; there are no voluntary contributions forthcoming from the masses.

Finally, by way of conclusion, it must be asked whether terrorism is likely to decline in the aftermath of the post-colonial era, on the one hand, and of New Left radicalism, on the other. Unfortunately, there seems to be no reason why that should be so. This pessimism follows from the starting point of the present paper, which was the advent of the ideological style of politics which now dominates the world. Since the essence of this style is to sacrifice experience, prudence and moderation to those dogmatic and inflexible visions of political and social change which have inspired the whole of the modern revolutionary tradition and the atrocities for which it has been responsible, it is appropriate to end by recalling the words with which Albert Camus ended his study of our contemporary situation. His words, which apply to the revolutionary in general, are even more apt when they are applied directly to the terrorist. These men, Camus wrote, 'forget the present for the future, the fate of humanity for the delusion of power, the misery of the slums for the mirage of the eternal city, ordinary justice for the empty promised land. They despair of personal freedom and dream of a strange freedom of the species; reject solitary death and give the name of immortality to a vast collective agony. They no longer believe in the things that exist in the world and in living man; . . . Impatience with limits, and . . . despair at being a man, have finally driven them to inhuman excesses. Denying the real grandeur of life, they have had to stake all on their own excellence. For want of something better to do, they deified themselves and their misfortunes began'.[38] It follows, of course, that the terrorism responsible for these misfortunes will only cease when men are content to abandon the revolutionary idealism which Camus is castigating; but there is as yet no sign that they are.

NOTES

1. C. Dobson and R. Payne, *Terror! The West Strikes Back* (London, 1982) p. 11.
2. *Ibid.* p. 192.
3. Quoted by Chalmers Johynson, in his report on a conference on the problems of terrorism sponsored by the Dept of State on 25–6 March, 1976. The report is reprinted in the *Terrorist Reader*, ed. W. Laqueur (London, 1979) p. 269.

4. *Ibid.* p. 243.
5. For an example of this way of proceeding *see* E. Hyams, *Terrorists and Terrorism* (London, 1975) chs. 2–4.
6. Franklin L. Ford, 'Reflections on political murder', in *Social Protest, Violence and Terror in Nineteenth and Twentieth Century Europe*, ed. W. J. Mommsen and G. Hirschfeld (London, 1982) p. 8.
7. Paul Wilkinson, *Political Terrorism* (London, 1974). Quoted here from W. Laqueur, *The Terrorist Reader op. cit.* pp. 243–4.
8. In Laqueur, *The Guerrilla Reader* (Philadelphia, 1977) p. 78.
9. *ibid.* pp. 68–70.
10. *ibid.* p. 158.
11. W. Laqueur, in *The Terrorist Reader op. cit.* p. 47.
12. *ibid.* pp. 53 and 55.
13. *ibid.* p. 59.
14. In W. Laqueur, *The Guerrilla Reader op. cit.* p. 167.
15. *See* W. Laqueur, *Terrorism* (London, 1977) pp. 49–50.
16. By Franklin Ford, in *Social Protest, etc. op. cit.*
17. *ibid.* p. 8.
18. Albert Camus, *The Rebel* (NY, 1962; original French edn. 1951) p. 168.
19. *ibid.* p. 169.
20. Ford *op. cit.* pp. 6–7.
21. *ibid.* p. 9.
22. G. Wardlaw, *Political Terrorism* (Cambridge, 1982) p. 176.
23. *ibid.* p. 178.
24. *ibid.* p. 180.
25. *Hitler's Children*, Panther edn. (London, 1978) p. 353.
26. London, 1982 (Eng. trans. by Lucy Forsyth and Michael Prigent).
27. *ibid.* p. 99; his italics.
28. *ibid.* pp. 99–100.
29. *ibid.* p. 76.
30. *ibid.* pp. 99–100. His italics throughout.
31. E. J. Hobsbawm, 'Political violence and political murder', in *Social Protest, Violence and Terror in Nineteenth and Twentieth Century Europe*, ed. Mommsen and Hirschfeld *op. cit.* p. 14.
32. G. Minnerup, 'West Germany since the War', *New Left Review*, Vol. 99 (Sept–Oct. 1976) p. 41.
    See also J. Sim and P. Thomas, 'The Prevention of Terrorism Act: normalizing the politics of repression', in *Journal of Law and Society*, Vol. 10, No. 1 (Summer 1983) pp. 71–84. The authors rightly stress the disturbing fact that the concept of terrorism is so vague that powers intended to combat it are easily used for purposes far different from those originally envisaged.
33. G. Minnerup *op. cit.*
34. *ibid.*
35. *The Wretched of the Earth* (Penguin Books, 1970) p. 18.
36. In his book *Revolution in the Revolution* (1967).
37. R. Clutterbuck, *Living with Revolution* (London, 1975) pp. 21–3.
38. Camus, *The Rebel* (Random House, 1956; first published 1951) p. 305.

2 Terror in the Theory of Revolution

Peter Calvert

In Ancient Greek mythology, terror (Phobos) and dread (Deimos) were the names given to the twin horses that drew the chariot of Ares (Mars), the god of war. War and revolution are intimately related. Not only is revolution like war in that it involves the convincing use of force or of the threat of force, but the 'great social revolutions' have been both influenced by and given rise to wars, and some recent theorists have sought to subsume the theory of revolution under that of war as 'internal war'.[1].

Terror, however, must be distinguished from dread, that is, fear. Fear is a generalized physiopsychological reaction to the strange, the unexpected or the hazardous. Some writers have argued that it is a necessary accompaniment of fear that it gives rise to aggression; others believe that aggression is a conditioned response, the chemical changes in the body elicited by fear equally permitting of 'fight or flight'.[2] Fear is a normal reaction to major political changes if they are seen as so significant as to threaten the physical safety of individual citizens; the 'Great Fear' which swept through France in 1789 was a massive example of such a fear being transmitted from one individual to another.[3] But fear of a threat to physical safety in most circumstances of political change is essentially confined to the political élite, including high-ranking military officers, civil servants and other dignitaries who may be the subject of reprisals by an incoming government.

Terror, on the other hand, is the systematic use of fear and in revolutionary circumstances to aid the establishment of a new government. It may be directed towards members of the former élite, other likely power seekers, or even towards the mass of the population to ensure their compliance. It is not a new phenomenon. Thucydides records that when the oligarchy of Corcyra was overthrown by its own citizens, the impetus of revolution spread to other cities, where the political struggles were accompanied by what he termed 'an elaboration in the methods of seizing power and by unheard of atrocities in revenge'.[4] Sulla used the terror engendered by proscriptions and executions against his political opponents in Rome, and under Tiberius and Caligula it was to be used both unpredictably and with a new permanence.

During this period governments rose and fell by violence, ultimately with significant political and social consequences, and the period has in consequence been fairly termed 'The Roman Revolution'.[5] The term 'revolution' is normally used by social scientists to designate such periods of fundamental social change. However, what makes them possible is the change of governments by force, either individually or in sequence, so that new groups rise to power, and it is the successful use of force that marks out revolution as a concept from all other related concepts such as revolt, insurgency, insurrection etc. As I have noted elsewhere, one of the consequences of this is that by definition a revolution can only be identified *after* it has taken place.[6]

The modern use of the concept of terror in revolutionary circumstances derives from the French Revolution of 1789. It is the name given to the period, after the most extreme faction, the Jacobins, had obtained power, in which physical violence was used in order to create the basis of a new social order. The most spectacular feature of terror was the execution of members of the aristocracy, not charged with a crime, not even with conspiracy against the state (although that was alleged in the case of some of them), but simply because they were aristocrats. Terror, furthermore, was seen as a method of rooting out opponents of the regime and eliminating them; of providing such an example to the others that they would be encouraged to give their wholehearted support to the new government; and of ensuring that no trace of the old order would be left. Robespierre justified the use of terror by the need to 'force men to be free'. Drawing as he was on the inspiration of Rousseau, Robespierre was nevertheless altering the thought which he had inherited, for Rousseau himself did not envisage the use of force in the sense in which it was actually employed in the French Revolution. Rather he assumed that with the removal of old social structures and restraints there would be no alternative left for individual human beings but to be free; they would, in effect, be forced to face up to circumstances.[7]

The French Revolutionary Terror was a spectacular feature, if not indeed the distinguishing feature, of that grand chain of historical events. It is important to realize, therefore, that the use of terror came in fact at a relatively late stage in the revolutionary process. The fall of the Bastille was accomplished with ease, as was the institution of a constitutional government and the development of a new system of laws, elaborating the Rights of Man and of the Citizen, which were to spread like wildfire throughout Europe. The ascendancy of the Jacobins resulted from the internal processes of political change. It was opposed, not from within, but from outside: by the development of a European-wide coalition designed to end extremism in France and to suppress the impetus to revolution elsewhere. Hence the Terror which came in response to this pressure, came at the period of consolidation of the Revolution, and would not have taken the form it did had it not been for the international dimension. Terror in the French Revolution was not employed in the period of preparation, and the actual changes that took place during it in political power were, even where moved by the force of the crowds of Paris, the series of political decisions taken by assemblies and not until a late stage the decision of a conspiratorial clique. Terror, therefore, represented the consolidation of the Revolution, not its inspiration nor its consummation. Lastly, the reason why it broke out when it did was closely connected with a single alarming event which erroneously led the Jacobins to conclude that the state itself was in danger from internal as well as external causes. This was the assassination of Marat, killed, as he sat in his bath to receive petitioners, by a young girl called Charlotte Corday. The assassination of Marat shocked the political leadership. It led them to conclude that they were all and each individually in danger, and its effect was to galvanize the National Assembly into creating the Committee of Public Safety, the twelve-man committee which had the self-imposed task of developing and directing terror as an instrument of the state.[8]

The crucial point about the Terror, however, is that it was not actually directed at the aristocrats. Those who were executed, and the many more who fled abroad, were both merely incidental victims of a process which was essentially directed towards other revolutionaries. Opposition to aristocracy, and zeal in rooting it out, became the test of loyalty to an extremist regime based on the shaky popular support of the crowds in the streets. The Terror was in fact a method of legitimating a minority government and justifying its continued maintenance of its position, and it was used in particular to enable Paris to colonize the provinces,[9] by sending out revolutionary zealots to create a new centralized order.

The Terror of the French Revolution is of crucial importance to the later development of the concept. First of all, the French Revolution has always been, and is still seen today, as the type example of a great social revolution. It was viewed in this light by its contemporaries, and it was viewed in this light by later theorists of revolution and above all by Karl Marx.

Marx and Engels ridiculed those who believed in terror as a means to initiate revolution. In Western Europe revolution would, Marx thought, be the product of the progressive development of class consciousness among the proletariat. In other parts of the world, particularly in Russia, he was inclined to be more tolerant of those who acted against tyranny in the only way open to them. Thus the assassins of Alexander II were praised by him for their heroism, and their action regarded as historically inevitable in the backward conditions in which they had to act.[10] The intensification of repression that followed was seen as dialectically necessary to further progress, as was the repression following the fall of the Commune in France.[11]

As a Marxist, therefore, Lenin did not see terrorism as having a role in the promotion of revolution, but as a Russian he did see it as having a role in its actual execution, once open resistance had begun. Thus he wrote in 1906 'that the party must regard the fighting guerrilla operations of the squads affiliated to or associated with it as being, in principle, permissible and advisable in the present period'. But he was specific that the purpose of all such operations must be 'to destroy the government, police and military machinery', and certainly always under the control of the Party to prevent effort being dissipated uselessly.[12]

Terror is after all merely a development of fear, and fear, as the first modern political theorist pointed out, is an instrument of government. '. . . since some men love as they please but fear when the prince pleases, a wise prince should rely on that which he controls, not on what he cannot control'.[13] The prince may well therefore choose to instil this fear through a sharp initial display of cruelty. Such a display is the essence of terror, a deliberate decision to employ force not for restraint or punishment of individual offenders, but simply to instil fear into the majority of the population, regardless of their beliefs or intent. In sixteenth-century Russia Ivan the Terrible (more properly 'Ivan the Dread') employed terror in this fashion, and the same was no less true of Nicholas I, whose notorious 'Third Section' adapted to Russian conditions the secret police, the classic governmental instrument of terror for the twentieth century.

The role of the secret police is derived from, though by no means identical with, that of police in general. In its continental mode, the police power is both negative and positive: the power on the one hand to arrest and to charge offenders, and on the other to enforce regulations designed to secure the greater good of the community as a whole. The secret police differ from regular police, not in their secrecy (for few people knew much about the internal operations of police forces before the days of television serials), but in the use of their powers to keep the government secure. All police forces have a certain latitude in the interpretation and application of the laws they nominally apply with rigorous impartiality. The secret police make use of this area of uncertainty to focus pressure on individuals believed to be politically unsympathetic to the regime. The use of informants, a normal part of police work, is extended in these circumstances into the systematic compilation of all information likely to lead to the disclosure of political dissent, and the arrest of suspects conducted in such a way that if the 'right' people have not been arrested, they will be in any event intimidated into conformity.

Terror used in this way can be of two kinds: discriminating and indiscrimate. It is important to understand that the use of terror by government in the nineteenth century, however wholesale, was normally still discriminating; that is to say, it was directed towards specific target groups and capable of being regulated in intensity according to the perceived needs of the situation. It was countered to some extent by political assassination, which, despite its apparent unpredictability, is also discriminating. The kings, tsars and presidents who fell to the assassins' bullets or bombs were killed in the vast majority of cases because they were the actual possessors of political power. When governments used indiscriminate force, as in Russia in 1905, it was taken as a sign of weakness, not of strength. Even then, despite the belief of the Bolsheviks that 1905 was in a sense a dress rehearsal for 1917, it was not a revolution in that it did not overthrow the government, nor did it bring about significant social or political change. And the lesson for revolutionaries was that good intentions were not enough; the seizure of political power was something that could not be achieved simply by instilling fear into an incumbent government; if anything that was likely to strengthen it in its resolve. What was needed was the precise direction of force towards specific political targets, and here, as in any other military operation, surprise and careful planning were crucial. This lesson was the main one which made the Bolshevik seizure of power in Petrograd in 1917 possible, and even then this would not have been possible without the impact of war on the social fabric and the corresponding weakness in all respects of the provisional government.

The fact is, the use of terror was associated less with the existence of revolutionary movements than with the actions of the forces of repression, until the events of 1870–1 in France brought the question of the use of terror by revolutionary governments again to the fore. After the failure of the Commune, far more people were shot by the provisional government headed by Adolphe Thiers than had died as a result of the purges of the Commune.[14] Yet it was widely accepted by those who wished to believe in governmental stability that the use of force to compel political obedience was something that only rebels against society went in for. Governments made use of only lawful physical constraint, and then only insofar as it was necessary to maintain the balance of law and order in the interests of society a large. They failed to realize that this was precisely the ground on which leaders of the French Revolution had made use of force: not to overthrow, but to maintain and consolidate and to stabilize.

Both aspects are very strongly present in the early phases of the Russian Revolution, the period now known in Soviet historiography as the period of 'war communism' (1917–21). Whereas the pre-French Revolutionary state had had no effective secret police, and the objectionable habit of locking people up arbitrarily in the Bastille had virtually fallen into disuse before that building was stormed in 1789, in Russia the use of terror and counter-terror was a recognized feature of 'a dictatorship tempered by assassination'. Again, the use of terror was not to be found either in the preparation, nor indeed in the execution of the October Revolution in 1917. Weakened by war weariness and led by an inefficient government with very minority support, the government troops had been extensively weakened by fraternization, and the seizure of the controlling levers of government was a relatively straightforward matter. The Winter Palace fell to a well-planned attack by a mere 200 troops.[15]

In the weeks and months immediately following the October Revolution the evidence is that a kind of euphoria prevailed among the Bolsheviks. Looking across a continent torn by war, they believed and confidently predicted the imminent European-wide social revolution which would consolidate and justify their own assumption of political power.[16] Hence, therefore, it was for the consolidation of the Revolution that terror began on Lenin's order to be employed as a governing device. Indeed, in the Russian case we see clearly the development both of the White Terror among the conservative forces and the Red Terror developed to answer it, the forces of each striving with the other in order to try and achieve ascendancy. Once more, as in the case of the French Revolution, three main purposes can be seen to have been served by the creation of the Chekas, which in turn to form the nucleus of the future Soviet secret police. The precipitant for their unleashing was the attempted assassination of Lenin himself (30 August 1918).[17] Again their purpose in the first instance was to rout out concealed enemies of the Revolution. Secondly, it was to defend the Bolshevik government from the threat posed by the simultaneous invasion of most of the Western powers and Japan, which was not ultimately beaten back until 1920. The Kronstadt Mutiny of 1921, which revealed sharply that despite the suppression of internal enemies and the beating back of the external invaders, challengers to the revolution might continue to exist even within the structure of government itself, led to the consolidation of their activities on a long-term basis.[18] They were thus available to be made use of when it was once again necessary to 'force men to be free', that is to say, at the time of Stalin's forced collectivization of agriculture from 1930 onwards, when he sought to make the peasants accept the superior virtues of the Soviet state and agree to inaugurate the new economic order which he was trying to create.

The Bolshevik ideology, however, gave the use of terror two additional dimensions, which the collectivization of agriculture threw into sharp relief. Firstly, it was a strategy in the class war, that is to say, the class war was seen as an armed conflict, in which the use of force was as natural as it would be in any other circumstance of belligerency. Secondly, since the basis of class lay in the relation of individual social groups to the forces of production, the achievement of class domination could only be attained by the economic restructuring of society. Neither coercion by troops, nor the elimination of the old aristocracy, was in any way original. What was original was the decision to create a new basis for the social order in which the old class conflicts simply could not exist.

Once the elimination of the small urban bourgeoisie was considered an accomplished fact, the proletarianization of the peasantry could proceed by the forcible collectivization of agriculture. Once again, as in the French Revolution, the town reconquered the countryside. Party committees centred on the Machine Tractor Stations enabled the regime to extend its surveillance permanently to the rural areas. It was no longer just a question of sending in the Cossacks on punitive expeditions, it was a permanent transformation in the social structure which brought the countryside into line with the cities, and it was carried through with a ruthlessness that was the greater for the fear that if the peasants continued to slaughter their cattle and to refuse to work, all might starve.[19] Once the decision to use force was made, therefore, the level of force deployed continued to escalate until the task could be pronounced at an end.

Turning the peasantry into employees of collective farms removed as far as possible those factors that differentiated them from the urban proletariat. Once in a common relation to the factors of production, the contradictions between the toiling classes could only be non-antagonistic. For the first time in history therefore, by a deliberate act of state policy, the basis for class conflict would have been eliminated.

By 1936, as we know, Stalin claimed to have achieved just that, and in that year the class struggle within the Soviet Union was declared at an end.[20] Terror and the show trials continued, for the recrudescence of violence, countered by mobilization of such large coercive forces, created within the Soviet state a new series of challenges. These the demonstration effect of the show trials was designed to eliminate, and so the Russian Revolution resumed the cycle a second time at an earlier stage and undertook a fresh consolidation of its hold on political power. The elimination of the 'Old Bolsheviks' was itself a further revolutionary act, making a transfer of power within the Soviet system to a new group absolutely and unconditionally loyal to Stalin himself.[21]

The establishment of pro-Soviet regimes in Eastern Europe in the period after the Second World War was accompanied by the creation of similar organs of coercion for the client states. All these states had lain in the part of Europe which in the inter-war period had been dominated by peasant-based political parties, or where peasant production was the major sector of the agrarian economy. Coercion of peasants, therefore, was something which the new regimes were prepared for, though by this time certain refinements were noticeable. Hoarding of food for private gain, previously dealt with by the execution of the food hoarders, was still so dealt with in serious cases. On the other hand, the regular demonetization of bank notes meant that any gains realized from this source could not be carried forward and made available at a later date and this technique was no less effective in removing the economic base of the former bourgeoisie.[22] The major purpose of the fear instilled by the secret police in Romania, Hungary and Czechoslovakia was to break the links that bound basic social formations such as the family and the peer group. The technique of the isolation of individuals from the reinforcement of the social groups to which they belong, of course, is in no way original with East European regimes. But the isolation of individuals was in the face of the unified will of the state much more effective, and required a much smaller use of actual force, than the cruder methods of the early stage of the Bolshevik revolution. It was therefore much more economical. A developed economy simply could not afford the luxury of a permanent state of civil war. It could operate very effectively despite the removal from time to time of certain individuals, even where they might separately be productively important.

Up to the Second World War terror remained a feature primarily of the consolidation phase of great social revolutions. It was once again a feature of consolidation both of the Chinese[23] and of the Cuban[24] revolutions, as well as in the consolidation of the power of the Islamic regime in Iran after 1979.[25] On each occasion terror was employed, not only against the military as supporters of the old regime, but against prominent members of the former oligarchy, and other people particularly identified with the maintenance of the old regime, but with a wide range of individuals regarded as economically undesirable, either because they were practising economic sabotage or because of the mere nature of their occupations.

The development of the technique of guerrilla warfare as a path to revolution, however, was to create an important additional role for terror in the theory of revolution. Mao's theory of the three stages of guerrilla warfare envisages a preliminary stage of preparation, a stage in which a guerrilla movement is established and expands its control over a wider and wider area, and thirdly a period in which the guerrilla force transforms itself into a regular army capable of defeating the forces of the government in a series of pitched battles.[26] In the Chinese case the Second World War offered the opportunity for the transition from the second to the third stage to be tested in actual combat against the Japanese, and with the supply of arms guaranteed from the Soviet Union. In the case of Cuba no real transformation occurred, since the regime succumbed to insurgency in the cities and the so-called Battle of Santa Clara was a largely formal affair significant because of its position and not because of what actually happened.[27] The expansion of the guerrilla forces in the second stage, however, is not a simple matter. It involves specifically the creation of a peoples' militia, the purpose of which is to expand ahead of the capacity of the active guerrilla forces and to undermine the will to resist among the government agents in the countryside. This technique, the 'oil-spot' technique as it is often called, from its similarity to the expension of a spot of oil on the surface of water, involves an element of finesse in the persuasion of individuals to accept the presence of guerrilla forces. Ideally this will be achieved, as Mao in his written work seems to expect, by persuasion and example, the 'guerrilla as teacher'. However, if the elements in the countryside, and particularly those who serve as headmen and other prominent figures in the villages are not willing to support the guerrillas, then terror enters the picture and it does so at a stage well before the revolutionary movement is fully afoot, let alone consolidated.[28] Thus in guerrilla warfare terror becomes an element of the actual campaign itself, of the achievement of power. It is, indeed, a feature of the entire process of a guerrilla revolution, and not simply of one aspect of it; it is integral to the way in which it operates, and not simply something that may be invoked when the revolution itself appears to be in danger.

A similar chain of reasoning lies behind the more recent attempts to use terror as a destabilizing factor in urban politics in Latin America. Deaths of prominent figures, the explosions of bombs in public places, and the like, are not designed actually to destroy the incumbent government, but to make it impossible to continue to carry out its functions because it has lost the confidence of its people that it is able to protect them. Violence is therefore a mere tool in the process of psychological warfare. Victims are random victims not individuals selected on the grounds of justice, revolutionary or otherwise. Indeed the less certain it is who may be subjected to such acts of violence the more unsettling—up to a point—it is from the point of view of the populace at large, since, if no one is safe, then everyone is in danger, and everyone has an interest in bringing the existing state of affairs to an end as quickly as possible.[29]

Thus though we must always distinguish between 'terror' as a *technique* and 'terrorism' as a *belief in the value of terror*, the two are in fact closely related, and indeed the historical myths of the efficacy of terror in earlier times and other situations have led to a diffusion of the techniques of terror into several varieties of political thought. Both Marxist and militant Islamic groups have used terrorist methods, and links have developed between revolutionary movements of very different backgrounds, including the Japanese Red Army, the Italian Red Brigades (Brigate Rossi), the PLO, the Basque nationalist movement ETA and the IRA.[30]

It follows therefore that in the period since 1945 terror has ceased merely to be a feature of the consolidation stage of revolutions, and even then something which may be invoked only when the challenges appear to be otherwise insuperable. It has become instead a feature of the actual achievement of power itself. Just as the stages of guerrilla warfare itself overlap so the use of terror has overlapped backwards into the earlier stages of revolution. At the same time it continued to be used in the actual processes of government. Rather more worryingly, it seems to have been assumed in many circles that its use by governments faced with revolutionary challenges is not only normal but natural, and critics have identified and criticized what has often been called 'the national security state'.[31]

Typically the 'national security state' is a Latin American military dictatorship. It originates in a decision by the armed forces that the political situation is becoming unmanageable as a result of challenges by either rural or urban guerrillas. The question of whether or not the challenge is a real one is immaterial. What matters is that if forms an excellent excuse for the military to assume supreme power. They do not, however, assume supreme power in the traditional mode in order to regulate political affairs and to retire again to the sidelines. Instead they see their society as threatened by a fundamental lack of strength and political will which they believe that they, in the embodiment of the state for the purposes of defence, have the right, and indeed the duty, to provide.

For this purpose they create a very large security apparatus. This security apparatus is not only large but unmanageable, partly because of the secrecy which surrounds all military operations, but also because of the impact on such circumstances of traditional inter-service rivalry. It was the Naval Mechanical School in Buenos Aires that was associated with the worse excesses of the period of the 'dirty war' and, earlier, in the 1960s, inter-service rivalry in Brazil helped the acceptance of the use of torture in the interrogation of political suspects.[32] The proliferating security apparatuses thus exist in competition with one another sustained by the overwhelming economic resources of the state and able to claim in the name of national security any degree of support which they may require from the nominal political authorities.

Once the apparatuses have come into existence, they may take a number of forms. The so-called death squads operating in Latin America in the late 1960s proliferated in the 1970s and have been above all a feature of the recent strife in Central America, particularly in Guatemala and El Salvador.[33] Charges and counter-charges of the use of terror have been exchanged between the countries in the region, but it at least is true to point out that in the case of Nicaragua, while there can be no doubt about the use of terrorist methods by the national guard under Somoza, the incoming provisional government, in an act without parallel in revolutionary circumstances, firmly abolished the death penalty, and the charges that the regime is holding a large number of political prisoners is something which has not been confirmed to the extent claimed by the United States.[34]

The most chilling examples of the use of terror as a permanent governmental device dedicated to the eradication of the possibility of revolution are, however, to be found in Chile and Uruguay.

Uruguay down to 1973 was the most democratic in the region and had the nickname of 'the Switzerland of South America'. Following the 'soft coup' of 1973, the Uruguayan military forces, in imitation of their Brazilian neighbours, established an effective military dictatorship, which set about the task of eradicating the roots of revolution from Uruguayan society. For this purpose, the entire population was classified into A, B and C categories. For important and governmental jobs it was essential to be A, known not only to be acceptable but also well disposed towards the regime. Category B, those acceptable to the regime but not active in its support, were excluded from the best jobs. Category C, however, namely those who came under any suspicion whatsoever, or proved politically unreliable—including many of the democratic politicians of pre-1973, were excluded from all jobs, subject to petty harassment, and might be arrested at any time and detained without trial on suspicion. At one stage there were more political prisoners in Uruguay per head of population than in any other country in South America, which in the circumstances is saying a lot.[35]

Within this system of terror, the most alarming and significant feature is the extent to which once again each individual, isolated in themselves, is left to stand along before the ruthless and uncontrolled power of the state. In such circumstances it is very easy to surrender to the official propaganda and to believe what one is being told, that every day things are getting better and that any actions that are being taken which might otherwise appear distasteful are in the higher interest of the state as a whole. Many Argentines, for example, simply could not believe the charges against their military rulers when these were first given international publicity in the latter days of the 1976–83 military government. Now that the bodies are being unearthed by the dozen in the cemeteries they have had to come to believe it.[36]

There is of course a long literature, stretching back to the days of the Ancient Greek writers, on regimes such as these. Aristotle describes systems in which self-appointed rulers used fear extensively and unpredictably to coerce their subjects into accepting the need for their rule continuing. There was no Greek word for a ruler of this kind, so the Greeks borrowed a Lydian one, and called them 'tyrants'. Later writers consistently agreed that the exercise of tyranny was illegitimate, and hence that it was lawful to overthrow a tyrant, if necessary by force. It things have come full circle and tyrants now justify their terror on the grounds that the alternative is that of revolutionaries, reasonable civilized human beings may well feel that there is no long-term hope for the human race. One or other of these propositions must be false and in fact both are. Nothing justifies the use of terror in any circumstances; it is always unjust and it is always morally unacceptable.

The question is, whether the vicious cycle of terror and counter-terror can in fact be broken, and if so at what point? The answer, of course, is that governments must come to exercise 'enlightened self-restraint'. Today even a relatively weak government has a staggering potential for violence and destruction, not only if it chooses to exercise it, but also if it fails to restrain those whose professional duty it is to use it. As the cycle of coups and military regimes in Latin America demonstrates, though, you can do everything with bayonets except sit on them.[37] The economy of force is like the credit of a bank, effective until there is a run on it, and it is disclosed that in fact there is not enough of the reserves to go round if everyone makes a call on them simultaneously. Hence a cynic may say that, though military governments are unlikely on the whole to listen to the voices of humanitarianism, they may perforce recognize the counsel of self-interest.

Once a government agrees to bind itself, and particularly if it agrees to limit its own term of office, the impetus to violence is much reduced. One does not have to agree with Che Guevara's other propositions to agree that his argument that revolution could not succeed until the possibilities for peaceful change were seen to be exhausted was fundamentally correct,[38] though some allowance has to be made for the clarity of perception and more perhaps for the excessive optimism of individuals.

Here too Uruguay offers a useful set of examples. For four years the military regime had been trying to establish a new constitutional order that would allow it to withdraw from the day-to-day task of government. It had not been successful, as the Uruguayan people had persistently refused to ratify by plebiscite the rigged constitutional devices set before them. The government had thus been forced to make further concessions, and in return massive demonstrations began to take place spontaneously in the latter part of 1983 at roughly monthly intervals. Contrary to the usual expectation in such matters, however, the government did not embark on massive physical repression of the demonstrations, and in consequence they remained peaceful. It was clear that the government would be forced to make many concessions that it did not want and did not like. But it did successfully negotiate a path to free elections in November 1984. And it is clear that as long as the possibility of such changes remains open, it is highly unlikely that the situation can attain the level of revolutionary spontaneity.

To sum up, therefore, there are many degrees of discriminating terror, and the fact that it is carefully directed and calculated does not make its impact on its target any less devastating. In the past few decades new methods have been devised for institutionalizing official terror and making it serve the purposes of the state. It has been used as a substitute for a military coup, to give the armed forces unchecked control over the people. It has been unofficially sanctioned in the form of 'death squads' of off-duty police and military against supposed enemies of the state, or at least of the regime, against whom evidence has not been found and may not even exist. It has been officially sanctioned by serving officers and men as a method of extracting confessions and so breaking up revolutionary organizations. It has even been used to eliminate whole social groups. In a latter-day Massacre of the Innocents youths aged fifteen to twenty-two were rounded up by Somoza's national guard and shot after the September offensive in Nicaragua in 1978. Lastly, the Pol Pot regime in Cambodia used terror as a sole instrument in the most wholesale attempt at social engineering in our time, and despite its appalling record is still recognized as the government of that unfortunate country by the major Western powers.

My argument, therefore, is that both in theory and in practice the factor most conducive to the use of terror by the political opposition is its use by govenment, and that, conversely, if terror is to be avoided, repressive measures on the part of government are to be eliminated and a satisfactory standard of governmental responsiveness established as rapidly as possible. There are undoubtedly some complex situations in which the best intentions are unlikely to eliminate the urge for terrorist activity, and Northern Ireland is possibly one of them. But then such cases are not ones in which there is any serious possibility of revolutionary change either.

NOTES

1. Peter Calvert, *Revolution* (London, Pall Mall Press, 1970) pp. 15, 127.
2. Ashley Montagu, ed., *Man and Aggression* (New York, Oxford University Press, 1973); T. R. Gurr, *Why Men Rebel* (Princeton, Princeton University Press, 1973).
3. Georges Lefebvre, *The Great Fear of 1789; Rural Panic in Revolutionary France*, trans. Joan White (London, NLB, 1973).
4. Thucydides, *The Peloponnesian War*, trans. Rex Warner (Harmondsworth, Middx., Penguin Books, 1956) p. 209.
5. Sir Roland Syme, *The Roman Revolution* (Oxford, Clarendon Press, 1939).
6. Calvert *op.cit.* p. 126.
7. R. R. Palmer, *Twelve who Ruled; the Year of the Terror in the French Revolution* (Princeton, Princeton University Press); cf. Joan Macdonald, *Rousseau and the French Revolution, 1792–91* (London, Athlone Press, 1965).
8. Palmer *op.cit.* p. 28.
9. Karl Marx and Frederick Engels, *Selected Works* (Moscow, Foreign Languages Publishing House, 1962) I, p. 133 (intro to 'The Class Struggles in France').
10. Palmer *op.cit.* pp. 128–9; *see also inter alia* Colin Lucas, *The Structure of the Terror; the example of Javoques and the Loire* (London, Oxford University Press, 1973).
11. Walter Laqueur, *The Terrorism Reader, A Historical Anthology* (London, Wildwood House, 1979) p. 198.
12. Walter Laqueur, *The Guerrilla Reader* (London, Wildwood House, 1978) pp. 178–8.

13. Niccolò Machiavelli, *The Prince*, trans. George Ball (Harmondsworth, Middx., Penguin Books, 1963) p. 98.

14. Stewart Edwards, *The Paris Commune 1871* (London, Eyre & Spottiswoods, 1971) p. 337 puts the number of hostages shot by the Commune at seventy and, p. 346, estimates the number of Communards shot in the aftermath by Government forces at 25,000. The French Revolutionary Terror, by comparison, killed 2,627 in Paris and at most 17,000 in the rest of France—D. Greer, *The Incidence of the Terror during the French Revolution* (Cambridge, Mass., Harvard University Press, 1935).

15. D.J. Goodspeed, *The Conspirators, A Study of the Coup d'Etat* (London, Macmillan, 1972) pp. 98–9 describes how the palace was almost totally undefended at its fall.

16. David Shub, *Lenin: a Biography* (Harmondsworth, Middx., Penguin Books, 1966) pp. 304–5.

17. Shub *op.cit.* pp. 344–50, 363–7.

18. Shub *op.cit.* pp. 408–15.

19. Robert Conquest, *The Great Terror; Stalin's Purge of the Thirties*, rev. edn. (London, Macmillan, 1973) pp. 41–7.

20. Milovan Djilas, *The New Class; An Analysis of the Communist System* (London, Thames & Hudson, 1957) p. 38.

21. Conquest *op.cit.* p. 123 ff.

22. Oscar Halecki, *Poland* (New York, Atlantic Books, 1957) pp. 426–7.

23. Jean Chesneaux, *China, the People's Republic 1949–76* (Brighton, Harvester, 1979) p. 41.

24. Boris Goldenberg, *The Cuban Revolution and Latin America* (London, George Allen & Unwin, 1965) p. 179; *see also Cuba and the Rule of Law* (Geneva, International Commission of Jurists, 1962).

25. *The Annual Register 1979*, pp. 265, 267.

26. W. Laqueur, *The Guerrilla Reader* (Philadelphia, 1977) pp. 189–97; *see also* Stuart R. Schram, ed., *The Political Thought of Mao Tse-tung* (London, Pall Mall Press, 1963) pp. 207–10.

27. Ernesto (Che) Guevara, *Episodes of the Revolutionary War* (New York, International Publishers, 1968) pp. 134–5.

28. David Wilkinson, *Revolutionary Civil War, the Elements of Victory and Defeat* (Palo Alto, Calif., page-Ficklin, 1975) pp. 59–60.

29. *See also* Richard Clutterbuck, *Protest and the Urban Guerrilla* (London, Cassell, 1973) pp. 245–6.

30. Grant Wardlaw, *Political Terrorism; Theory, Tactics and Countermeasures* (Cambridge, Cambridge University Press, 1982) pp. 55–7; *see also* B. M. Jenkins, 'International terrorism; trends and potentialities', *Journal of International Affairs*, Vol. 38, No. 1 (1978) pp. 115–23.

31. For its origins *see* Alfred Stepan, *The Military in Politics, Changing Patterns in Brazil* (Princeton, NJ, Princeton University Press, 1971) p. 227.

32. Stepan *op.cit.* pp. 260–2; *see also* George-Andre Fiechter, *Brazil since 1964; Modernization under a Military Regime* (London, Macmillan, 1975) pp. 147–9.
33. *Guatemala, a Government Program of Political Murder* (London, Amnesty International, 1981. *Guardian*, 4 July 1983, gives estimate of the number killed in El Salvador since the civil war began as 42,000, most by the 'death squads'.
34. Henri Weber, *Nicaragua, the Sandinist Revolution* (London, Verso, 1981) pp. 62, 65, 108–9.
35. The *Guardian* (7 Feb. 1984).
36. Before going out of office the Argentine military government tried to pardon itself—*Guardian* (29 Sept. 1983). First news of exhumations of bodies in unmarked graves coincided with the repeal of the amnesty by the new civilian Congress—*Guardian* (29 Dec. 1983).
37. 'A man may build himself a throne of bayonets, but he cannot sit on it': Dean Inge, cited in *The Oxford Dictionary of Quotations*, 2nd edn. (Oxford, Clarendon Press, 1970) p. 267.
38. Ernesto (Che) Guevara, *Guerrilla Warfare* (New York and London, Monthly Review Press, 1967) p. 15.

Part II
European Terrorism

3 From Regeneration to Terror: the Ideology of the French Revolution
Norman Hampson

Historians are usually apprehensive about attributing to the actions of the men they study an ideological dimension of which the actors themselves may have been unaware or to which they were indifferent. Historians of the French revolution need have no such qualms. The revolutionaries inhabited a mental world that had been defined for them by Montesquieu and Rousseau, to whose writings they continually referred. Barnave and Roederer reproached the Right with treating Montesquieu as their oracle but disregarding his more inconvenient ideas.[1] Mounier drew attention to the paradox confronting the Rousseauists: 'We recognize the need to entrust legislative power to representatives and we blindly invoke the maxims of a philosopher who thought the English were only free while they were electing their representatives' (4 September 1789). It was, of course, true that the revolutionaries did not always have a very clear idea of what their mentors had intended, especially where the general will was concerned. They quarried the sacred texts for what suited their political convenience and ignored what did not. As practising politicians they often took whatever action seemed appropriate to a particular tactical situation and then decorated it with a suitable ideological gloss. It is none the less true that their conception of their goals was derived from the works of the two theorists. To that extent, ideology helped to determine political choices as well as to justify those already made. Any account of the contribution of ideology to the revolution must therefore begin with a brief reference to what the revolutionaries believed that Montesquieu and Rousseau had said.

The early part of *De l'Esprit des Lois*, with its justification of the power of corporate aristocratic bodies, had been much invoked by French *parlementaires* for a generation or more, but had become politically irrelevant by 1789. The men of the Constituent Assembly saw Montesquieu rather as the advocate of a pluralist society, in which government should reflect pre-existing social values. Rulers were free to try to modify these values, indeed good rulers were under an obligation to do so, but only to the extent that this could be achieved by precept, example and consent. All societies ought to pursue liberty, justice and the provision of tolerable living standards for all their members. Such values were universal and external to the configuration of any particular society, but the extent to which progress could be made towards implementing them would vary with circumstances and any attempt to impose them by decree would be self-defeating. Granted the inclination of anyone with power to extend it indefinitely—which could only lead to tyranny, however altruistic the motives—sovereignty had to be divided and good government was a matter of contriving a balance between the competing interests within a society, so that all were held in equilibrium. Montesquieu believed this to be exemplified in England and his followers could be identified by their penchant for referring to British principles and practice.

Rousseau, at least in the minds of the revolutionaries, stood at the opposite pole. To be legitimate, government must correspond to the general will, which was what was best for society, and not necessarily what its members believed themselves to want. By definition, the general will—like the future republic—was one and indivisible. It was infallible and morally binding on all citizens. The function of government was therefore not to reflect the diverse interests within a society but to serve as the vehicle for its moral improvement. As Duport said on 29 March 1790, this meant providing society with *habitudes heureuses*. However happy the outcome, those who were to be reformed might not see the need for their re-education and, as Rousseau said, they would have to be forced to be free. Since the vicious habits of a society were both the cause and the effect of its corruption, it could not be expected to will its own regeneration. What it needed was a 'legislator' whose main function was to devise the institutions that would confirm citizens in the habits of *vertu*. As examples of the kind of men he meant, he cited Moses, Mahomet and Calvin. If a government actually did reflect the general will, opposition to it was not merely illegitimate but a source of moral corruption that must be suppressed in the name of liberty itself. Rousseau and his followers tended to be somewhat dismissive of the British, whom Montesquieu had idealized. They found their own inspiration in an equally unrealistic vision of the classical republics of Rome and Sparta. Where Montesquieu had been almost provocatively cosmopolitan, the Rousseauists, as befitted neo-Spartans, felt that patriotism could never acquire the power to spur men to heroic deeds unless it was confined within the frontiers of a particular state. The general will, in any case, was the product of a particular society and no one was entitled to appeal from it to principles of universal morality. Whether he knew it or not, the royalist deputy, Cazalès, was following Rousseau (and paraphrasing *Emile*) when he said on 20 May 1790, 'The *patrie* should be the exclusive object of our love. Love of the *patrie* creates more than men, it creates citizens'.

Almost without exception, the men of 1789 tried to have the best of both worlds, to achieve Rousseau's regenerative ends by Montesquieu's libertarian means. All of them disregarded Rousseau's warning that the general will could not be represented. They were convinced of the need for the separation of the powers, on which Montesquieu had insisted. Despite all this, they found themselves irresistibly drawn in the direction of Rousseau. Even ultra-royalists like the abbé Maury found it impossible to deny that, in some sense, sovereignty was located in the people. From this it was a comparatively easy step—especially for those whose ideas about the general will were even hazier than Rousseau's—to assert that the will of the people was embodied in that of their representatives. At its most general, this need mean little more than that everyone ought to prefer the common good to his own self-interest. This was the political equivalent of being against sin. When the proposition took on more specific shape, it encouraged people to believe that their opponents were positively encouraging the sinners. When the general will was equated, not with the divided Assembly as a whole, but with a parliamentary majority, it tended to generate the feeling that opposition was morally pernicious as well as politically indefensible. Generations of French historians who have insisted that 'the revolution' was a *bloc* have in practice also identified it with the general will, which has allowed them to damn all those who could not accept the way that things were going as 'counter-revolutionaries'.

To appreciate the interaction between politics and ideology in 1789, some familiarity with at least the outline of events is necessary. Louis XVI, in the theoretical plenitude of his power and the practical need to find a way of balancing his budget, had summoned a meeting of the Estates General to advise him on his problems. All those liable to direct taxation—a majority of the adult male population—had been eligible to vote in the election of the representatives of the Third Estate. Each constituency provided its deputy with a *cahier* or list of grievances. Some of these imposed limitations on the freedom of action of the deputies; some noble *cahiers*, for example, prohibited the noble deputies from debating and voting with the other two Orders.

The opening of the Estates General produced deadlock, when the Third Estate insisted on joint meetings of the three Orders and the other two refused. When the king eventually intervened and demanded the separate meeting of the Orders, he was defied by the Third Estate, which had begun to call itself the National Assembly. When the clergy began to go over to the Assembly the king, to buy time, ordered the nobility to join them, until he could surround Paris with troops. His dismissal of his more conciliatory ministers, on 11 July, was presumably intended as a prelude to the dismissal of the Assembly itself. Paris, however, revolted and was followed—or in one or two cases, preceded—by other important towns. Rather than begin a civil war, the king capitulated and returned his troops to the frontier. In October, a Parisian expedition to Versailles brought the royal family back to the capital.

This course of events meant that at no time had there been a decisive contest between the king and the Assembly. It was therefore possible to pretend that all the differences had been due to misunderstanding. The king had been temporarily misled by wicked ministers—ministers were always wicked—but his good intentions had been proved by his summoning the Estates General in the first place, everything had come right in the end and the Assembly declared him to be the 'Restorer of French liberty'. The flight of a handful of irreconcilables meant that it was possible to regard everyone who remained as accepting the new order. This was more than a pious fiction: for a few months, debates were actually conducted on this basis. The Assembly, encouraged by the expectations aroused by the Enlightenment, assumed that it was entitled—and had indeed been convened—to provide France with a new constitution, and the king was in no position to assert a contrary view. This was a situation rich in ambiguity; the freedom of action of the deputies had not been forfeited by the limited violence of July and what they chose to do depended to an unusual extent on the kind of way in which they thought.

The first theoretical problem concerned the imperative mandates that some of the noble electors had imposed on their deputies, forbidding them to vote in common with the other two Orders. By the second half of July this was a nuisance to everyone. It was, however, difficult for Rousseauists to argue that electors were not entitled to impose their will on those who represented them. The solution was to distinguish between sectional groups, who possessed merely a *volonté particulière*, and the nation as a whole. This got the Assembly off the hook, but at the price of considering it to be, not a group of men chosen to advise the king, or even an elected legislature, but the voice of the general will itself. This was asserted, not merely by radicals like Mirabeau and Sieyès and by moderates like the archbishop of Aix, but even by royalists like de Sèze, who was later to risk his life defending the king in 1792. De Sèze then went on to argue in favour of the kings having an absolute veto—presumably in order that he could frustrate the general will whenever he felt disposed to do so. He was not the only one to find his ideology at variance with his politics.

Conservatives were inclined to emphasize that the Assembly was not creating a new society from scratch. The monarchy existed, the king was personally popular and he still disposed of a residual authority that it might be unwise to challenge too openly. Few, if any, of the deputies wanted to do so. Montesquieu and Rousseau had taught them that in big states executive power should be concentrated in the hands of one man and Louis XVI, if not as enthusiastic a convert to the new order as one might have wished, was pliable enough and could generally be induced to endorse what he did not feel strong enough to prevent.

Those who came to form the majority in the Assembly, convinced that the revolution was regenerating French society (if it had not already done so), were inclined to assume that whatever had happened must reflect the general will. The way things stood in the autumn suggested that that mysterious force must therefore have entrusted executive power to the king and legislative power to the Assembly, each enjoying the same sort of legitimacy within its own sphere. As Mirabeau was to remind his colleagues somewhat later, after he himself had negotiated a secret deal with the king, legislative power— which belonged to the general will alone—should not be confused with the legislative body (22 May 1970). At the time, most of the deputies would probably have agreed with the duc de Liancourt when he said on 1 September that to change the form of government would have requred a convention, 'nothing less than the expression of the general will'.

In practice, the belief of the majority that the king shared in the legitimacy derived from the general will did not do him much good. When it came to drafting a constitution, someone had to decide the extent of royal authority. If, as had been generally assumed when the Estates General was elected, its function was merely advisory, the king was free to resume as much of his former authority as he chose. This was obvious political nonsense and almost all the deputies agreed that he had no right to veto the constitution itself. This meant that it was for the legislature to define the powers of the executive. Whatever the deputies thought about Louis XVI, they were outspoken in their dislike of his ministers. Since his orders had, under the new dispensation, to be signed by a minister, anything he did could be, and much of it was, opposed. To preserve the achievements of the revolution, the Assembly therefore continually encroached on what should theoretically have been the territory of the executive, both in terms of the constitution and of day-to-day administration. Some went a good deal further than that. Mirabeau, while he was still in his radical phase, argued that the Assembly, as representative of the sovereign people, could overrule the king. On 2 November he argued that, as a constituent body, it possessed the same powers as the men who had provided French society with its first political institutions. By the spring of 1790 he was saying the exact opposite, but his old tunes had been taken up by others. The Protestant pastor, Rabaut Saint-Etienne, claimed as early as 4 September that the king, unlike the Assembly, was not a representative of the nation, but merely its mandatory. For a Rousseauist, this was true of all representatives, but Rabaut claimed that the nation had delegated is own authority to the Assembly. He would have been embarrassed to explain when and how. Robespierre, supported by Barnave and Pétion, claimed on 5 October that the executive (it was more polite to put it that way than to name the king) was no more than an emanation of the constituent power.

It was natural that the Assembly, in its constitutional debates, should tip the scales every time against the executive. More interesting, as regards the future, was its view of its own nature and of its relationship to those who had elected it. Garat, the future Minister of Justice after the overthrow of the monarchy, maintained that the Assembly, as representative of the nation, had the same powers as the people itself in a direct democracy (21 May 1790). This meant that, in the name of the general will, the Assembly need take no heed of precedent or prescription. On 2 November Mirabeau told his colleagues, 'There is no legislative action that a nation cannot repeal; if it wants, it can change its laws, its constitution, its organization and its machinery . . . whatever is merely a consequence of the general will must cease to exist as soon as that will changes'. That was one of the problems of trying to apply Rousseau's theories to practical politics: the general will was liable to turn into a will o' the wisp—but it is perhaps worth remembering that the absolute sovereignty of the British Parliament presents the same difficulties. Pétion applied the principle to a specific issue when he claimed on 21 January 1790 that the people's will took precedence over existing international treaties. Rewbell, the future director, maintained that 'The only allies we recognize are just peoples; we recognize no family compacts or ministerial wars' (15 May 1790). Conservatives were not slow to point out that a foreign policy that reposed entirely on what a fluctuating majority in the Assembly believed to constitute the general will, was unlikely to commend France to her former allies.

Where its successors were concerned, the Assembly had no inhibitions about distiguishing between the general will and the legislative body. Its own constituent status gave it special powers: by 1790 some of the deputies, in cheerful disregard of its actual origins, were claiming that it was a convention. This entitled it to do more or less what it liked in relation to the king, the constitution and even the people who had elected it. The king was given a suspensive veto over the decisions of *future* assemblies; the enactments of the Constituent Assembly itself were 'constitutional'. It need therefore pay no more than prudential attention to any signs of opposition amongst the public. When the royalist, d'Esprémesnil, accused his colleagues of suppressing petitions from towns that did not like what the Assembly was doing, on 8 June 1790, he missed the point. As Alexandre de Lameth explained a week or so later, those who opposed the decisions of the Assembly, since they were *ipso facto* setting their sectional interests against that of the public, did not count as citizens. He did not actually say that they would have to be forced to be free, but that was what he meant. On 28 October Mirabeau had spoken of the need to fit men to the laws that they should obey, by revolutionary fêtes and similar psychological conditioning, which implied the indoctrination of the majority by those who knew what was best for them. This was to anticipate Robespierre and Saint-Just. Duquesnoy explained on 17 June 1790 that the demands of the public should always be discussed, even though one might have to reject them for the good of the people themselves, and Charles Lameth hinted that the people should be grateful for all that the Assembly had done for it. That was to become familiar too. In 1790 these were no more than straws in the wind. Such principles were not invoked in support of totalitarian measures. They are important only as an indication that totalitarian attitudes, which were perhaps implicit, not so much in what Rousseau had actually said, but in the practical application of his theories, were already in some men's minds.

The Right fought a rearguard action, rather badly handicapped by the fact that it shared some of the Rousseauist assumptions of its opponents. Montlosier pointed out, on 17 May 1790, that the king was the *commis*, not of the Assembly but of the nation. If the Assembly personified the general will, that was neither here nor there. The only radical opposition came from a different quarter, when the deputies set about the reorganization of the Church, towards the end of May 1790. Those of the clergy who remembered their canon law could only accept popular sovereignty in matters temporal. A curé answered the demand for total obedience by the Assembly, on 31 May, with the equally uncompromising claim that the powers of the Church were divine in essence, inalienable and imprescriptible. One imperative was answered by another. Behind Rousseau's theories lay the belief that men were born good as well as free and that their corruption by society was not irremediable. Committed to a belief in original sin, this was something the clergy could not accept, although they need not have been quite so insistent on the particular corruption of the eighteenth century. Faced with this challenge, the Rousseauists could only reply with an aggressive assertion of the sovereignty of the general will, in morals and belief, as well as in politics. Treilhard, on 30 May, said that 'When the sovereign believes a reform to be necessary, nothing can oppose it'. On the following day Robespierre maintained that 'ecclesiastical officials' were established for the good of society. Le Chapelier supported him when he argued, ten days later, that to object to the election of bishops on the ground that the voters could not be relied on to choose the best men, was to challenge the entire elective process. That was logical enough, although Robespierre was to modify his views about the wisdom of the electorate when he himself was

in office. Camus who, until 1789, had represented the clergy
in the Paris Parlement, claimed that the Assembly, as a
convention, could prescribe a different religion if it chose.
Presumably the clergy were expected to be grateful that it did
not. The archbishop of Aix tried in vain to distinguish
between the temporal and the spiritual. This had little effect
on a secular-minded and anti-clerical audience which knew
that the general will encompassed both. The bishops were
even deserted by a fair number of the parish clergy who
avenged themselves for the slights of the past. The
comparatively easy victory of the anti-clericals in the
Assembly did nothing to suggest that things were going to be
very different in parts of the countryside, where *voltantés
particulières* were to become bloodily apparent in the coming
years.

When the constitution was finally completed in the summer
of 1791 it bore a superficial resemblance to the Montesquieu
model of a parliamentary monarchy, with power divided
between executive and legislature, and an independent
judiciary. By this time, some of the former radicals were
looking for a compromise with the king and, in different
circumstances, the constitution might have provided it. In fact
it established a republic with a king. A unicameral legislature
had been allowed to encroach on the sphere of the excutive,
but skilful manoeuvring by a more clever man than Louis
XVI, during a long period of peace and stability, might have
done something to alter that. More important was the fact
that the monarchy was isolated within a system where every
post that conferred any kind of authority was elective.
Popular sovereignty ruled everywhere outside the Tuileries.
Given the prevailing opinion, any attempt by the king to
assert such powers as he retained was bound to be seen as the
attempt by one individual to thwart the general will. There
were good political reasons for this. The king had not
accepted the revolution and if the Assembly had had more
confidence in him it would have allowed him more scope. To
some extent, all the tortuous theorizing gave an air of
respectability to hard political calculation—but only to some
extent. The deputies would not have gone so far, notably in
their treatment of religion, which had not got much to do with

royal power, if they had not been the devotees of a theory that made them the omnipotent creators of a new moral order. As Robespierre said on 15 May 1790, 'It is from France that must emanate the freedom and happiness of the world'. People who thought in those terms were unlikely to be content for long with the compromise of 1791. The sequel was not inevitable, but it was implicit in what had gone before.

When the first—and last—legislative assembly met in September 1791 it accepted its position as a constituted rather than a constituent body, but those of its members who hoped for a genuine partnership with the king were challenged by a noisy minority, impatient of any compromise and intent on the enforcement of the uniformity that Rousseauist doctrines implied. Their immediate targets were the *émigrés*, now in substantial numbers, and those of the clergy who rejected the religious settlement. The favourite language now was less about regeneration than the cutting off of gangrened limbs, that is, the exclusion of dissidents from the body politic. When the king vetoed the punitive legislation voted by the Assembly, which was, of course, within his constitutional right, this was denounced as an act of hostility towards the revolution. Brissot then decided that the only way to end the deadlock between legislature and executive was to start what he intended to be a limited war. This was designed to force the king to capitulate to the Assembly or to expose him as the ally of France's enemies, in which case he would presumably be deposed. Brissot's calculations proved correct, but when the crisis that he had engineered came to a head and August 1792 found a Prussian army preparing to invade France and liberate the royal family, Brissot and his friends lost their nerve. The king hoped for a French defeat, the majority in the Assembly was not prepared to save the revolution by violating the constition and the crisis was resolved by a popular insurrection in Paris. The Tuileries were stormed and the king, in effect, overthrown. The Assembly, almost as discredited as the monarchy, voted its own replacement, as soon as possible, by a new constituent body; this time it was actually to be called a convention. When the new assembly met in September, one of its first actions was to declare France a republic.[2].

For Rousseauists, the significance of the August insurrection was obvious: faced by a situation in which both executive and legislature were flouting the general will, the people of Paris—the only section of the sovereign in a position to apply pressure to both—had resumed the powers it had delegated and disposed of an illegitimate government. The elections to the Convention were the endorsement of its action by the nation as a whole. What had happened made good political sense, but it raised the interesting ideological question of whether or not Paris was entitled to do it again. For the Girondins, who initially enjoyed a majority in the Convention, it was not; the Convention, like the Constituent Assembly, as its name implied, was a sovereign body and the incarnation of the general will. For their Montagnard opponents, sovereignty continued to reside in the 'people' who retained their right to 'save' the assembly once again, as they had done in July 1789 and August 1792. Both sides agreed that monarchists of every complexion had excluded themselves from the national community, which consisted of republicans only—Brissot even argued, on 6 December 1792, that the electorate was not entitled to discuss the restoration of the monarchy. Once again, this was politically inevitable, since the victors could not be expected to allow the defeated to recover at the hustings what they had lost by force of arms, but it constituted one more step in the process by which the general will was divorced from what Frenchmen actually wanted. By implication, it also legitimized future purges.

The republic was much more than a form of government that dispensed with a king. For Montesquieu, who had eventually rejected it as both unattainable and illiberal, it was a regime that depended for its functioning on the *vertu* of the citizens, in other words, on the population as a whole putting the collective good above the satisfaction of personal interests and ambitions. This was also Rousseau's view. In the first issue of the newspaper, *Lettres à Ses Commettans*, that Robespierre started in October 1792, he told his readers that the fact that France was now a republic meant that it was qualitatively superior to all existing states, but that its survival depended on the *vertu* of the citizenry. The problem was that 'To draft our political institutions we should need the *moeurs* that the institutions themselves must eventually produce'. For the time being, since he was in opposition, he could convince himself that *vertu* came naturally to ordinary working people; if only the ambitious and self-seeking could be excluded from power, a democratic republic would therefore be self-sustaining and coercion need only be applied to the minority of monarchists who had excluded themselves from the *polis*.

Girondins and Montagnards, despite differences of opinion within each of these loose groups, originally shared the same ideas on all the main political issues.[3] If they became bitter enemies within the Convention, this was because of personal and political rivalry. What was really at issue was the claim of each to be the custodian of the general will. Despite their agreement on policy—except as regards the fate of the king—each was therefore bound to regard the other as illegitimate and a source of moral corruption that had to be eliminated if the democratic republic were to survive and prosper. Once again, politics and ideology were mutually reinforcing. The feud between the two prevented the government from waging the war effectively and by the spring of 1793 the revolution was once more threatened with destruction by the allied armies. Eventually the issue was resolved, as it had been in July 1789 and August 1792, by a third recourse to Parisian insurrection. On 2 June 1793 the Convention was surrounded by National Guards and the deputies intimidated into arresting the leading Girondins. This time there was no appeal to endorsement by a national electorate. Although the attempts to organize armed revolt in the provinces fizzled out, there cannot be much doubt about the unpopularity of the Montagnards. Those who now claimed to embody the general will had lost the support of much, if not most, of the actual population. This tended to make them more sceptical of the electoral process.

The summer of 1793 saw a decisive change in the political situation. The Committee of Public Safety emerged as the first effective government since 1789, capable of both winning the war and imposing its authority in Paris. There was not going to be any fourth revolution. Inevitably, the prosecution of what might reasonably be described as total war, with its mobilization of men and resources, control of wages and prices, requisitioning of war materials and ruthless repression of defeatism and dissent, created many enemies. For the more dogmatically Rousseauist members of the Committee, Robespierre and Saint-Just, this produced a worrying paradox. Conscious of their own disinterestedness, they were totally convinced that France had at last a government dedicated to the implementation of the general will. This should have ensured it the enthusiastic support of the greaty body of citizens, uncorrupted by wealth, personal ambition and the false conventions of an artificial society. When this failed to happen and the two men realized that the revolution was, as Saint-Just put it, 'frozen', they came, in the autumn of 1793, to see that they had underestimated their problem. The corruption of *ancien régime* society had penetrated the entire population. To quote Saint-Just again, on 26 February 1794, 'A revolution has taken place within the government; it has not yet penetrated civil society'. If a democratic republic could only be based on the *vertu* of the people, the people would have to be made *vertueux*. This was perhaps not very surprising: even the paragons of ancient Greece had had to be moulded into shape by Solon and Lycurgus and as far back as April 1793, paraphrasing Rousseau, Saint-Just had told the Convention, 'It is for him [the legislator] to make men what he wants them to be'.

This implied social conditioning that would not bear a full harvest for at least a generation, during which time those who were being somewhat vigorously regenerated might not appreciate the experience. Robespierre advocated compulsory education for all children in state boarding schools where they would be preserved from the corrupting influence of their parents and submitted to a discipline that was Spartan in every sense of the word. By the spring of 1794 both men were becoming increasingly desperate as they seemed to be making no progress towards their goal. Political faction was increasing in the Convention, munition workers were striking for higher wages; nothing, in fact, seemed to have changed very much apart from the repressive powers available to the government. Robespierre turned to the kind of state religion that Rousseau had advocated in the penultimate chapter of his *Social Contract* and Saint-Just became increasingly obsessed with the need for what he called 'republican institutions' which involved, amongst many other acts of state interference of a more or less Utopian nature, keeping children away from their parents from the ages of five to twenty-one.

Social engineering on this scale would obviously involve a fair amount of coercion, of the selfish and indifferent, as well as the politically hostile. In a fascinating speech on 5 February 1794 Robespierre, always intellectually honest after his own fashion, wrestled with the theoretical implications of the problem. 'It has been said that terror was the activating principle of despotic government.' It had indeed, and most of his audience must have been well aware that it was Montesquieu who had said so. Robespierre accepted this where 'constitutional' government was concerned. 'Revolutionary' government, however, was something different, since it involved the destruction of those who were barring the way to the Promised Land. It was, in fact, the 'despotism of liberty against tyranny', which was not a bad anticipation of the democratic dictatorship of the proletariat. Robespierre then went on to salute the vigour of the revolutionary people 'which takes on the vigour of youth as it escapes, so to speak, from the arms of death'. Only the experts were likely to recognize that: the only passage in the *Social Contract* where Rousseau had admitted the possibility of regeneration for an old and corrupt society. Understandably, Robespierre left out the first part of the sentence, where Rousseau had said that this could only be a product of civil war. Destroying counter-revolutionaries and political opponents might be a messy business, but it was likely to be short. Regenerating an entire people meant that the terror would have to last for a very long time. Whereas Robespierre, in his speech, had lost himself in contemplation of the moral perfection of the new order, Saint-Just, three weeks later, was both more laconic and more ruthless, as became a neo-Spartan. 'We want to establish an order of things such that a universal tendency towards the good is established and the factions find themselves suddenly hurled on to the scaffold.'

It was the logical end of the road. The general will, which

had originally been supposed to reside in the people as a whole, had been progressively restricted to the republicans, the Convention, the Montagnards, the Committee of Public Safety and eventually a minority within the Committee itself. A Manichean conception of politics which meant, as Robespierre said, that 'what is immoral is bad politics and what corrupts is counter-revolutionary', excluded any possibility of compromise with political sin and implied the destruction of all the unrighteous if the virtuous were ever to inherit the earth. Of course, revolutions are violent things that occur when consensus has broken down and the victors in a revolution are likely to do all they can to ensure that their defeated opponents do not get a second chance. The French revolutionaries had to contend with both foreign invasion and civil war. If none of them had ever heard of Rousseau, there would still have been a revolution and it would have been a bloody business, but it would have been different. Ideology played its part in suggesting extreme solutions, in making compromise more difficult and in emboldening men to pursue fearful goals with easy consciences. For a long time politics and ideology had pointed in similar directions. By the spring of 1794 the political objectives had been largely achieved: the revolutionary armies had gone over to the offensive on all fronts, the civil war was under control and the Committee of Public Safety dominated the Convention. Politically speaking, the time had come for a relaxation of the dictatorship and a gradual return to more normal government. It was precisely then that the Terror was enormously intensified. This was not entirely the responsibilty of Robespierre, Saint-Just and Couthon, indeed there are some ground for thinking that Robespierre and Couthon at least were considering a return to moderation. They were, however, the prisoners of an ideology that had made them responsible for the regeneration of everyone else. This had been implicit from the early days. Circumstances had allowed it to bear frightful fruit and circumstances were to destroy it. When Robespierre split the Committee of Public Safety he enabled the frightened Convention to recover its hold over the government. That was the end of Robespierre and, for the time being at least, of his ideology. There is a profound sense in which historians who chose to end their accounts of the revolution with the 9th of *thermidor* knew what they were doing.

The French revolution, therefore, provides an introduction to any study of terrorism and its justification. On the whole, the revolutionaries denied the legitimacy of individual acts of terrorism. When one or two of them flirted with the justification of tyrannicide, they relied on old and familiar arguments. What was to be of more lasting significance was that when they proclaimed, for the first time in modern European history, the right of all men to self-government, they welded on to their conception of the Rights of Man the belief that the elect (whether in a majority or not) were not merely entitled, but morally obliged, to repress dissent, in the name of a transcendental general interest of which they were the custodians. Although the logical premises of this were already apparent in the early years of the revolution—for example, on 7 december 1790 when Alexander Lameth proclaimed that opposition to the general will was disastrous, sacriligious and had to be silenced—such attitudes could at first be confused with the 'legitimate' repression by the majority of a defiant minority that was prepared to resort to force. In practice, although the Constituent Assembly tolerated a good deal of disorder and intimidation, it did not invoke the principle of terror. That came later, when war and invasion had generated a national crisis and the beleaguered Montagnards were fighting for survival against domestic and foreign enemies. On 30 August 1793 the Jacobins were urged to make Terror the order of the day. In his speech of 5 February 1794 Robespierre defined revolutionary government as resting on the twin bases of *vertu* and Terror.

The word 'terror' was therefore given *droit de cité* by the French revolutionaries, but Terror was not the same thing as terrorism. It implied something more akin to a political version of martial law, administered by the government, in accordance with rules that placed the supposed interests of society above those of the individual. If, in practice, this often provided a pretext for lawless violence, there was nothing particularly new about that. What *was* original, and was to live on as part of the burgeoning myth of the French revolution, long after the demise of the 'reign of terror', was the idea that it was legitimate to resort to methods of this kind to regenerate a society that was not fully aware of what was good for it. In a moral Armageddon, those who understood the issues and fought on the right side were entitled to resort to methods that were illegitimate when used by their opponents. The attainment of the messianic end must not be jeopardized by the constraint of constitutional means. Up to a point, hard-pressed politicians had no doubt always used some of the methods of the revolutionaries, if not on the same national scale. What was to matter for the future was the revolutionaries' sense of commitment to a new moral order and their legitimation, in order to achieve it, of means that were abominable when employed by anyone else.

NOTES

1. Debate of 6 May 1790. Unless otherwise indicated, all references are to reports of debates in the *Moniteur*.
2. I have discussed at some length, in *Will and Circumstance: Montesquieu Rousseau and the French Revolution* (Duckworth, 1983) the implications of the events of August 1792 and the subsequent Terror. What follows is, in the main, a summary of that argument.
3. *See* the appendix to *Will and Circumstance* for a comparison of the opinions of Brissot and Robespierre.

4 The Origins, Structure and Functions of Nazi Terror
Jeremy Noakes

The use of terror was an integral aspect of Nazism from its very beginnings. However, the functions terror performed, the forms that it took, and the personnel who employed it underwent significant change over time. Nazi terror took two main forms. The first predominated until 1933–4 and was mainly associated with the paramilitary sections of the Nazi movement, the SA and its then junior partner the SS. It involved physical violence and intimidation exercised on the Party's political and ideological opponents which, though condoned by the leadership, were largely practised by local organizations and rank and file members on their own initiative and in an *ad hoc* fashion. From 1933–4 onwards, however, terror was practised more systematically and placed on an official footing. This occurred in the context of emergency legislation which freed the authorities from legal restraints. It was also facilitated by the take-over of the political police departments of the various German states by the SS and their consolidation into one political police network for the whole of Germany—the Secret State Police (*Geheime Staatspolizei*) or Gestapo. This new form of terror, whose main weapon was internment in a concentration camp, operated through an elaborate bureaucracy and according to official rules and regulations which, though sometimes ignored in practice, provided a degree of system and control. This new emphasis on functional rationality and quasi-legality associated with the Gestapo terror not only improved efficiency but also facilitated the acceptance of terror by other parts of the bureaucratic apparatus and its tolerance by the population. The turning-point for the transition from the one form of terror to the other came during 1934 and was particularly connected with the destruction of the SA as a power centre, the result of a purge which began with the notorious 'Night of the Long Knives' of 30 June 1934. Nevertheless, the change did not come overnight. The emphasis had already begun to shift from informal to formal terror during 1933. However, informal and arbitrary terror carried out by sections of the Nazi movement continued until the pogrom of 8 November 1938—the *Reichskristallnacht*.

Although the two forms of Nazi terror were in many ways distinct from one another, their respective practitioners came to share to some extent a common mentality. Even under the Weimar Republic the traditional bureaucratic outlook of the police with its stress on the defence of the established order through the upholding of the law, the observance of official regulations, and the avoidance of involvement in party politics had been undermined by the intense politicization characteristic of those years. This was particularly true of the younger generation of police officers. Now, with the take-over of the police by the SS in the years after 1934 and the influx of SS men and of Nazi ideas and attitudes which followed, this process accelerated rapidly and took an extreme form. Thus, while the emphasis on hierarchy remained, the corresponding concern to operate within a framework of law and rules and to adopt a non-partisan approach was superseded by the demand for political commitment in the sense of a new and overriding priority of destroying those who were regarded as hostile to the new 'national community' (*Volksgemeinschaft*) through the ruthless exercise of unrestrained power. This new mentality regarded individual human rights and due process of law with contempt. Politics were seen in quasi-military terms involving a complete polarization between friends and enemies, who were considered to be at war with one another. In this political perspective there was no room for bargaining, compromise, or the coexistence of a plurality of political ideologies or parties. Political and ideological opponents were considered to have forfeited the right to be considered as fellow citizens and were regarded as enemies against whom the use of physical violence or even annihilation was entirely legitimate.

In part this new mentality represented a radical extension

of the glorification of state power and the contempt for individual rights characteristic of the dominant German constitituional tradition. However, it departed in crucial respects from this tradition—above all in its rejection of the state as the embodiment of the true interests of the nation in favour of the *Volk* as represented by the Nazi movement and above all its leader. The origins of this mentality lie in the *völkisch* movement of the radical Right of pre-1914 Germany of which the pan-German League was the most influential expression. It was, however, the First World War and its chaotic aftermath which provided the favourable climate in which this mentality could flourish.

The Nazi movement was born and passed the first and formative years of its existence in a climate saturated with political violence and terror. Four years of a war of unprecedented ferocity and destruction had accustomed those involved to carnage on an enormous scale, dulling sensibilities and blunting inhibitions about the moral acceptability of violence. Defeat had nullified all the sacrifice of life and effort, and this provoked bitterness and a hunt for scapegoats, particularly since defeat had come as a complete surprise to the German people. Scapegoats were not hard to find, for the humiliation of national defeat had been accompanied by the revolution of November 1918 and broad sections of the upper and middle classes found the temptation to explain the one in terms of the other irresistible. However, the legend of the 'stab in the back' by subversive 'Jewish–Bolshevik agitators' not only provided a convenient alibi for the bankruptcy of the previous regime; it also enabled the upper and middle classes to cloak their unwillingness to come to terms with the new democratic order with the mantle of patriotism. In the eyes of these groups the 'November criminals' had merely confirmed their treason with the acceptance of the humiliating peace settlement of Versailles.

Thus the new Weimar Republic failed to establish its legitimacy.[1] Founded in the wake of defeat and revolution by those political forces—the Social Democrats, the Catholic Centre Party, and the Left liberals—whom Bismarck had already dubbed 'enemies of the Reich' and who were responsible for accepting Versailles, it acquired few active supporters and many enemies. Members of the lower middle class felt isolated and vulnerable since they were now deprived of the status and economic protection they had enjoyed under the empire. Fragmented into numerous parties and pressure groups, they found themselves at a relative disadvantage *vis-à-vis* their political and economic rivals, the organized working class. Even more serious was the fact that partially displaced élites resented the reduction in their power through the introduction of parliamentary government. For many within the army, the civil service, the legal profession, business, and the universities the new democratic republic was merely a temporary aberration. During its first phase of 1919–23, a period marked by hyper-inflation, foreign incursion and latent civil war, these groups evolved a distinction between the existing regime, to which their loyalty was a matter of temporary necessity or convenience, and their concept of the German state, of which the army and the civil service in particular saw themselves as the true embodiment and to which their loyalty was absolute. In their eyes the Weimar Republic with its pluralist parliamentary democracy governed by divisive political parties undermined the state whose role was to stand above a fragmented society and represent its true interests.

The failure of the new regime to establish its legitimacy in the eyes of substantial and influential sections of the population not only undermined respect for law and order, it also contributed to its inability to establish a complete monopoly of the use of force, a weakness which was crucial to the spread of political violence and terror during the early years. After the demobilization of the armed forces at the end of the war a power vacuum had emerged. The new government failed to create an effective force loyal to the new order. Instead armed 'self-defence' organizations sprang up all over Germany composed of middle class citizens determined to defend their property against Bolshevism.[2] These so-called 'civil guards' totalled over one million members. Moreover, the government itself, fearful of Communist subversion, cooperated with the old military authorities to organize volunteer forces of so-called 'Free Corps' whose membership fluctuated between 200,000 and

400,000 men. They were modelled on the élite commando units or 'storm troops' which had emerged during the war. These had been small, self-sufficient, well-armed and highly mobile units designed to storm the enemy defences and so create a breakthrough for the regular infantry. They were characterized by a particularly close relationship between officers and men. Their officers, who formed a high ratio to the enlisted men, were required to be under twenty-five years of age, unmarried, extremely fit, and above all utterly ruthless. In 1919 these and other young officers who found it more than usually difficult to settle down to peaceful civilian existence during the turbulent post-war period now found in the Free Corps much more important commands and freedom of action than in the army. They recruited their membership mainly from middle and lower middle class young men, many of whom had played little or no part in the war itself and had felt cheated of action. The functions of the Free Corps were twofold: first, to crush left-wing uprisings against the new Reich and state governments and, secondly, to defend Germany's borders against the threat of foreign, particularly Polish, incursions.

The mentality of these Free Corps fighters is well expressed in the following quotation from one of the most notorious leaders, Gerhard Rossbach, who became closely involved with the Nazi movement during its early years:

It was the beautiful old Freebooter class of war and post-war times . . . organizing masses and losing them just as quickly, tossed this way and that just for the sake of our daily bread; gathering men about us and playing soldiers with them; brawling and drinking, roaring and smashing windows—destroying and shattering what needs to be destroyed. Ruthless and inexorably hard. The abcess on the sick body of the nation must be cut open and squeezed until the clear red blood flows. And it must be left to flow for a good long time till the body is purified.[3]

One of the main areas of activity of the Free Corps was in the Baltic states where they fought against the Bolsheviks during 1919 with the hope of gaining land for German settlement. It was a campaign of exceptional brutality described by one of the participants, Ernst von Salomon, who was eighteen years old at the time:

We were cut off from the world of middle class norms . . . The bonds were broken and we were free. The blood surging through our veins was full of a wild demand for revenge and adventure and danger . . . We were a band of fighters drunk with all the passions of the world; full of lust, exultant in action. What we wanted, we did not know. And what we knew we did not want! War and adventure, excitement and destruction. An indefinable, surging force welled up from every part of our being and flayed us onward . . . We roared our songs into the air and threw hand grenades after them . . . We saw red. We no longer had anything of human decency left in our hearts. The land where we had lived groaned with destruction. Where once peaceful villages stood, was now only soot, ashes and burning embers after we had passed. We kindled a funeral pyre and more than dead material burned there—there burned our hopes, our longings; there burned everything . . . And so we came back swaggering, drunken, laden with plunder.[4]

Even after the official dissolution of the Free Corps during 1920 they continued to poison the political atmosphere of the Republic. Many of them went underground, adopting various disguises, notably that of labour camps on the estates of Conservative landowners in eastern Germany where they helped to intimidate agricultural workers who might have participated in political and trade union activity. The most significant development, however, was the creation of a secret terror organization, the Organization Consul or OC, by Captain Ehrhardt, who had led the Free Corps mutiny in the abortive Kapp putsch.[5] On the basis of his experience during that affair Ehrhardt decided that the most effective method of bringing down the Republic would be to assassinate prominent Republican politicians with the aim of provoking a left-wing uprising such as had followed the Kapp putsch, which would then provide the pretext for a right-wing coup.

The OC, though relatively small (never more than 5,000), recruited many of the most ruthless Free Corps members. Its campaign of terror during 1921–2 included the assassination on 26 August 1921 of the leading Catholic politician, Matthias Erzberger, a signatory of the Treaty of Versailles, an attempt to blind the leading Social Democrat, Philipp Scheidemann, with prussic acid on 4 June 1922, and the murder of the Foreign Minister, Walther Rathenau, a Jew, on 24 June 1922. However, the activities of the OC and the assassination of prominent Weimar politicians represented merely the most striking examples of the terror campaign waged by the extreme Right during these years. The Free Corps revived the mediaeval practice of the *Vehmgericht*—vigilante justice— which had originated during a period when there was no effective judicial system. Three hundred and fifty-four political murders were committed by the Right in the period 1919–June 1922[6]. Apart from a few prominent politicians, the main victims were those who had fallen foul of the Free Corps particularly by revealing the existence of arms caches to the Allied Control Commission and disclosing military activities to the government.

It would be difficult to overestimate the significance of the Free Corps in preparing the ground for Nazi terror. Many of the leaders of the Nazi stormtroopers (SA) and of the SS as well as other Nazi leaders had been one-time members, and the Free Corps leaders provided role models for many young Germans who were members of the flourishing youth movement during the 1920s and were to acquire influential positions in the terror apparatus of the Third Reich. It was in the Free Corps that many of the characteristic features of Nazi politics were first practised: the leadership principle, the military forms and style, the contempt for humane values and civic virtues, and the cult of violence and of struggle for its own sake. These values crystallized in the ideal cultivated by 'revolutionary conservative' theorists of the 1920s of the 'political soldier' for whom the traditional distinctions between military organization and civil society, war and peace had disappeared, an ideal to which SS members were trained to aspire.[7]

The significance of the activities of the Free Corps and other paramilitary formations during the years 1919–23 lay not only in the creation of a mentality and style which was crucial in shaping the outlook and behaviour of the future Nazi cadres. These years were also important in determining the response to terror on the part of substantial sections of the population and, in particular, of the élites. This response was ambivalent. For, despite the fact that the possession of arms and military activities were unlawful according to state law, the extreme Right regarded such law as illegitimate since it had been passed at the behest of the Allies. Obedience to such law, therefore, in their eyes represented treason, a view that was quite widely shared. Moreover, the authorities themselves also tended to turn a blind eye to the activities of the former Free Corps men because they regarded them as a potential source of military strength in the event of foreign incursion. This view was confirmed by the important role played by the Free Corps in resisting Polish attempts to seize parts of Silesia in 1921, attempts which the Reich Government was powerless to counter because the Allies would not tolerate intervention by the *Reichswehr*. Finally, after the French and Belgian invasion of the Ruhr in 1923 the former Free Corps were actually taken under the wing of the *Reichswehr* and given access to weapons and training, forming the so-called 'Black *Reichswehr*'.

In short, the fact that the Allies were enforcing military restrictions on Germany, combined with the threat of foreign incursion on the one hand and internal Communist subversion on the other, prompted the authorities to adopt an ambivalent attitude towards the activities of the paramilitary formations throughout the period 1919–23. Indeed, in the view of many members of the upper and middle classes, even their subversive and terroristic activities at home were patriotic since they were directed against an illegitimate state and in defence of the established socio-economic order. This ambivalence in the attitude of the authorities towards the Free Corps was reflected in the behaviour of the courts. Members of paramilitary formations of the Right who were convicted of terrorist offences were invariably treated much more leniently than those on the Left. Of the 354 murders committed by the Right only the defendants in the Rathenau case received heavy sentences and were later amnestied; the remainder received brief prison terms or were fined a few inflated marks.[8] Thus a climate developed in which political violence and terror was condoned or even glorified by many 'respectable' citizens.

This situation was most extreme in the state of Bavaria, which was the centre of right-wing paramilitary activity and terror in Germany during the years 1919–23. In the years 1920–23 Bavaria became the haven for ex-Free Corps men and the headquarters of the terror organization, OC, whose leader, Captain Ehrhardt, had actually been invited to Bavaria by the chief of the Bavarian police, Pöhner. Pöhner channelled police funds to the OC and provided false passports to terrorists on the run. Above all, of course, Bavaria provided the context within which the Nazi movement developed during its first and formative phase of 1919–23, a context characterized by an extensive paramilitary subculture and the brutalization of politics. The Party soon developed its own strong-arm squad to defend its own meetings from left-wing harassment and to break up those of its political rivals.[9] By the autumn of 1921 it had acquired the appropriate title of 'Storm Detachment' (*Sturmabteilung*) or SA. During 1923, however, the SA increasingly diverged from this subordinate role, becoming instead a semi-autonomous paramilitary formation, part of the 'Black *Reichswehr*' organized by the army leadership out of the ex-Free Corps units as a military reserve with which to resist possible foreign incursion. This development culminated in the abortive Munich Beer Hall putsch of 8–9 November 1923 through which Hitler tried to use the SA to launch a 'March on Berlin' along the lines of Mussolini's 'March on Rome' of the previous year, a miscalculation which led to the banning of the whole party and imprisonment for some of its leaders including Hitler.

After the refounding of the Nazi Party in February 1925, Hitler determined that the role of its paramilitary organizations, the SA and the SS, must be neither a military one such as they had adopted during 1923 nor that of a secret terror organization such as Ehrhardt's OC. They must return to their original role as propaganda and strong-arm squads 'conquering the streets' from the Left. Thus he concluded his first order to the new SA leader, the former Free Corps leader, Captain Franz von Pfeffer:

The training of the SA must be carried out not on a military basis, but in accordance with the needs of the Party . . . What we need is not a hundred or two hundred daring conspirators but a hundred thousand and hundreds of thousands more fanatical fighters for our *Weltanschauung*. We must not work in secret conventicles but in huge mass marches, and neither by dagger nor poison nor pistol can the path be cleared for the movement, but only by conquering the streets. We have to teach Marxism that national

Socialism is the future master of the streets, just as it will one day be master of the state.[10]

Even during the relatively peaceful years 1924–29 clashes between various paramilitary organizations, now linked more or less closely to political parties, helped to sustain and entrench violence as a significant feature of Weimar political culture so that when the Republic plunged once more into political and economic crisis between 1930 and 1933 political conflict increasingly found expression in violence and terror. During 1930, the Prussian state police intervened nearly 2,500 times to restore order at political meetings.[11] During the first seven weeks of the two-month campaign preceding the July 1932 Reichstag election campaign there were 461 political riots in Prussia resulting in 82 deaths and 400 serious injuries. With the SA and its junior partner, the SS, the Nazi movement was well equipped to encourage and exploit this trend and their casualty rate reflected the extent of the Party's involvement. Thus between 1924 and 1929 there were thirty Nazi deaths as a result of political violence, in 1930 seventeen, in 1931 forty-two, and in 1932 eighty-four.[12]

Nazi terror during the phase prior to the take-over of power culminated in a campaign of unprecedented violence in the late summer of 1932 concentrated mainly in the eastern provinces of Prussia.[13] It reflected the movement's frustration at its failure to achieve power after the July election and took the form of arson and other attacks on SDP publishing houses and trade union offices in which the rank and file went on the rampage or the local leadership acted without authority. However, the results of the November 1932 Reichstag election, which saw a significant fall in the Nazi vote, particularly in those areas most affected by Nazi terror, suggest that its escalation in the late summer and early autumn had been counterproductive, alienating some middle class voters. Nevertheless, violence and terror performed several positive functions for the Nazi movement during the years prior to its take-over of power. First, they had the effect of weakening its political opponents by hampering their propaganda activities and intimidating their supporters. Secondly, they helped to destabilize the political system by creating an atmosphere of disorder in the context of which the movement could project its promise of a return to order under a Nazi regime. On the whole, the Nazis were careful to confine their terrorist attacks to their political opponents, in particular the Left, and to avoid confrontations with the state. They also generally exercised restraint in their attacks, avoiding major assaults on property or the large-scale use of firearms. Where they went beyond those limits, as in East Prussia during August 1932, the state responded with tough action, unlike the Italian situation during 1921–2. Indeed, before 1933, the SA generally followed Hitler's instructions and represented a movement of organized hooliganism harnessed to a political party, whose main functions were propaganda and intimidation, rather than a clandestine organization bent on subversion through terror.

Recent research into the social background of the members of the SA suggests that there was a marked distinction between the leadership and the rank and file.[14] Most of the leaders belonged to the pre-war generation, whereas the rank and file had generally grown up in the post-war years. Most SA leaders had been involved in the war and/or the Free Corps and regarded the SA as a career, an alternative to the Army from which they had been excluded by the restrictions of Versailles. According to the analysis of one large sample, their background was overwhelmingly middle class and their level of education was considerably higher than that of the average of the population, though below that of the SS leadership.[15] Forty-four per cent were white collar workers, nearly four times the proportion among the population as a whole, and around 25 per cent were self-employed. However, their most striking social characteristic was their extreme social mobility either in terms of their own career or in inter-generational terms. Between 60 and 70 per cent of the white and blue collar workers were downwardly mobile, whereas the civil servants among them tended to be upwardly mobile. Both groups were, therefore, characterized by an ambivalent social position between the status groups and classes, inevitably a source of acute social anxiety and a situation in which the Nazi ideal of a 'national community', in which class and status divisions would be superseded by a sense of national comradeship, had a strong appeal.

The rank and file, on the other hand, were characterized above all by their extreme youth and their social heterogeneity. Although they contained a larger proportion of working class members than the Party as a whole, many of whom were unemployed, the working class was still under-represented in terms of its proportion of the population as a whole. Moreover, some of those defined as 'working class' appear to have been downwardly mobile members of the middle class with a very different mentality from that of typical blue collar workers. For most of these young men membership of the SA did not constitute engagement in an ideological crusade. Their ideology, such as it was, was primarily negative, fuelled by social resentment and taking the form of violent hostility towards stereotyped enemies, perceived as responsible for their plight. For some, membership of the SA provided a badge of identity, a means of self-assertion otherwise lacking in their lives. Their loyalty to the movement and its leader was in certain respects similar to that of English football supporters to their club. SA activity provided a means of proving one's manhood through conflict with outsiders.[16] For some, particularly in the big cities, it was virtually a new form of gang warfare for control of territory against rivals—the Reichsbanner (SPD) and the *Rote Frontkämpferbund* (Communist) who came from a similar social background.

The social composition and mentality of the SS were at this stage in some respects similar to those of the SA. However, since his appointment as *Reichsführer SS* in 1929 Himmler had endeavoured with some success to recruit members of the upper and middle classes, and in particular graduates, into the SS—law graduates were particularly prevalent—so that its leadership corps was becoming on average better educated and of a somewhat higher social status than that of the SA.[17]

With Hitler's appointment as Chancellor on 30 January 1933, and more specifically with the appointment of Frick and Göring to head the Reich and Prussian Ministries of the Interior respectively, Nazi terror entered a new phase. This phase was marked by a continuation of the informal and arbitrary terror of the pre-1933 period but within a new context which saw the introduction of various forms of legitimation for the exercise of terror by the Nazi movement and a corresponding shift towards a more formal, systematic, and bureaucratic form of terror.

Terror tactics employed by the SA and SS played a crucial role in the Nazi take-over of power during the first months of 1933.[18] During the spring of 1933 the two organizations renewed the attacks on trade union offices and on the party headquarters and publishing houses of their left-wing opponents which had erupted briefly in the eastern provinces of Prussia in the autumn of 1932. They rounded up party and trade union officials, subjecting them to severe beatings and confinement in *ad hoc* concentration camps established in derelict factories and warehouses. These attacks rapidly succeeded in destroying the political and economic organization of the working class and depriving it of any means of independent expression. At the same time, the SA and SS launched sporadic attacks both on bourgeois political opponents, particularly those who had adopted an overtly hostile stance towards the movement in the past, and on ideological enemies, notably the Jews. Finally, during the early months, the SA and SS played a crucial role in imposing Nazi domination at state and local government level, intimidating their political opponents into resigning their offices.

Much of this terror appears to have been unplanned and uncoordinated, depending on the initiative of local Party leaders and SA and SS units seizing the opportunity for revenge on political enemies or giving expression to socio-economic resentments and ambitions. Initially, however, it operated in the interests of the take-over and consolidation of power by the new regime and hence was condoned if not encouraged. By the Summer of 1933, however, the Nazi 'seizure of power' was largely complete and the new regime was firmly in control. In this situation the main functions of the SA—propaganda and intimidation—had become superfluous. The SA, by now swollen to over two million men, was obliged to seek a new role for itself. The Chief of the SA, Ernst Röhm, aimed to turn the SA into a mass army which would absorb the existing professional army, the

Reichswehr, and assume the dominant position in what would become a garrison state. However, this ambition brought him into direct conflict with the *Reichswehr* leadership. Moreover, in the mean time, members of the SA were expressing their frustration at their failure to secure significant benefits from the new regime in acts of hooliganism. These alienated public opinion in general and the traditional élites in particular, with whom the Nazis had formed a tenuous alliance, and threatened to jeopardize economic recovery on which the future of the regime depended. This situation provided the context for the 'Night of the Long Knives' on 30 June 1934 in which the top leadership was purged and the SA subsequently restricted to pre-military training and ceremonial parades.

The emasculation of the SA by no means put an end to terrorist actions on the part of the Nazi rank and file. With their left-wing opponents confined to concentration camps or intimidated into silence, and with the Nazi leadership now in alliance with former Conservative opponents, rank and file militants focused their discontent on the main ideological enemy—the Jews.[19] Acts of violence against the property and persons of Jews continued sporadically throughout Germany in the 1930s. They reached a peak in a great wave of anti-Semitism in the summer of 1935 and then culminated in the great pogrom on the night of 8–9 November 1938, the notorious *Reichskristallnacht*. Much of this violence appears to have been spontaneous, initiated by the bottom echelons of the Nazi organization without prompting or explicit authorization from above. On the other hand, there were clearly periods, such as the summer of 1935, and specific incidents, such as the *Reichskristallnacht*, when terror was expressly encouraged or—in the case of the pogrom of November 1938—initiated from above. Rank and file terror against the Jews in the 1930s appears to have been regarded as a useful safety valve for the disappointment and frustration of Nazi party activists, who had failed to secure anticipated benefits from the regime, and also as a means of maintaining pressure on the Jews at a time when political and economic constraints prevented a more comprehensive implementation of official anti-Semitic measures. At the same time, rank and file terror operated to some extent as an autonomous force, putting pressure on the state bureaucracy to implement official anti-Semitic measures in order to pre-empt this pressure from below and maintain control over the situation in a process of 'cumulative radicalization'. Despite this continuation of terror from below, however, the emasculation of the SA in 1934 marked a turning-point in a trend in which informal and arbitrary terror by the Nazi rank and file and lower echelons was increasingly replaced by official and systematic terror implemented from above by official organs of the state.

What then were the functions of official terror in Nazi Germany? Its major role was envisaged by Himmler as the defence of the regime against subversion. However, the nature of Nazism and of its goals ensured that this role was interpreted in an extraordinarily extensive fashion. For the Nazis saw themselves as representing the true interests of the German *Volk* in a life and death struggle for survival. In their view, to succeed in this struggle Germany would require a restoration of her unity and morale after decades of racial and moral corruption. This could only be done by creating a 'national community' (*Volksgemeinschaft*) governed by the rules of race, eugenics, and social efficiency. To be accepted as a 'national comrade' (*Volksgenosse*) one was required to be of the correct racial type (Aryan), to be genetically healthy, to be socially efficient (*leistungsfähig*), and to be ideologically reliable. If one was unsatisfactory in any of these respects then one was outside the national community and subject to the various penalties enforced by the agencies of terror responsible for protecting the national community against biological or ideological corruption. Thus, the objects of Nazi terror fell into three main categories: political offenders, social offenders, and racial offenders. Of the political offenders by far the most numerous were the Nazi Party's enemies on the Left and in particular the Communists. The suppression of the traditional representatives of the working class was crucial to the regime, first, as part of its implicit bargain with the existing élites and, secondly, because its economic policy was geared to a major shift in national resources from consumption to rearmament. The Gestapo was the stick to complement the carrot of full employment and 'Strength through Joy'. Other political offenders were disillusioned Conservatives, liberal intellectuals, and Churchmen. This category, 'politicals', wore red triangles on their concentration camp uniforms. Secondly, there were the social offenders—habitual criminals (green triangles), 'asocials' (black triangles), and homosexuals (pink triangles). And, finally, there were the racial enemies—the Jews (yellow triangles) and the gypsies.

The mechanisms of coercion came to be controlled by a section of the Nazi movement—the SS. The official system of Nazi terror consisted of three main components: a security police network which, though officially part of the state machine, was in effect controlled by the SS; a concentration camp system which, though financed by the state, was also controlled by the SS; and, finally, a legislative framework which ensured the security apparatus the maximum freedom of action while remaining nominally within the law.

The success of the SS in achieving dominance over the terror apparatus of the Third Reich owed much to the ambition and the political and bureaucratic skills of its leader, Heinrich Himmler.[20] Since his appointment as *Reichsführer SS* in 1929, Himmler had followed a plan of developing the SS as the élite order of National Socialism for which his models were the Jesuits and the Knights of the Teutonic Order. He saw the role of the SS as that of 'political soldiers', militant exponents of Nazi ideology owing absolute loyalty to the Führer. He regarded its key function as the defence of the new regime against ideological infection and internal subversion. For this purpose he envisaged the creation of a Reich security network under the control of the SS in place of the fragmented police forces of the various federal states. As early as 1931 he had established an intelligence section (IC) within the SS, to head which he appointed a young ex-naval officer who had been dishonourably discharged for breach of promise, Reinhard Heydrich.[21] An able and ruthless organizer, Heydrich built up this Security Service (*Sicherheitsdienst*) or SD by recruiting agents, often graduates, throughout Germany. Their role was to gather intelligence on political opponents and also to police the Nazi movement itself.

Following the Nazi take-over in Bavaria in March 1933, Himmler and his deputy, Heydrich, acquired control of the Bavarian political police. Over the next year, with the aid of Heydrich's SD apparatus, Himmler managed to secure his appointment as chief of the political police of all the German states with the crucial exception of that of Prussia. As Prussian Minister of the Interior, Göring had created out of the small political police department bequeathed by the Weimar Republic an enlarged Prussian Secret State Police (Gestapo) directly subordinate to himself. Initially he had resisted an SS take-over of his Gestapo. By April 1934, however, Göring had decided to ally himself with Himmler against two men whom he saw as his main rivals: Frick, who as Reich Minister of the Interior was trying to take over responsibility for Prussian affairs, including its police, and, above all the SA leader, Röhm, whose ambitions appeared to pose an even graver threat. Göring, therefore, handed over the Gestapo to Himmler, enabling him to coordinate all the political police departments in Germany. In June 1936, Hitler crowned Himmler's achievement by appointing him to the new office of Chief of the German Police and he in turn united the Gestapo and the Criminal Police to form a new 'Security Police' under Heydrich who now assumed the title of 'Chief of the Security Police and SD'.

The members of the Nazi terror apparatus were remarkably young.[22] Of the leaders of groups and minor departments exercising authority in this field and identified in the organizational plans of 1941 and 1943, nine were born before 1900, thirty-two between 1900 and 1910 and five even later. Also, apart from those promoted from subordinate positions, their level of education was high. Of 135 officials examined in one sample, forty-six had a degree in law, eight in literature, five in economics, four in theology, two in medicine, and one in agriculture. Among these sixty-six graduates, only ten had been born before 1900. Among the non-graduates in leading positions, twenty-three came from subordinate positions in the police or the administration. Twelve officials indicated other professions. Many of these had been forced to abandon their studies for financial reasons. Among these former subordinates were colleagues of Heydrich from the Bavarian political police, professional policemen like the new Gestapo chief, Heinrich Müller, who had had no previous connexion with the Nazi Party.They were now given the opportunity to carry out their police role freed from the restrictions previously imposed by the need to respect individual rights under the law. At the same time, SS men were also integrated into the police and police recruited into the SS with the result that the ethos of the terror apparatus became one of cool, rational, technocratic efficiency deployed in the service of irrational ideological dogma.

In addition to their take-over of the German police the SS also acquired control of their own independent prison system—the concentration camps.[23] A considerable number of concentration camps had been set up in the spring of 1933 by both the SA and the SS to house the thousands of political prisoners captured during the seizure of power. The ordinary prisons were overwhelmed and in any case the Nazi organizations preferred to 'look after' their own prisoners themselves. In July 1934, as a reward for its role in the purging of the SA, the SS was officially recognized as independent of the SA and was given responsibility for the SA concentration camps. The SS leadership seized the opportunity for a drastic rationalization of the camps, both reducing their numbers and introducing uniform procedures modelled on those developed by Theodor Eicke, commandant of the SS concentration camp at Dachau outside Munich. Under Eicke as Inspector, the concentration camps formed a separate section of the SS. Thus, while the Gestapo was responsible for the consignment of prisoners to the concentration camps and for ordering their release, it had no control over the camps themselves. And, although the camps were financed by the state, no state agency had any influence over them.

Prisoners arrested by the Gestapo and confined to concentration camps could legitimately be held indefinitely and had no right of appeal, except to the Gestapo itself. This situation, which formed the third major component of the official Nazi system of terror, derived above all from the so-called Reichstag Fire Decree issued on 28 February 1933, the day after the Reichstag Fire, which was blamed on the Communists. This emergency Decree for the Protection of People and State suspended the basic rights of the individual enshrined in the Weimar Constitution.[24] Although in practice many political offences were tried under Nazi laws specifically designed for them and the offenders sentenced to terms of imprisonment in state prisons, under this decree the Gestapo was always able either to avoid the courts altogether or to rearrest offenders after the completion of their sentences and consign them to concentration camps.

Between 1934 and 1939 the need to employ terror was limited by the significant degree of consent in Nazi Germany and by the fact that where dissent existed both on the part of individuals and social groups it was normally only partial rather than total. In this situation only a limited use of terror or even simply public awareness of its potential proved sufficient to prevent the organization of fragmented and isolated sources of dissent to form a serious threat which might then have required more drastic action. However, with the outbreak of war consent was progressively eroded and the use of terror correspondingly increased with, for example, a marked and accelerating rise in the number of death sentences and in those consigned to concentration camps.

Finally, the fact that the Nazis increasingly saw society in terms of a rigid dichotomy between those who were loyal members of the 'national community' and those who were either outside it *per se* on the grounds of racial origin or hereditary defect or placed themselves outside it either through overt resistance or through their failure to conform to its (often unclear) norms and values, ensured a growing politicization of life in the Third Reich, through which all offenders tended to be increasingly regarded as 'enemies of the people'. In particular, criminal matters, especially during the war, came in greater degree to be considered as quasi-political offences since they were seen as directed against the 'national community' in its struggle for survival. Moreover, as it became increasingly evident that the Nazis' utopian vision of an ideological and racially homogeneous 'national community' bore little relation to reality, so the bureaucratic ambitions of the terror apparatus to expand its sphere of

competence were reinforced by an increasingly paranoid
search for subversive elements and 'community aliens'
(*Gemeinschaftsfremde*), a definition which was continually
expanding to include almost any sign of non-conformity.[25]
The assumption was that if the regime could 'eradicate'
(*ausmerzen*) these negative forces, then the 'national
community' would come into its own and Germany finally
triumph.

NOTES

1. The literature on the Weimar Republic is vast. The most substantial
   study is K. D. Bracher, *Die Auflösung der Weimarer Republik: Eine
   Studie zum Problem des Machtverfalls in der Demokratie* (4th edn.
   Villingen/Schwarzwald, 1964).
2. For the following *see* James M. Diehl, *Paramilitary Politics in Weimar
   Germany* (Bloomington/Indiana, 1977) and Robert G. L. Waite,
   *Vanguard of Nazism. The Free Corps Movement in Postwar Germany
   1918–23* (Cambridge, Mass., 1952).
3. Quoted in Waite *op.cit.* pp.51–2. For an illuminating if not always
   convincing psychoanalytic analysis of the mentality of the Free Corps
   see Klaus Theweleit, *Männerphantasien* 2 vols. (Frankfurt, Main,
   1978). For an interesting work of autobiography *see* Ernst von
   Salomon, *Die Geächteten* (Berlin, 1930) and of fiction *see* Richard
   Hughes, *The Fox in the Attic* (London, 1961).
4. Quoted in Waite *op.cit.* p.108.
5. cf. Gabriele Krüger, *Die Brigade Ehrhardt* (Hamburg, 1971) pp.73ff.
6. cf. E. J. Gumbel, *Verräter Verfallen der Feme, Opfer-Mörder-Richter
   1919–29* (Berlin, 1929) pp.386–9. On the right-wing terror during
   these years *see also* the same author's *Vier Jahre Politischer Mord*
   (Berlin, 1922).
7. cf. Bernd Wegner, *Hitlers Politische Soldaten: Die Waffen SS 1933–45*
   (Paderborn, 1982) pp.36–7.
8. *See* the books by Gumbel cited in note 6 and David Southern, 'Anti-
   democratic terror in the Weimar Republic: the Black Reichswehr and
   the Feme-Murders' in Wolfgang J. Mommsen and Gerhard
   Hirschfeld, *Social Protest, Violence and Terror in Nineteenth- and
   Twentieth-century Europe* (London, 1982) pp.330–41.
9. On the development of the SA *see* Andreas Werner, 'SA und
   NSDAP. SA: "Wehrverband", "Parteitruppe", oder
   "Revolutionsarmee"? Studien zur Geschichte der SA und der
   NSDAP 1920–33' (Dissertation Erlangen 1964) and Wolfgang Sauer,
   'Die Mobilmachung der Gewalt' in K. D. Bracher *et. al.*, *Die
   Nationalsozialistische Machtergreifung: Studien zur Errichtung des
   Totalitären Herrschaftssystems in Deutschland 1933–4* (Cologne,
   1960) pp.830ff.

10. cf. Jeremy Noakes and Geoffrey Pridham, *Nazism 1919–45. Vol. 1. The Rise to Power 1919–34* (Exeter, 1983) p.56.

11. cf. Diehl *op.cit.* p.287.

12. cf. Peter H. Merkl, *The Making of a Stormtrooper* (Princeton, 1980) pp.96–7.

13. For the following *see* Richard Bessel, *Political Violence and the Rise of Nazism. The Stormtroopers in Eastern Germany 1925–34* (London, 1984) pp.85ff.

14. For the following *see* Merkl *op.cit., Bessel op.cit.* and Conan Fischer, *Stormtroopers. A Social, Economic and Ideological Analysis 1929–35* (London, 1983).

15. cf. Mathilde Jamin, *Zwischen den Klassen. Zur Sozialstruktur der SA-Führerschaft* (Wuppertal, 1984).

16. For a similar mentality and pattern of behaviour among the Italian squadristi *see* Adrian Lyttelton, 'Fascism and violence in post-war Italy: political strategy and social conflict' in W. Mommsen and G. Hirschfeld *op.cit.* pp.257–74.

17. cf. R. L. Koehl, *The Black Corps. The Structure and Power Struggles of the Nazi SS* (Madison, Wisconsin, 1983) pp.51–3 and Gunnar Boehnert, 'The Jurists in the SS Führerkorps 1925–39' in G. Hirschfeld and L. Kettenacker, eds., *Der "Führerstaat": Mythos und Realität. Studien zur Struktur und Politik des Dritten Reiches* (Stuttgart, 1981) pp.361–74.

18. cf. W. Sauer *op.cit.* pp.855ff.

19. *See* the reports on antisemitic terror in the *Deutschland-Berichte der Sozialdemokratische Partei Deutschlands 1934–40* 7 vols., (Frankfurt, 1979).

20. On Himmler *see* J. Ackermann, *Heinrich Himmler als Ideologe* (Göttingen, 1970).

21. For the following *see* S. Aronson, *Reinhard Heydrich und die Frühgeschichte von Gestapo und SD* (Stuttgart, 1971) and H. Buchheim, 'The SS' in H. Krausnick *et. al.*, *Anatomy of the SS State* (London, 1968).

22. cf. Friedrich Zipfel, 'Gestapo and the SD: a sociographic profile of the organizers of terror' in Stein U. Larsen *et.al.*, *Who were the Fascists?* (Oslo, 1979) pp.308–9.

23. cf. Martin Broszat, 'The concentration camps 1933–45' in H. Krausnick *et.al.*, *op.cit.*

24. For the text of this decree *see* J. Noakes and G. Pridham *op.cit.* p.142.

25. On this point *see* I. Kershaw, *Popular Opinion and Political Dissent in the Third Reich: Bavaria 1933–1945* (Oxford, 1983).

26. cf. Detlev Peukert, 'Arbeitslager und Jugend-KZ: die "Behandlung Gemeinschaftsfremder" im Dritten Reich' in D. Peukert and J. Reulecke, eds., *Die Reihen fast geschlossen. Beiträge zur Geschichte des Alltags unterm Nationalsozialismus* (Wuppertal, 1981) pp.413–34.

5 The Process of Terror in Irish Politics
Charles Townshend

Despite a mass of writing and untold seminar-hours of discussion over the last twenty years, the concept of terrorism still evades definitive analysis. If it seemed that the original and penetrative essays of T. P. Thornton and E. V. Walter had established dominance over the whole field, the most substantial recent study shows that this is not entirely the case. Cautious and collative, Grant Wardlaw's *Political Terrorism* seeks to overlay their sharp insights with a new definition of terrorism; and implants into this definition its own characteristics: 'political terrorism is the use, or threat of use, of violence by an individual or a group, whether acting for or in opposition to established authority, when such action is designed to create extreme anxiety and/or fear-inducing effects in a target group larger than the immediate victims with the purpose of coercing that group into acceding to the political demands of the perpetrators'.[1]

Yet, curiously, even this compendious formula is not altogether satisfactory. This is not just because it ends with such an unexpectedly loaded word—as if clinical detachment belatedly bows to the need for moral judgement. Nor is it because it breaks with precedent and common sense alike in using the word 'coerce', which means direct physical compulsion, to describe a function which cannot be merely physical. (On the question of 'use or threat' of violence, Martha Crenshaw has rightly pointed out that the act of terrorism 'is a combination of use and threat: the act implies a threat'.[2]) Nor is it the avoidance of 'terror' itself as an effect of 'terrorism'. This is certainly not unprecedented: Thornton similarly excised it (in favour of fright and anxiety), and many others have preferred the prosaic 'fear' to highly-charged words like terror, dread, or awe. Still, it remains a serious

88

problem to specify how fear, once induced, translates into political action.

TERRORISM AND WAR

The central weakness of Wardlaw's definition, which it shares with most others produced in recent years (including that used in British legislation such as the Prevention of Terrorism Acts), is that it fails to discriminate between the particular concept of terrorism and the general concept of war. Too many definitions of terrorism are in effect definitions of war, and consequently of little or no special value, unless one accepts the state's own view that 'violence' is illicit force. This very fact underlines the formidable difficulties in the way of clear thinking about terrorism. The problem is to get away from the value-loaded use of the term by states (for instance 'irrational' versus 'rational' violence) without falling back upon anodyne terms which do not fix the moral properties of terror.

The relationship between terrorism and war is crucial at several levels, and is vital to the analysis presented here. The starting-point must be the Clausewitzian definition of war as 'an act of violence [*Gewalt*] intended to compel our opponent to comply with our will'[3] (in effect, coercion). Clausewitz recognized the moral and political dimensions of war as paramount, and technical military dimensions as secondary ('grammar' rather than 'logic'). The opponent's 'power of resistance' is a product of two inseparable factors, the 'total means at his disposal' and the 'strength of his will'.[4] Thus we are immediately presented with a perspective both physical and psychological. (One could add that even in dealing with the technical aspects of warfare, Clausewitz always laid stress on the moral determinants of action.)

Terror has a definite place in war as such. Indeed that place was so evident in the Second World War that one recent analyst of the Ulster problem, unwilling to create a definition of terrorism but taking 'atrocious behaviour' as a 'necessary defining condition', finds by this criterion no operative distinction between the RAF's and the IRA's indiscriminate bombing of civilians.[5] To avoid defining terrorism in this way is to be drawn too far in the direction of relativism. It is possible to distinguish the element of terror in conventional military action, but it is a terminological confusion to call the induction of fear by military action 'terrorism'. This is to lose sight of what is distinctive about terrorism as a concept and a strategy, which is that fear-inducement is a means sufficient in itself.

The clue to understanding the relationship between war and terror is provided, as Walter saw, by Clausewitz himself in his insistence that war 'is always the collision of two living forces', not 'the action of a living force upon a lifeless mass'.[6] In other words, war is a reciprocal activity between like (though not necessarily equal) forces. Terrorism is a one-way relationship between unlikes. It might most straightforwardly be defined as the use of violence by the armed against the unarmed. Only because the targets are unarmed, undefendable, unprepared by organization or training to cope with the shock of violence, are they put into terror. Conventional military action against military forces, though it may well terrify them, is not terrorism.

This is not to disavow entrely the distinction commonly drawn between the physical (war) and the psychological (terrorism). But as the basis for contextual analysis it is of limited use. The interrelationship of the two was obvious to Napoleon—'in war the moral is to the physical as three is to one'—and the increasing use of guerrilla warfare in the twentieth century can only have reinforced it. All war is both political and psychological. Even the distinction between internal and international war, whilst obviously an important one, is insufficient. The strategy of terrorism cannot be restricted to the sphere of internal war, even by the device of adding the adjective 'revolutionary'. As Thornton recognized, colonial wars are structurally different from internal wars; but they have produced some of the major exemplars of terrorist strategy.

THE DEFINITION OF TERRORISM

The point of this argument is not to deny the validity of terrorism as a concept. There may, of course, be dispute about the limitations of such a general category. Historians will be content to identify a general pattern or tendency; political scientists look for specific predictors with universal application, regardless of period or culture. To a historian such a quest is foredoomed. So although the utility of terrorism as a concept will be assumed here, this paper will make no attempt to categorize types or causes of terrorism— an endeavour which usually seems to result in linear lists freighted with provisos and exceptions.[7] On the parallel assumption that the only interesting form of terrorism is political, it will examine the operation of the phenomenon in one specific context.

How can the concept of terrorism be delineated? In the first place, by emphasizing (as Thornton and Walter did) the centrality of fear itself. Second, by stressing the systematic nature of the fear-inducing violence used.[8] Third, by insisting that the mark of terrorism as a method is its reliance on the sufficiency of non-physical effects. Fourth, by recognizing that it is a relationship of unlikes. It seems useful to ask, not why terrorism occurs, but how well it works (which may help to answer the more popular question). It is necessary to follow, in Walter's terminology, the 'process of terror'. So as to provide some initial framework for contextual analysis, terrorism will be defined here as 'the systematic use of violence by armed people to put unarmed people in fear, in the belief that this will deliver political results'.

To assess the political results of fear, it does not seem absolutely necessary to insist on Thronton's idea of terrorist action as symbolic. But it seems necessary to accept his criterion of 'extranormality'. The violence of terrorist acts must go beyond what is normal in a given society. The quality of 'outrageousness' rightly identified by Heskin is part of this; so is departure from conventional political strategies. Here it is also necessary to clarify the purpose of particular terrorist actions. The broadly-accepted distinction between governmental and anti-governmental terrorism is relevant.

Thornton distinguished 'agitational' from 'enforcement' terror, Walter the 'siege of terror' from the 'regime' or 'reign of terror'. This paper will suggest that this primary distinction cannot be pressed too far, but it remains important analytically. (Crenshaw has refined these concepts in her perceptive work on the Algerian FLN by showing that the 'support' generated by terrorism can be both 'compliance' and 'endorsement'.)[9] Some terrorist actions can only have effect as part of a struggle for change, others—probably the vast bulk—as part of a struggle to preserve.

On the basis of his rigid separation, Thornton went on to argue that agitational terror was more effective the more indiscriminate it looked. This argument has been sensibly challenged,[10] though one may note that Thornton's idea of disorientation still seems to require some quality of arbitrariness. What Thornton did was to conflate 'discriminate' and 'predictable' ('terror must always have at least some element of indiscrimination, else it becomes predictable').[11] Yet predictability is, at one level, what terrorists, as much as governments, must aim for. Indeed the state's law itself meets Thornton's terrorist criterion in that it has some element of randomness in its actual enforcement. To avoid the sort of predictability that could be damaging to their survival, terrorists need not indiscrimation but unpredictability in mode—timing, method, and so on. Otherwise agitational and·enforcement terrorism would be mutually exclusive, whereas this paper will try to show that they can be functionally identical.

For terror to be transformed into terrorism, it is necessary not only that it be systematically used, but also that its users should believe in its utility or necessity. In other words, there must be some sort of terrorist philosophy, no matter how primitive. It must be consciously adopted as a process with an intended effect, whether it be elimination, disorientation, publicity, catalysis (these last two fused in the idea of 'propaganda by deed'), provocation, or even mere vengeance. Thornton's central argument was that agitational terrorism achieved effect through disorientation. This is a sophisticated concept, designed to be applicable to complex modern societies.[12] In theory it supplies the key to engineering a revolution by terrorist means alone. The extremism of its goal, however—to 'remove the structural supports that give society its strength'—means that it has rarely if ever been achieved in practice.

Indeed the question needs to be raised whether terrorism can, in fact, have revolutionary political effects. It is common to speak of the 'threat' of terrorism to Western societies. But analysis of this threat is habitually vague. The second (and larger) part of Wardlaw's book is taken up with measures for countering terrorism, on the grounds that 'contemporary terrorism constitutes a potential threat to the stability, and, in the extreme, the existence of democratic states'.[13] But the first part of the book produces no concrete examples of such a threat, except in the over-reactions of governments themselves. The widespread apprehension that democracy is peculiarly vulnerable to terrorism seems to have little concrete basis. It is certainly odd to contend that terrorism is a threat to the state, when all commentators agree that it is the resort of those who are physically too weak to do this.

TERRORISM IN IRELAND

Lest one be tempted to throw over all functional explanations and dismiss terrorism as activism for its own sake, it may be wise to turn at this point to analysis of terrorist actions in Ireland in order to supply some answers to the question 'What can be achieved by putting people in fear?'. In the following sections the forms of fear-inducing violence which have been used in the last century will be examined in relation to the intentions and achievements of the groups which used them. In the interests of clarity, two broad periods will be distinguished: (A) before and (B) after the creation of the Irish Republican Army (an event which cannot be dated with real exactness, but which will be placed at the beginning of 1919). Within these periods violent action will be related to the concepts of (i) enforcement and (ii) agitational terror.

A(i) enforcement terror
The first thing to notice about the earlier period is the prevalence of agrarian struggle and the relative infrequency

of overt political violence. The distinction between enforcement and agitational terror is particularly clear, even leaving out of account all the actions of the British administration. Killings, woundings (including torture such as 'carding'), and demonstrative violence against animals and property (houghing of cattle, firing into houses, burning of haystacks) were repeatedly used to enforce a social code often called the 'unwritten law'. These acts were carried out by small oathbound groups, under the names of mythical leaders like Captain Rock, Captain Thresher, or Captain Moonlight, which can be seen as agents of the close communities from which they sprang. The 'unwritten law' was designed to secure tenant farmers against unfair eviction by landlords (especially for inability to pay rents in times of bad harvest or low prices). It operated by directing deterrent violence against the unprotected—farmers who took up tenancies from which the former occupants had been evicted—rather than against landlords or their armed agents.[14] 'Whiteboyism', as the system was generally called, was remarkably successful. It may be seen as a diffuse form of insurgency, and was of course labelled 'terrorism' by the government.

This label was, in an important sense, justified. At the centre of the secret societies' method was a process of terror. The punishments meted out were strikingly violent and destructive. In the view of a pioneering observer, the 'singular cruelty' of the agrarian groups stemmed from their need to 'give their opinion the weight of the law of the state' by using sanctions at least as painful as those of the criminal law.[15] In this may be noted a major element of terrorism: the compensation for inferiority of means by extravagance of violence. And the terror process worked on a clearly designated target group which could easily understand the action it had to take (or refrain from taking) in order to escape the fear of violence.

But it must be repeated that this terrorism was not in any strict sense agitational. It had no conscious reference to politics. Its source was internal, not external to the mass of the rural people. Albeit Whiteboys were often forced into membership of their societies, the force was that of their peer-group. And if outsiders were often summoned to carry out violent acts, to make police investigations more difficult, they would not come from far away. In general the activity of the Whiteboy movements was deeply conservative, not to say reactionary. It clearly conveyed an unconscious political message, but the government was woefully wrong to read in such communal reflexes signs of a national conspiracy. Even when the agrarian terrorist groups coalesced into structures more like 'rival governments', the objective always remained local control of land occupancy.[16] There was no conception of achieving change by putting pressure on the state, much less of overthrowing the state as such. And relatively little violence was needed to achieve the desired results, in part because, as Sir James Stephen contemptuously observed, 'a very small amount of shooting in the legs will effectively deter an immense mass of people from paying rents which they do not want to pay'.[17] The unwritten law was in the interest of the peasantry.

More important still, from the perspective of terrorism generally, the agrarian intimidation system had credibility. It was believed to work because it had worked for so long. Punishment, even if erratic or capricious in application, was widely believed to be inevitable. The power of the societies was assiduously publicized, as a hostile witness observed as early as 1806, by 'alternate terror and delusion, hope and fear, vain and wicked promises, daring and atrocious threats, amplified and false reports of the numbers and strength of the association . . . '.[18] This is surely of the essence of terrorism.

A(ii) agitational terror
If there was something akin to a 'reign of terror' in the Irish countryside, the 'siege of terror' was fitful and comparatively ineffectual. The main reason for this was that no durable organization committed to the use of terrorist methods emerged in the nineteenth century. It is a serious mistake, repeated several times recently, to place the Fenian/IRB organization in this category.[19] The 'physical force tradition' cannot be equated with terrorism. The Irish Republican Brotherhood was a revolutionary secret society committed to achieving Irish political independence by physical force. It

was élitist in its arrogation of the right to decide the nation's destiny, violent in rhetoric, and hostile to constitutional (parliamentary) politics. But it was not terrorist. Quite the reverse: its leaders always strove to maintain the unsullied purity of their insurrectionist principles. They wanted a fair fight in which Ireland's national honour would be tempered and restored. Even the guerrilla strategy suggested in the mid-1860s by Irish–American veterans of the Civil War was looked at askance.[20]

Partly in consequence, their one effort at open insurrection in 1867 was a fiasco. The only undoubted success of that year was achieved, ironically, by terror—but by accident rather than design. The Clerkenwell prison explosion was the prototypal urban bombing, but it was intended to release Fenian prisoners by the crude method of blowing down the prison wall. Bungled execution caused the deaths and injuries which sent a shockwave through English society. The extent of the national panic can be measured in the surge of vigilantism as hundreds of thousands enrolled as special constables. The political results were equally dramatic: Gladstone attributed the feasibility of his Irish reform programme after 1868 to the 'sense of insecurity' which produced an uncharacteristic 'attitude of attention' amongst the English people.[21] Yet the IRB leadership was not prepared to repeat this terror process, or to acknowledge that such terror could be justified.[22] The planned use of terror was left to other, more transient organizations.

The shortest-lived of these was the mysterious Irish National Invincibles, a group which appears to have recruited from frustrated rank and file IRB activists, but whose direction came from a different quarter, the Land League.[23] The President of the IRB Supreme Council, Charles Kickham, expressed the same contempt for the Invicible terrorists as for the squalid vendettas of the Whiteboys, to whom they were in his view closely related. It is by no means easy to be sure what the Invincibles were trying to achieve. Like many other Irish terrorists they were far from being what Martha Crenshaw calls 'a fragment of the élite'. (It is an error to confound élitism with membership of the existing élite). Artisans and small traders, they wrote little about their ideas.

The only certain contemporary expression of their thoughts is James Carey's declaration that they wanted 'to make history'. A more elaborate rationalization of their plans is contained in P. J. P. Tynan's discursive memoir written over ten years after their single successful attack, the Phoenix Park assassinations.[24] At that remove Tynan showed an awareness of the use of terrorism in Russia, though little of *Narodnaya Volya's* philosophy. His own philosophy was a compound of elimination, propaganda, vengeance, and perhaps martyrdom. His *leitmotiv* was 'suppression'. British offices of state were to be suppressed by the systematic killing of their incumbents. He does not make it clear whether this was intended to paralyse the government or simply to punish it for its crimes against the Irish people. He is unclear, too, about the precise public impact of the killings: he preserves a Fenian hope that the spectacle of blood he envisions at the (imaginary) assassination of the Viceroy, Earl Spencer, would not only heighten Irish national consciousness but trigger an open national uprising.[25]

The attack actually carried out, in which the senior civil servant in the Irish Executive and his newly-appointed minister were stabbed to death with surgical knives, has always provoked speculation because of its timing. It was widely interpreted as a direct blow against Parnell's recently-adopted policy of accommodation with the British government (the so-called Kilmainham Treaty).[26] However, what is known of the machinery of the Invincible organization, even the favourable picture presented by Tynan, suggests that such precise timing would not have been technically feasible. There is no direct evidence that such political reasoning occurred, either. What we are left with is an indubitably shocking act, whose intended effect is almost impossible to discern. This makes an important comment on the concept of 'propaganda by deed'.[27] Everyone recognizes the spectacular nature of terrorist acts—and some analysts have tried, not very systematically, to draw on the theory of drama to explain their impact. (There has been some very loose thinking about 'terrorism as theatre'.)[28] The real question is not how such outrageous acts gain publicity, but whether they have a chance of conveying an intelligible political message. An inherent limitation of agitational terror is that while actions speak louder than words they are far more open to misinterpretation. To speak loud and clear, a terrorist group must be far more articulate than the Invincibles.

The other groups using terrorist methods in this period were more articulate, at least in that they saw the point of announcing their policy. This was, as the Irish–American *Clan na Gael* declared, that while 'we cannot see our way to an armed insurrection in Ireland this side of some great foreign war with England . . . in the meantime we shall carry on an incessant and perpetual warfare with the power of England in public and in secret'.[29] By this logic many adherents of the physical-force idea were drawn into the sporadic bombing campaign mounted by the Clan and by O'Donovan Rossa's 'Skirmishers'. The latter stuck to old-fashioned black powder, but the Clan bombers led by William Lomasney were true dynamiters, sharing some of the anarchist sense that the phenomenal destructive power of the new explosives had a purgative, regenerative quality. Dynamite was an exciting, revolutionary weapon which seemed to offer unprecedented power to opponents of the state.

Unfortunately, technical sophistication was accompanied by relatively undeveloped organization and doctrine. Like the security forces who pursued them, the bombers were at a primitive stage. Even allowing for structural weaknesses, their campaign was flawed in conception. Their early attacks caused terrific alarms, but thereafter the government kept a level head and perceived the limited proportions of the terrorist threat. In spite of the Home Secretary's hawkish tendencies, no special legislation abrogating civil liberties was brought in. When Lomasney was finally killed by his own bomb while trying to blow up London Bridge in December 1884, the campaign sputtered out. It is hard to see what he would have achieved had he succeeded. London Bridge was a symbolic target, and thus meets Thornton's criterion, but this very fact tends to suggest that symbolism is not enough. There is, too, surely great force in the view that terrorist campaigns lose their impact the longer they are protracted.[30]

The failure of the Irish–American bombers discredited terrorism on the utilitarian level. On the moral level, the IRB in Ireland (and the sage John Devoy in America) remained steadily opposed to it. When the geriatric Fenian organization was revitalized in the early twentieth century it began a movement towards a new form of action. The idea of 'defensive warfare' recognized that the effectiveness of physical force was dependent on moral justification, which only a defensive posture could provide. Rebels must wait for the government to strike the first blow.[31] (It would be a short step from waiting to inducement or provocation.) This progress was temporarily interrupted in 1916 when an old-style Fenian insurrection was engineered by a group of activists impatient to take advantage of 'England's difficulty', who saw it as propaganda by deed in the authentic Malatestan sense. In the wake of this a diffuse guerrilla campaign took shape, heralding the modern age.[32]

B(i) guerrilla warfare and terrorism: enforcement

The relationship between terrorism and guerrilla warfare is very close, because of the irregular nature of guerrilla methods. Hardly a single major guerrilla theorist or practitioner has claimed that a guerrilla strategy alone can produce decisive results.[33] It is characteristically seen as either auxiliary to the action of regular armies (as by Clausewitz, on the original models of Spain and Russia during the Napoleonic wars) or preparatory to a decisive phase of conventional strategy, as by Mao. The guerrilla method is political rather than military in that it starts from and operates through public opinion. Its military actions are essentially propagandist. At the same time they are recognizably military: in this lies their propaganda value. The symbiotic relationship of people and guerrillas (not quite accurately captured in Mao's ubiquitous 'water and fish' metaphor) requires that the latter operate in ways seen by their society as 'honourable', or at least acceptable. Outrageousness and indiscriminate violence self-evidently have no part in the building of public sympathy (or 'endorsement').[34]

The function of terror for guerrillas is strictly delimited. Tom Barry, leader of the 3rd (West) Cork Brigade IRA flying column in 1920–21, made it as clear in his memoirs as Che Guevara was to in his.[35] It is to preserve the security of the insurgents: to deter the people from collaborating with or giving information to the government. This can be achieved only by pinpoint attacks, sometimes called 'targeted assassination'. Each individual attacked must be recognized by the people as having been a collaborator or informer. 'Revolutionary justice' (Guevara's phrase) must be perceived as fundamentally just, if necessarily rough and ready in application. It must also be believed to be 'regular', in the sense of being inevitable.

Building up a credible enforcement (or 'compliance') system of this sort from scratch is a major task. The IRA, however, as it emerged in 1918–19, was in the enviable position of being able to draw on the long tradition of agrarian terrorism. Its strength lay in its local roots rather than its formal revolutionary ideology.[36] It did not need to convert the people, and it could rely on its messages being deciphered unambiguously. At root it was the last and most powerful of the 'associations', though it added an overtly political ideology and an organizational superstructure imitative of its opponents'. Its claim to represent a counter-state or 'rival government' secured immediate recognition (if not instant endorsement) in the popular consciousness. The people knew how to react to its demands. IRA terror was a notable hybrid of enforcement and agitation.

In this it foreshadowed Mao's doctrine on counter-enforcement terror, and the practice of the Vietminh. The incidence of targeted assassination in Vietnam dwarfed anything seen in Ireland either in 1919–23 or since 1970, but the Irish system was analogous in structure (and at least as effective). Agitational terrorism as such was uncommon in the first Anglo-Irish war, or was fused with the function of enforcement—which not only defended the IRA but at the same time enhanced its prestige and power. Targeted assassination was extended into attacks on the British forces which could bear a terrorist aspect. Thus the systematic assassination of detectives of the political branch of the Dublin police had a progressive psychological effect on the survivors. The set-piece attacks on military officers on

'Bloody Sunday' again produced observable impact on the intelligence service as a whole.[37] Essentially, though, these attacks were instrumental rather than demonstrative: their object was the elimination of intelligence systems which threatened the IRA. They cannot strictly be compared with terrorist attacks on officials and ministers.

Such attacks were noticeably absent (unless one includes attacks on magistrates under this head) during the first conflict, and infrequent during the civil war. The assassination of Sir Henry Wilson in 1922 may be seen as an overhang from the Anglo-Irish war, as that of Kevin O'Higgins in 1927 was from the civil war. In both cases the actors remained obscure, and their motives unclear. (Revenge seems the strongest.) More clearly articulate was the shooting of two Free State Dáil members by Republicans in 1922, though this was not followed by the systematic campaign which it seemed to herald. Whether such a campaign would have worked is impossible to judge. The response of the Free State government was the ruthless use of counter-terror, including the shooting without trial of four Republican prisoners (symbolically selected from each of the provinces of Ireland), and the taking of hostages by the Free State forces. Events reached an awesome pitch of grimness in county Kerry when a group of hostages were stood on a landmine and blown to pieces. This was enforcement terrorism on a grand scale, an extremity of violence which shattered the IRA's support and seemed almost demoniacal to its stunned recipients.[38]

The ingrained tradition of enforcement terror extends from this period into the conflict which has developed since 1969. The enabling communal assumptions were muted in the interim, but those who saw evidence of their disappearance were seriously mistaken. The shift of geographical focus from the rural south-west to the urban north-east superimposed a further set of conflict mechanisms which had developed over a century within the polarized communities of Belfast and Londonderry. This machinery was tripped as soon as Protestants reacted defensively against the Civil Rights movement. (Indeed the Loyalist UVF had re-established the currency of terror in the campaign it launched even earlier, in

1966, against the north–south *démarche*.) It was the traditional display of Protestant mastery in Londonderry, the Apprentice Boys' march, which triggered the 'battle of Bogside' and showed how, in Richard Rose's somewhat baffled phrase, 'time past and time present can fuse together in an explosive way'.[39] Communal terrorism is not an easy concept to fit into conventional political-science taxonomies, but the adjustment must be made.

It is hard to see what Martha Crenshaw intends to convey when she asserts that the IRA 'posed as the defender of Catholics' in this crisis.[40] Her implication is that this was a ruse. Yet all Ulster history points the other way—to the consistency with which 'defenderism' under one name or another was thrown up by each succeeding communal crisis.[41] The 'Provisional' IRA (PIRA) set out specifically to take up once more a traditional role that had allegedly been abandoned by the doctrinaire socialists who had official control of the organization. At this level the hybrid of control and demonstrative terror—to recast slightly the enforcement/ agitation duality—was self-sufficient. It did not need to serve a political programme in order to achieve legitimacy. It could maintain a steady state in virtual isolation from politics.

B(ii) Guerrilla warfare and terrorism: agitation

The truly unprecedented aspect of the PIRA campaign since 1970 has been the high incidence of agitational terror action. This is not to say that it has been a terrorist campaign. According to the analysis presented here that would be a misconception. Crenshaw's rather lofty assertion that 'the IRA is an interesting example of an organization that would like to think of itself as practising "guerrilla warfare", that is, attempting to defeat the enemy's military forces by unconventional tactics, but actually uses a combination of guerrilla warfare and terrorism, which aims at undermining the enemy's will to fight, primarily through influencing public opinion'[42] seems erroneous at several levels. In the first place, guerrilla fighters do not use unconventional *tactics* as such, they merely adopt the unconventional *strategy* of avoiding decisive military combats. Secondly, guerrilla strategy seeks decision through public opinion. Third, the undermining of the enemy's will is the object of all warfare. Following the canons established by the struggles in China, Vietnam and Cuba—not to mention Ireland itself—the PIRA is a guerrilla organization fighting a guerrilla war, with an admixture of terrorist means.

The ethnic limits of the Republican movement are plainer than they were in 1919–21, but there should be no doubt that within those limits the function of the IRA is inherently representative. Whether or not one approves of his terminology, Frank Burton's central contention that 'the IRA represents a political isomorphism of the ideological meanings of Catholicism' should command assent.[43] Too much should not be made of the periods in which the IRA's commitment to the use of force demonstrably lacked popular support (such as the final phase of the civil war, or the years of operation 'Harvest' between 1956 and 1962). The fish/water relationship is subtle, complex and apparently anomalous—visibly troubling to many political analysts.

At the level of strategic choice, the matter is fairly straightforward. Although the physical force tradition survived the Republican defeat in the civil war, it could never again take the pure Fenian form. The feasibility of a mass insurrection disappeared in 1922. As the Free State stabilized, the only possible battleground for future Republicans lay across the border in the six counties. Unification remained a popular cause, but the people ceased to accept that war should be waged for it. In consequence Republican military means shifted towards terrorism, even if the term was not accepted or its implications discussed. In the marches of Fermanagh and Armagh the IRA could (and can) still operate by 'true' guerrilla methods. But Protestant terroritory was impenetrable: only action against Britain offered a mechanism for achieving unity. So argued Seán Russell in the 1930s, when as IRA Chief of Staff he led the ill-prepared campaign of indiscriminate bombing on the British mainland. So, again, argued Seán Cronin in laying out the blueprint for operation 'Harvest'.[44]

It is of course an important fact that 'terrorist' is now an epithet used by governments to illegitimize their opponents. Few practitioners of terror today dare to embrace the term as the *Narodovolt'sy* did. But the terms they prefer (whether 'rebel', 'freedom fighter', 'guerrilla', or in the Irish case the technical title 'volunteer') do not always accurately describe their function. (Much the same can be said of the label 'partisan', which gained currency during the Second World War to describe groups using methods which, had they not been directed against the Germans, would undoubtedly have been called 'terrorist' by the Allied governments. Rather better are the Lawrentian 'irregular', the ambivalent 'gunman', and the increasingly-current 'paramilitary'). As a result there is an element of self-deception in their self-image. It would be useful, at least in analysing its function, to have a neutral term for the violent action which has become characteristic of the IRA. Such a term should recognize the inherently political nature of this action, and at the same time indicate the gulf between it and conventional political means. Elsewhere I have used the term 'demonstration politics' to denote this mode of using violence to assert a political belief. It is a short-circuiting of the political process, a substitution of rhetorical gesture for exegesis, debate and compromise. It simplifies issues and offers simple solutions, in the Fenian case the proposition that England is the cause of all Irish problems.

As many commentators have noticed, this mode is intensely élitist, and maybe also authoritatian.[45] Whether it is undemocratic naturally depends on one's definition of democracy. Pearse and de Valera were notable exemplars of Robespierre's version of Rousseau's democracy, in that they believed in the representative nature of their own moral instincts. If they were militarists in the sense that they were prepared, if it could be done, to impose their vision by force, they were not militarist in the conventional sense. Much less were they *anti*-democratic, as their opponents within the national movement alleged. They merely believed that it was possible for the majority to be wrong in the short run (or in Rousseau's terms, for the will of all to conflict with the general will.)

Their form of militarism has been transmitted to their successors in the Republican movement. The élitist anti-parliamentary attitude is deeply ingrained. The Fenian preference for secret conspiracy as against mass organization, no doubt originating in self-defence against police surveillance, eventually became a habit of mind. The very idea of an 'advanced' nationalist suggested that most people lagged behind and would somehow have to be led or driven on. Fenian hostility to parliamentary politics as an engine of Anglicization, compomise and betrayal is too well known to be rehearsed here.[46] But it should be noted that a series of 'betrayals' in the twentieth century have powerfully reinforced this aversion to the politics of 'politicians', an aversion which Sinn Féin has seldom overcome since 1926. The IRA has been marked by its independence from all political groups and institutions.[47] The present (1985) conditional espousal of the ballot box is unlikely to outlast its nuisance value in embarrassing the British government.

The independent IRA has experimented with mass social movements, notably Peadar O'Donnell's *Saor Eire* in the early 1930s, but has always reverted to the physical force idea. Its demonstration politics have included, alongside sporadic military action, the focusing of mass emotions through hunger–strikes and funerals. (It is a serious question whether in such contexts suicide should be classified as a terrorist act.) Only in the 1970s did indiscrinate killing emerge as a major form of action. This departure from a relatively narrow traditional repertoire may be seen as a desperate recognition of the IRA's limited guerrilla potential. Such a commonsense view cannot, however, be tested in the absence of documentary evidence. In interpreting the intentions of the PIRA, reliance has to be placed on the handful of memoirs which have, against the odds, been published.[48] Few safe conclusions can be drawn from these except that little rigorous thinking has gone on about the use of terror methods. No comprehensive or logical theory has underpinned the strategy, which seems to have been developed on an *ad hoc*, opportunist basis. The tidy lists drawn up by military intelligence officers and social scientists are the contribution of outsiders.

This lack of concern with theoretical paraphernalia, like the general vagueness of Republican ideology, reveals much about the real sources of the IRA's resilience. Before finally turning to this important issue, however, it will be useful to survey the functions of IRA demonstration politics, using a variant of Thornton's list of 'proximate objectives'.[49] Two of these, 'morale building' and 'elimination', are sufficiently self-evident not to need further discussion. 'Provocation', a function especially associated with the ideas of Carlos Marighela, has in one sense presented no problem in Ireland, where the British government has characteristically conformed to the repressive image built up by nationalists. But in a triangular struggle provocation can also function indirectly—for instance, Republican action can provoke Loyalist reactions which necessitate British intervention. Thornton's central concepts of 'advertising' and 'disorientation' are more questionable. The first of them, more often labelled publicity, is usually rated very important by commentators. It is not uncommon to see the contention that 'media exposure' is vital to terrorism (now enshrined in Mrs. Thatcher's showy phrase 'the oxygen of publicity'), and even that the reporting of terrorist acts has a 'contagious' effect and can legitimize terrorist aims. This may seem a logical extension of Thornton's view that advertising was the most characteristic (though not the most important) terrorist objective because 'it is of the very essence of terror that it be noticed'.[50]

But the question arises whether such notice is a simple, multipliable factor. The facile assumption that modern mass media increase the impact of terrorism certainly does not bear scrutiny.[51] Notice will in any case be taken, and alarming messages conveyed—perhaps more alarmingly—by rumour and other primitive communicative means. It is indeed possible that the reassuring banality of the mass media may reduce rather than heighten public alarm.[52] And the central problem remains whether alarm and anxiety are directly coupled to decision-making and political change. It seems clear that public anxiety diminishes somewhat as terrorist campaigns go on, and that if there is a direct reaction it is as likely as not to run counter to that intended. If the use of violence is illegitimate, even unarmed people can respond with defiance rather than compliance.

As for disorientation, nothing resembling Thornton's process of total dissolution of social bonds, followed by rebonding to the insurgent structure, has been seen. But here it is relevant to remember that Thornton was specifically excluding colonial wars from his definition of internal war. It is hardly conceivable that the IRA could achieve this effect in Britain or even in county Antrim, or the UVF in west Belfast or south Armagh. Within their ethnic areas, the redefining of structures has scarcely been novel, but rather a re-emergence and strengthening of long-established allegiances.

One or two possible objectives may be added to Thornton's list. Some writers see 'catalysis' as an illuminating metaphor, and others speak of terror as a 'precipitant' of change. The trouble is that chemical metaphors are no more accurate than organic ones in explaining the operation of societies. IRA action has led the British government to accede to public (or media?) demands for 'initiatives' and has thus revealed a serious weakness—the inability to find 'solutions'. But the process is not regular or repeatable. Bombs might produce the fall of Stormont, but not internationalization or British withdrawal. Timing and mood are vital. The impact of terror is so varied according to context that one could argue that the only concrete effect of apparently agitational terrorism is to reinforce the position of the IRA (or each of the three rival sections of the Republican movement). In other words, only enforcement terror really works. But of course enforcement terror *can* produce the impression of 'ungovernability' which can lead to political change.

We are left at the end with the more primitive motives rightly stressed by Crenshaw: revenge—which has demonstrably governed the timing and perhaps the form of many attacks—and the urge to action for its own sake. This last is important because it draws attention to the organizational basis for the persistence of terrorism. A physical-force activist who cannot wage open war must turn to covert warfare. That is obvious. The necessity is to explain how the physical-force idea persists. In the case of the IRA this seems directly related to the persistence of the organization itself, a feature which has uniformly impressed outside observers (though Crenshaw surely goes too far in calling it 'the longest-lived organization in history').[53] The survival of the organization mirrors Irish nationalists' image of their cause as a 'phoenix flame'—an image which not only embraces the metaphor of fire beloved of all revolutionaries, but also enshrines the ceaseless renewal of the struggle even in the ashes of death and failure.

The organization's formal origins reach back to the Phoenix Society of the 1850s, its claimed spiritual ancestry to the United Irish Society of the eighteenth century. Its informal, unclaimed origins encompass the earthier ubiquity of the agrarian secret societies. The survival of the independent IRA through the lean years of the 1930s and 1940s suggests that the organization had by then become permanent and self-sufficient. Violence had also become more than merely a habit: rather a means in itself, self-validating even though its presumed ends may be unattainable. The most significant result of T. G. Carroll's research on 'disobedience' in Northern Ireland is that while exposure to violence emerged (as most social scientists would expect) as the strongest indicator of disobedient attitudes, it was a much weaker predictor of approval for violent methods. The overwhelming factor here was what Carroll labels 'justifications for violence'.[54]

Thus, in conclusion, Gurr's idea that there must be both normative and utilitarian justification for the adoption of violent strategies may be questioned. It is common to say that 'violence pays', and up to a point it clearly does so. Beyond that point, it can be dysfunctional. The IRA has reached an *impasse* in the six counties. But there is no reason to suppose that its commitment to the use of physical force will therefore be modified, much less abandoned. The IRA has been castigated by social scientists as well as by governments, perhaps for its failure to fit what Chalmers Johnson calls the revolutionary paradigm of the age. (Which, ironically, it helped to create.) If this misleading path is followed, its actions will necessarily appear irrational or repellent. The evidence suggests that its actions are effective to the extent that they are perceived by a section of the people as legitimate. Such legitimacy is the product of a long communal tradition validating the use of violence, and, crucially, enabling its message to be understood. Where terror works it will surely persist.

NOTES

1. E. V. Walter, 'Violence and the Process of Terror', *American Sociological Review* vol. 29, 1964; *Terror and Resistance. A Study of Political Violence* (New York, 1969); T. P. Thornton, 'Terror as a Weapon of Political Agitation', in H. Eckstein, ed., *Internal War. Problems and Approaches* (Glencoe, 1964); G. Wardlaw, *Political Terrorism. Theory, tactics and countermeasures* (Cambridge U.P., 1982).
2. M. Crenshaw Hutchinson, 'The concept of revolutionary terrorism', *Journal of Conflict Resolution*, Vol. XVI, No. 3 (1972) p. 385.
3. K. von Clausewitz, *On War*, bk. I ch. I. Compare the translations of Graham and Howard and Paret; note that there is no moral discrimination here between 'force' and 'violence'.
4. Howard and Paret's translation.
5. K. Heskin, 'The psychology of terrorism in Northern Ireland', in Y. Alexander, ed., *Terrorism in Ireland* (London, 1984) pp. 88–91.
6. Howard and Paret's translation. Walter used his own translation: 'the shock of two living forces colliding'. Graham's translation is inadequate at this point.
7. cf. M. Crenshaw, 'The causes of terrorism', *Comparative Politics*, July 1981; P. Wilkinson, *Political Terrorism* (London, 1974).
8. In Crenshaw's words, 'neither one isolated act nor a series of random acts is terrorism' (1972) p. 384.
9. *Revolutionary Terrorism. The FLN in Algeria 1954–62* (Stanford, 1978) pp. 40–60.
10. H. E. Price, jr, 'The strategy and tactics of revolutionary terrorism', *Comparative Studies in Society and History*, Vol. 19, No. 1 (1977) p. 54.
11. Thornton *op. cit.* p. 81.
12. Thornton *op. cit.* pp. 83–6.
13. Wardlaw *op. cit.* p. 65.
14. M. R. Beames, *Peasants and Power. The Whiteboy Movements and their Control in Pre-Famine Ireland* (Brighton, 1983) pp. 127–36.
15. G. Cornewall Lewis, *Local Disturbances in Ireland* (London, 1836; new edn. Cork, 1977) p. 77.
16. cf. C. Townshend, *Political Violence in Ireland. Government and Resistance since 1848* (Oxford, 1983) pp. 14–24.
17. J. F. Stephen, 'On the suppression of boycotting', *The Nineteenth Century* No. cxviii (1886) p. 773.
18. Evidence of Mr Moore, *Proceedings of Special Commission in cos. Sligo, Mayo, Leitrim, Longford, and Cavan, Dec. 1806* (Lewis, 1836) p. 34.
19. Most recently by M. Crenshaw, 'The persistence of IRA terrorism', in Y. Alexander *op. cit.* p. 249.
20. Townshend *op. cit.* p. 33.
21. *ibid.* p. 37.

22. J. Devoy, *Recollections of an Irish Rebel*, new edn. (Shannon, 1969) p. 250.

23. C. Townshend, 'Introduction', reprint of P. J. P. Tynan, *The Irish National Invincibles and their Times* (New York, 1983) pp. vi-vii.

24. For a modern study of the attack *see* T. Corfe, *The Phoenix Park Murders* (London, 1968).

25. Tynan, *Irish National Invincibles* p. viii.

26. Parnell himself so interpreted it. F. S. L. Lyons, *Charles Stewart Parnell* (London, 1977) pp. 208ff.

27. Tynan does not use this (then novel) phrase, though his ideas about the impact of violent acts bear some resemblance to those of Malatesta and Brousse.

28. e.g. in A. McClung Lee, 'The dynamics of terrorism in Northern Ireland, 1968–1980', *Social Research* Vol. 48, No. 1 (1981).

29. Clan na Gael memo. (Sept. 1883) in Anderson to Harcourt (3 Nov. 1883). Bodleian Library, Harcourt papers 105.

30. Hutchinson *op. cit.* p. 27.

31. Bulmer Hobson, *Defensive Warfare. A Handbook for Irish Nationalists.* (Sinn Féin, Belfast, 1909).

32. C. Townshend, 'The Irish Republican Army and the development of guerrilla warfare 1916–21', *English Historical Review*, Vol. XCIV (1979).

33. The most notable exception being T. E. Lawrence's argument about his (very exceptional) campaign, 'The evolution of a revolt', *Army Quarterly* (Oct. 1920).

34. See Hutchinson *op. cit.* p. 49–60.

35. T. Barry, *Guerrilla Days in Ireland* (Dublin, 1949) ch. XVI.

36. Townshend *op. cit.* (1983) pp. 332–3.

37. But this impact can be exaggerated; for discussions *see* T. Bowden, 'Bloody Sunday—a reappraisal', and C. Townshend, 'Bloody Sunday—Michael Collins speaks', *European Studies Review*, Vol. 2, No. 1 (1971) and Vol. 9, No. 2 (1979).

38. D. Macardle, *Tragedies of Kerry 1922–1923* (Dublin, 1924); C. S. Andrews, *Dublin Made Me* (Cork, 1979) pp. 250-71.

39. R. Rose, *Governing Without Consensus. An Irish Perspective* (London, 1971) p. 354.

40. Crenshaw *op. cit.* (1984) p. 248.

41. A. T. Q. Stewart, *The Narrow Ground. Aspects of Ulster, 1609–1969* (London, 1977) pp. 113–22.

42. Crenshaw *op. cit.* (1984) p. 268.

43. F. Burton, *The Politics of Legitimacy. Struggles in a Belfast community* (London, 1978) p. 68.

44. Townshend *op. cit.* (1983) pp. 386–8.

45. Heskin *op. cit.* p. 94.

46. For a study of the quintessential Fenian intellectual *see* R. V. Comerford, *Charles J. Kickham* (Dublin, 1979).

47. Townshend *op. cit.* (1983) pp.374–8.

48. Most notably Maria McGuire, *To Take Arms: A Year in the Provisional IRA* (London, 1973); S. MacStiofain, *Memoirs of a Revolutionary* ((?) Edinburgh, 1975).

49. Thornton *op. cit.* pp. 82–8.

50. *ibid*. p. 82.

51. P. Schlesinger, 'Terrorism, the media and the Liberal Democratic State: a critique of the orthodoxy', in Alexander (ed.) *op. cit.* An essay notable not least for its attack on the editor of the ramshackle collection in which it appears.

52. The 'media boredom' with Ireland, castigated by some commentators, is itself evidence of the limits of terrorism.

53. Though she is certaintly correct to stress the importance of 'myth' in Fenian history. Crenshaw *op. cit* p. 249. Cf. R. V. Comerford, *The Fenians in Context. Irish Politics and Society 1848–82*. (Dublin 1985), pp. 41–2, 49–51.

54. T. G. Carroll, 'Disobedience and Violence in Northern Ireland'. *Comparative Political Studies*, Vol. 14, No. 1 (1981) pp. 3–29.

Part III
Terrorism in New Contexts

6 Terrorism and Islam
David Capitanchik

Terrorism has been defined as 'a specific weapon in the struggle for political power, employed either by groups of the extreme Left or the extreme Right but also quite frequently by national minorities'.[1] There is nothing new about it as a general phenomenon, nor is it confined to a particular group, philosophy or continent. The weapon is violence, says Laqueur, but it is not identical with civil wars, peasant uprisings, brigandage, military coups, wars of liberation or blockades.[2]

The fact that terrorism occurs in relatively stable social milieux means that it can be contrasted with the 'constitutional procedures prescribed for established state representatives'.[3] Put in another way, constitutional government is, among other things, a subsitute for violence in intra-state relations, just as international law and international agreements of various kinds are substitutes for violence in the relations between states.

The purpose of terrorism, whether national or international, is to murder political enemies, to deter potential foes and to destabilize society. In recent decades it has come to be regarded as a major menace by governments, and among the academic community of social scientists and others it has come to be regarded as a subject meriting serious study. However, the efficacy of terrorists in achieving their goals is a matter of some dispute. Walter Laqueur insists that 'their exploits, however unpleasant for the victims, are more or less irrelevant'. Yonah Alexander, on the other hand, has said that having been treated as just a nuisance for many years, it is now clear that terrorism is the new mode of warfare, and worthy of study in strategic terms.[4] Indeed, in 1983, according to one source, the total number of incidents of terrorism (defined as the threatened or actual use of force and violence to attain a political goal through fear, coercion

115

and intimidation) amounted to 2,838.[5]

Whichever view one takes of its significance, there is no disputing the increase in the incidence of terrorism in recent decades and the ubiquitousness of the contemporary ideological politics[6] which is propounded in mitigation of the most heinous acts of violence. Many of the more dramatic and violent incidents of recent decades have been perpetrated either in the Middle East or elsewhere by groups involved in the domestic and inter-state conflicts in that region. Groups such as the Palestine Liberation Organization and most of its constituent factions are defined by their opponents and victims as 'terrorist' bodies, and therefore any act of warfare or violence conducted in their name must be 'terrorist' by definition.

Others, however, especially those who sympathize with their cause, would regard them as fighting a war of national liberation and, therefore, by the definition used above, the PLO, say, would not be regarded as a terrorist group.

Nevertheless, even if it has been less significant than is popularly supposed, terrorism has been a prominent feature of the politics of the Middle East. Its intensity in terms of the scale of the atrocities committed in pursuit of some political, religious or other ideological goal has prompted scholars to seek for some explanation in the beliefs, values and ethics of the dominant religion of the region, namely Islam, and in a combination of the history, culture and contemporary conditions of the Middle East. These issues provide the focus for the remainder of this chapter.

In a recent article, Professor Elie Kedourie has referred to that Western ethos which regards politics as 'an ordinary kind of life, an ordinary kind of activity; that to engage in politics, to pursue the political life, is beneficial to oneself and to society at large'. It is a view, Kedourie argues, which is grounded in tradition and in a broad range of social and political arrangements. However, he goes on to suggest that in the context of the Middle East, 'the aspiration to engage in politics in the hope of "making things better" seems inevitably to lead to oppression, torture, murder, and terrorism'.[7]

Terrorism, as it is defined in this essay, has found its most menacing expression in the context of the resurgence of Islamic fundamentalism so evident during the past decade. However, both terrorism and movements for fundamentalist Islamic reform have frequently appeared in times of political, social or economic crisis. They represent no new or modern phenomenon. In any kind of upheaval—during man-made or natural disaster—men turned to Islam and the mosque which served both as the fortress of the most conservative, reactionary and xenophobic elements of society, and, at the same time, as the custodian of the only true vision of the just society, which offered hope and guidance to the poor, the disenfranchised, and the disillusioned.[8]

Two recent examples will suffice to illustrate this duality of purpose. In 1981, those responsible for the assassination of President Anwar Sadat of Egypt explicitly combined their demands for a thorough moral cleansing of Egyptian society by a return to basic Muslim principles with an attack on the corrupting influences of the West, for whose introduction they blamed Sadat. The same charges were levelled against the rulers of Saudi Arabia on 20 November 1979, by those who seized control of the Grand Mosque at Mecca. The Saudi Princes were accused of Western degeneracies and were therefore judged to be unfit to guard the Holy Cities.[9]

The recent 'Islamic revival' has enhanced the political significance of Islam to an extent rarely witnessed in modern times, hence the strong anti-Western sentiment in many Muslim countries and the various attempts in such countries as Iran, Pakistan and the Sudan, to reimpose strict Islamic law. Another feature has been the intensification of the traditional enmity between the various Muslim sectarian forces, and in particular between the two main groups, the Sunnis and the Shi'as.

Islam never has been simply a spiritual community. Instead, from its rise in the seventh century it developed as a religio-political movement, and the belief that Islam embraces faith and politics is rooted in its bible, the Koran, and the example (*Sunnah*) of Muhammed, its founder and prophet. This belief has been reflected in Islamic doctrine, history and politics.[10]

In 622, Muhammed was invited to emigrate from Mecca to

Medina where he was to consolidate his political power by establishing a state based upon his prophetic message. The importance of the community (*Ummah*) in Islam and the importance of its establishment as a state were emphasized by the fact that the Muslim calendar is dated from 622 rather than from 610, the year of God's first revelation to Muhammed.

During the following decade, under Muhammed's guidance, the Muslims extended their hegemony over much of the Arabian heartland. In the process, the disparate Arab tribes were welded into a single polity with common institutions and a common ideology.

However, this new-found unity was not enough to prevent successive crises of political authority following the death of Muhammed in 632. The Prophet's death was the prelude to the Caliphate Period (632–1258) during which Islamic ideology and institutions as they are understood by Muslims today were formed and developed. Of particular importance in the present context is the rule of the first four caliphs since it is the period to which both conservative and radical Islamic activists today turn for guidance in attempting to define the Islamic character of the modern state.

Muhammed died without designating who was to succeed him and neither did he establish any mechanism for the selection of his successor. Eventually, following a brief but tense interlude, the Prophet's companions chose as their leader one of their number, Abu Bakr, who was the father of Muhammed's youngest wife Aishah. Abu Bakr took the title of Caliph (successor) to the Prophet of God, which made him the political and military leader of the community. He was not regarded as a prophet himself, although he enjoyed a certain religious prestige symbolized by him leading the Friday congregational prayers and the mention of his name in prayer.

During his brief caliphate (632–4), Abu Bakr dealt swiftly and brutally with a series of tribal revolts brought on by Muhammed's death. For many Arab tribal chiefs, their participation in the Islamic political community was based upon a personal pact with the Prophet himself. Now the long-standing tribal sources of political and social identity challenged the unity of the new Muslim state. Employing the brilliant generalship of Khalid ibn al-Walid, Abu Bakr soon crushed the tribal revolt, thus consolidating Muslim rule over the entire Arabian peninsula.

The second caliph, Umar (634–44), sought to avoid future succession crises by appointing an 'election committee' to choose his successor. The committee duly elected Uthman ibn Affan to be the next caliph. However, Uthman was a member of a leading Meccan family, the Umayyad, who had been among Muhammed's strongest opponents before they converted to Islam. Uthman's election, therefore, was resented by many Medinans and he was accused of weakness and nepotism. In 656, Uthman was assassinated in the first of a series of rebellions and religious assassinations that were to mark the political development of Islam.

The issue of succession, highlighted by Uthman's assassination, was matched by a consequential problem of equal importance, namely Muslim civil war. Uthman was succeeded by the fourth caliph, Ali, who was a cousin and son-in-law of the Prophet. Indeed, Muhammed himself had been brought up in the household of Ali's father. Ali is regarded by many of his followers as the Prophet's first convert and the relationship between them was sealed by his marriage to the only one of Muhammed's children to have survived into adulthood, Fatima. Ali and Fatima had two sons, Hasan and Huseyn.

Ali's supporters had always believed that the political succession should be through the Prophet's family and in their view Ali was the true legitimate heir of Muhammed. Thus they regarded the first three caliphs as usurpers and they saw Ali's election to the caliphate as a sign of divine vindication of their belief. However, their triumph was to be short-lived. During his brief five-year rule (656–61), Ali was challenged by two rebellions, both of which used his failure to find and prosecute the assassins of Uthman as a pretext for their opposition. The first revolt was by a coalition led by the Prophet's youngest wife Aishah, whom Ali had once accused of infidelity. It was crushed by Ali in the 'Battle of the Camel' (656), near Basra, in which the fighting took place around a camel upon which Aishah was mounted. This was the first time a caliph fought against another Muslim army.

The other challenge to Ali's authority was led by Muawiyah, the govenor of Syria and a cousin of the caliph Uthman. Muawiyah called for vengeance for his cousin's murder and he had also refused to be replaced as Governor of Syria by one of Ali's generals. In 657, Ali led an army against Muawiyah at the Battle of Siffin (in Syria). According to tradition, in that battle Ali is said to have killed 523 men in one day with his own hand. Remarkable feats were attributed to him by his followers. He had waited unmoved for the enemy attack and knocked down fifty-three attackers simply by extending his arm. When it looked as though Ali's forces had the upper hand, Muawiyah called for peaceful arbitration as laid down in the Koran. Ali agreed, but with unfortunate results for him personally and for those among his supporters who opposed the idea of the caliphate.

A group of Ali's followers, the Kharijites ('seceders'), fell out with their leader. For them, Muawiyah had been guilty of a grave sin in opposing Ali's authority. He could no longer be considered a Muslim and was therefore the lawful object of *jihad* (holy war). By agreeing to arbitration, they contended, Ali had failed in his sacred duty to subdue the rebels. The Kharijites were the first sect in Islam to contend that the leadership of the Islamic community belonged to the most observant of Muslims, regardless of his socio-economic status and family relationship. Not only had Muawiyah not been subdued, but following the battle of Siffin, he continued to govern Syria and even extended his authority to include Egypt as well. In 661, Ali was himself assassinated by a Kharijite and Muawiyah was able to claim the caliphate and establish his capital in Damascus.

With this, the age of Muhammed and the Rightly Guided Caliphs of Medina came to an end. This is regarded by all Muslims as the exemplary period of Muslim life. It was the time when God sent his final and complete revelation for mankind and his last prophet. The Islamic state, with a common religious identity and purpose, was created with the Koran as its guidance. There was the importance of Muhammed's exemplary behaviour (*Sunnah*) and narrative stories (*Hadith*) reflecting the extent to which the Prophet, his family and companions served as models for Muslim life. Above all, it is a period which serves as a reference point for all Islamic revival and reform, whether traditionalist or modernist, conservative or radical.

The early history of Islam is essential for any understanding of the contemporary Muslim world and the role of violence in general and terrorism in particular in Islamic politics. The schism which opened up in the first civil war between the caliph Ali and General Muawiyah led to a second round of violence during the reign of Muawiyah's son and successor Yazid. It was from the revolt against Yazid by Ali's son Husayn that the major division in Islam between Sunni and Shia emerged.

When Yazid came to power in 680, Husayn refused to recognize his legitimacy and he was persuaded to lead a rebellion against him. However, Husayn failed to win popular support for his revolt and he and his small army were utterly vanquished at the Battle of Karbala. Their slaughter and martyrdom gave rise to a movement of political protest centred on the martyred family of the Prophet. It provided the paradigm for Shi'a Islam. The supporters or partisans of Ali (after whom Shi'a Islam takes its name) link the injustice that denied Ali his rightful succession to Muhammed with the martyrdom of his son Husayn. The violent deaths that father and son both suffered has instilled in Shi'as an admiration for martyrdom and a deep desire to emulate that martyrdom. However, it is of the utmost importance to point out that neither Ali nor Husayn are regarded as martyrs either in the Christian sense of the term, or in the same sense as the 'kamikaze' truck drivers who bombed the headquarters of the American, French and Israeli forces in Lebanon in 1983 and attacked the withdrawing Israeli army in 1985. Ali and Husayn are venerated for having fought bravely in battle and having fallen to the enemy. The unfortunate Iranian soldiers who have died in battle with the Iraqis in the recent Gulf War are similarly regarded.

This outlook, that Ali and Husayn were martyrs to injustice, has provided Shi'a Islam with its major theme—the battle of the forces of good (Shi'a) against the forces of evil (anti-Shi'a). Their goal is to establish righteous rule and social justice through martyrdom and protest under the political leadership of the imam, hence the fundamental political and legal difference between the majority Sunni stream of Islam and the minority Shi'a denomination.

Nowadays, there are about 800 million Sunni Muslims throughout the world. They derive their name from Sunna, the practice of the Prophet as defined in the Hadith. Sunnis follow one of four schools of Islamic law, Shafa'i, Maliki, Hanbali and Hanifi, for all of whom the practice of the Prophet and his immediate successors (the Righteous Caliphs) is the primary source of guidance after the Koran. The religious significance of the caliphs is limited, their real importance being in their political and military leadership of the Islamic community.

Sunnis are in the majority in all Islamic countries except Iran, Iraq, Lebanon and Bahrein. Within the Sunni community, two smaller sects exist in the Ibadhis and the Wahhabis. The more puritanical Wahhabism was adopted by Ibn Saud and it is now the main Sunni stream in Saudi Arabia.

In contrast to the Sunnis, Shi'as believe that both the spiritual and temporal leadership of the Muslim world were vested by divine ordinance in Ali's descendants and that successive leaders were to appoint their successors by divine inspiration. Consequently, Shi'as appear for the most part to be more intensely religious than Sunnis. The two streams of Islam have different interpretations of the meaning of history. For Sunni historians, success and power were signs of a faithful community and validation of Islam, its beliefs and claims. For Shi'as, history was a struggle of a righteous remnant in protest and opposition against the forces of evil in order to realize its messianic hope and promise, that is, the establishment of the righteous rule of the Imam.[11]

However, as Islam developed after the demise of the caliphate with the fall of Baghdad to the Mongols in 1258, through the period of the sultanates of the medieval Muslim empires down to the twentieth century, the reign and just social order of the imam was in fact to remain a frustrated hope.

Shi'ism, however, has survived to embrace some 110 million of the world's Muslims. Shi'as are opposed to all Arab kings and ruling sheikhs because their doctrine preaches that monarchies are unlawful in Islam. Since the principal figure should always be an imam or ayatollah, all Arab monarchs fear overthrow by Shi'a subversion, especially since the Iranian revolution of 1979.

However, as we have seen, regicide was a familiar phenomenon from earliest Islamic political history. Of the four Righteous Caliphs, three were murdered, including the second caliph Umar, who thanked God on his death-bed that he was struck down by a Christian slave with a private grievance rather than by one of the faithful.[12] In the cases of Uthman and Ali, the perpetrators saw themselves as tyrannicides, freeing the community from an unrighteous ruler. Ali's supporters justified his inaction against the murderers of Uthman on the same grounds: that his death was a justified execution, not murder.

Over the centuries, Shi'a Islam produced offshoots among which one of the best known is the relatively small Ismaili sect. There are no more than a million or so Ismailis in the world today. The majority of Shi'as, approximately 60 million, are Ithna' Asharis (Twelvers) who claim that the twelfth imam disappeared in the ninth century, but that he will return to establish the righteous rule of perfect justice. Meanwhile, they regard all governments as corrupt, although those which accept the guidance of religious leaders might be tolerated. The Twelvers' doctrine has been the state religion in Iran since 1502. Under Khomeini, it became an extremist activist ideology that inspired both the overthrow of the Shah and it has since served as the doctrinal basis of the new Islamic republic.

Ismailis are also known as 'Seveners' because they restrict the number of 'visible' imams to seven and take their name from the last of these, the imam Ismail. It was the Ismailis who gave the world the concept of 'Assassin' in the 13th century. Known for centuries as a 'gang of drugged dupes led by scheming imposters, as a conspiracy of nihilistic terrorists, or as a syndicate of professional murderers',[13] the Ismaili Assassins caught the imagination of Europeans from the time mention of them was first made in the chronicles of the Crusades.

In his famous historical essay,[14] Professor Bernard Lewis
has reviewed the evidence concerning the Assassins and their
role in the history, culture and ethos of Islam. They did not
invent assassination, he insists, but merely gave it their name.
Murder began when the son of Adam and Eve murdered his
brother and political murder came with the emergence of
political authority. When power, says Lewis, is vested in an
individual, the removal of that individual is seen as a quick
and simple method of effecting political change. Such
murders are commonplace in autocratic kingdoms and
empires of both East and West.

The idealization of tyrannicide, Lewis reminds us, became
part of the political ethos of Greece and Rome and found
expression in the murders of Philip II of Macedon, Tiberius
Gracchus and Julius Caesar. It finds a clear echo in the 'new
ideological politics' of post-eighteenth century Europe.[15]
Since, as we have seen, a similar Islamic tradition could be
invoked by the Ismailis in sending their emissaries to kill the
unrighteous, they appear little different from any such group
in European, let alone Oriental history. Indeed, after the
death of Ali and the accession of Muawiyah, the assassination
of rulers becomes rare and when it does occur it has more to
do with dynastic rivalries than revolution.

The Assassins then, drew their inspiration from a variety of
sources. They shared with other groups of many different
religions and cultures the ancient ideal of tyrannicide and the
religious obligation to rid the world of an unrighteous ruler.
But they also regarded such killings as a ritual with a virtual
sacramental quality. They were, perhaps, the world's first
professional terrorists. The Assassins always used a dagger,
even when other weapons would clearly have been safer.
According to Lewis, they were invariably caught and, indeed,
few Assassins made any attempt to escape capture. There is
even a suggestion that to survive a mission was somehow
shameful. Again, as we have already noted, this type of
martyrdom has no place in Islamic tradition in general nor in
the particular beliefs of Shi'a Islam. However, as Lewis points
out, such practices and beliefs of the Assassins are ancient and
deep rooted in human society. They predate Islam, but
reappear in unexpected places. It is worth quoting him in full:

As custodians of esoteric mysteries for the initiate, as purveyors of salvation through knowledge of the Imam, as bearers of a promise of messianic fulfilment, of release from the toils of the world and the yoke of the law, the Ismailis are part of a long tradition, that goes back to the beginnings of Islam and far beyond, and forward to our own day—a tradition of popular and emotional cults in sharp contrast with the learned and legal religion of the established order.[16]

The victims of the Assassins belonged to two main groups: princes, officers and ministers on the one hand, and religious dignitaries on the other. With only rare, occasional exceptions the victims were all Sunni Muslims. Normally, other Shi'as, including 'Twelvers', as well as Christians and Jews were immune. Even the Crusaders seemed to escape the Assassins' daggers, except on a few occasions following Ismaili agreements with Saladin and with the caliph. The enemy was the Sunni political, military, bureaucratic and religious establishment. Their murders were not opportunist killings but were carefully planned and carried out. They were designed to frighten, to weaken and ultimately to overthrow the Sunni authorities.

The ancient Assassins were believed to be inescapable. One important leader who wore armour at all times and surrounded himself with loyal bodyguards was nevertheless struck down while at prayer. Referring to their Sunni victims, a prominent Assassin is reported as saying: 'To kill these people is more lawful than rainwater. To shed the blood of a heretic is more meritorious than to kill seventy Greek infidels'.[17]

Throughout the medieval period, the Assassins were regarded as a profound threat to the existing social, political and religious order. They were one of a long series of messianic movements and, as such, they were by no means unique. Ismailism, however, had begun as a major intellectual force in Islam, attracting poets and philosophers as well as theologians. It became an unparalleled social movement of the dispossessed, the deprivileged and the unstable. The Assassins were the product of the mobilization by the Ismaili leadership of the frustration and anger of the discontented into an ideology and an organization exemplary in its cohesion, discipline and purposive violence.

It is also true to say, though, that the failure of the Assassins to overthrow the Sunni order was utter and complete. They failed to capture any city of any size and even the remote mountain strongholds they did rule for a while were overrun. Their followers have become small peaceful communities of peasants and merchants, a small minority sect under their revered leader, the Aga Khan.

However, the undercurrent of messianic hope and revolutionary violence that impelled the Assassins has survived to inspire new movements in the Muslim world of today. Their methods and ideals have found their imitators among those for whom modernization and contemporary conditions have given new cause for resentment and anger.

What are the most common themes that inspire the modern 'Assassins' and fuel their resentment? For among the Muslim fundamentalists in Iran and the various groups elsewhere who have been responsible for, among other things, the assassination of President Sadat, the take-over of the Grand Mosque at Mecca, anti-American rioting in Pakistan and bomb plots in Kuwait, certain grievances are clear. In common with each other, they all decry the ungodliness and corruption of most contemporary societies. They argue that man's only hope of salvation lies in making society conform strictly to the word of God as revealed in the authoritative sources of the Faith. In practice, this means restricting political leadership to devout Muslims and establishing the *'Sharia'* (Islamic Law) as the law of the state. Only then will society be saved from sin and cured of the ills visited upon it in retribution for deviations from the path of righteousness. As we have seen, this theme is not new; movements inspired by a fundamentalist drive have appeared throughout Muslim history. If anything they are a traditional aspect of the inseparability of the secular and the religious in Islam.

The fundamentalist revolution in Iran owes its legitimacy to its secular success in overthrowing the regime of the Shah and replacing it with Khomeini's version of an Islamic theocracy. This version is based upon a blend of radical Shi'ism, anti-Westernism, leftist radicalism and religious extremism.[18] Khomeini's theocracy is based squarely on Shi'a belief, recognizing, as described above the successors of Ali as the true heirs of the Prophet's authority to govern after his death. Until the reappearance of the twelfth Imam, Shi'as rely on the extensive knowledge of religious jurists in order to interpret Islamic rule. These learned men (*mujtahids*) were bound to fall foul of temporal rulers and to avoid the inevitable and invariably unpleasant consequences of such conflict, the *mujtahids* adopted the practice of *Taqiyya* or 'counsel of caution'. Over time, *Taqiyya* became an article of faith leading imams, as well as *mujtahids*, to refrain from a direct challenge to the established order.

Khomeini abolished this practice in seeking to restore the early activist drive of Islam. Citing the Prophet and the first three imams (Ali and his two sons Hasan and Huseyn) as his example, he insisted that the jurist (*Faqih*) must rule as only he could save Islam from the dangers of the West and modernizing élites in Muslim countries. Thus in the Islamic theocracy, government would be based on the revealed law (*Shari'a*) with sovereignty resting with God. The jurist-governor as the 'trustee of the Prophet' would be able to exercise the same power as the Prophet or the imams.

Since he exercises the power of the Prophet, the rule of the jurist-governor is by definition just and therefore no system for ending his rule is necessary. Not so with an impious or presumptuous ruler (*Taghut*). Thus Khomeini calls upon his followers to 'create suitable conditions to facilitate the emergence of a generation of believers who would destroy the thrones of despots, just as Imam Huseyn attempted to do at Karbala in 680'.[19] It is this dimension of the Khomeini creed which might well underlie the Iranian attitude towards the war with Iraq; it certainly causes considerable disquiet among Iran's neighbours in the Persian Gulf; and it seems also to have inspired the fanaticism of the Shi'a fighters in Lebanon.

For the political objective of Khomeini's activism is to attain Muslim unity, regardless of the conventional boundaries of nation-states and even ignoring the ancient schism between the Shi'a and Sunni sects. A combination of the steady growth of authoritarianism and autocracy in the Middle East since the 1950s, the lack of economic development and poverty, and the pursuit of power for Muslims so that Muslim communities can govern themselves according to the law of

God and thus lead proper Muslim lives,[20] has created the conditions for conspiracies to bring about political change. The seeds of such a process, as we have seen, lie deep in Islamic religion, history, culture and psyche.

Non-Muslims probably exaggerate the extent to which Islam is a religion of holy war (*jihad*). Indeed, the concept of *jihad* refers to the vocation of Muslims to 'strive or struggle to realize God's will, to lead a virtuous life'.[21] But this includes the universal mission and obligation to spread God's will and rule. This obligation came to be formulated during the third phase of the caliphate, the Abbasid era (752–1258) with the division of the world into Islamic (dar al-Islam, land of Islam) and non-Islamic (dar al-harb, land of warfare). Importantly, however, the hundred-year period following the death of Muhammed was marked by the conquest of the Byzantine and Persian empires by Arab armies driven by a combination of religious zeal and opportunities for plunder. Their success, it has been argued, brought religious, political and economic rewards. To die in battle was not to fail, but instead meant becoming a martyr with the reward of immediate entry to Paradise.

The advancing Muslim armies offered their vanquished enemies three alternatives: (i) voluntary conversion to Islam, (ii) acceptance of Muslim rule as a 'protected' people, and (iii) battle or the sword. In latter times, the majority of peoples encountered by the Muslims are thought to have accepted the first option, and to have been converted peacefully by missionaries.[22] But it still remains the case that there was a powerful militant strand in Islam from the very beginning and that it characterized the initial period of expansion, including the era of the Righteous Caliphs to which contemporary Islamic reform movements, in common with their predecessors over the intervening centuries, refer for guidance and inspiration.

Professor P. J. Vatikiotis has discussed the relationship between the commitment to the restoration of power to the Islamic nation, or community of believers, and contemporary terrorism. He points to an 'unbridgeable gap' between Islam and those who claim to represent it and all other social and political arrangements. Vatikiotis suggests that 'the dichotomy between the Islamic and all other systems of earthly government and order is clear, sharp and permanent; it is also hostile'.[23] The basically Western and therefore un-Islamic state system and man-made political order can be legitimately attacked. Indeed, says Vatikiotis, when 'its architects, current guardians, representatives, and institutions are attacked, this is not considered to be either unethical or immoral, let alone criminal. In the common parlance of the fanatic, 'spilling the blood of the infidel has God's blessing'. Terrorism, therefore, has its place among the means employed by extremist Muslim fundamentalist factions. What is novel is its use by rulers or states. However, this does not alter the fact that for the actual terrorist, the enemy or target is the 'non-Muslim', the 'unbeliever', the 'infidel'.

Finally, an important distinction needs to be drawn between 'Islamic' terrorism and terrorism emanating from the Middle East. Middle Eastern conditions, we have already noted, seem to lead inevitably to extreme violence among those who aspire to engage in politics, in contrast to the ethos of politics in the West. However, the model for the spread of terrorism since the 1960s, both within the Middle East and in the wider world outside has been the Palestine Liberation Organization (the PLO). Nobody would argue that the doctrine and practice of the PLO derive from Islam. It draws its inspiration very much from European sources. The PLO at first sought to emulate the guerrilla tactics of the Chinese and Vietnamese Communists and only when these failed did it turn to terrorism proper. Its ultimate aim, the establishment of a secular state in Palestine is, of course, totally removed from any Islamic aspiration.

The success of Khomeini's revolution in Iran has provoked a resurgence of Islamic militancy. The consolidation in power in various Middle Eastern countries, such as Libya, Iraq and Syria, of autocratic military rulers bent on total domination at home and abroad has produced the relatively novel phenomenon of state terrorism. The relative abundance of wealth from oil revenues and the consequent abundance of weaponry has caused the proliferation of terrorist groups from among the many elements in the Middle East with a real or imagined grievance.

Thus, the experience of the Middle East, both historically as well as today, seems to support both of the views of the efficacy of terrorism that were expressed at the beginning of this paper. It is at once an irrelevance and a menace. What links the PLO with the medieval Assassins is the absolute failure of its methods to achieve its goal, which, if the Organization survives, will have, at best, to be a politically negotiated compromise. The Islamic groups have so far been more successful, but only where support for the existing regime was already crumbling. The powerful, autocratic military rulers of the Middle East have, to date, largely been able to suppress them when they appeared seriously threatening. In practice then, terrorism has been little more than an irrelevance.

But this is not to say that, unlike the Assassins of old, terrorist groups are not to be regarded as a profound threat to the 'existing order, political, social and religious'. Among the countries of the Middle East, whether the small principalities of the Gulf, the great Arab states like Egypt or, last but by no means least, Israel, they are so regarded. It is for this reason that all the states in the region, from the most extreme to the most moderate, seek either to eliminate them altogether or to ensure that they are firmly and securely under their strict control.

NOTES

1. Walter Laquer, 'International Terrorism', *Washington Post* (29 Apr. 1984).
2. *ibid.*
3. Noel O'Sullivan, 'Terrorism, ideology and democracy', p.3 (see above).
4. David Shribman, 'The textbook approach to terrorism', *New York Times* (22 Apr. 1984).
5. *ibid.*
6. Noel O'Sullivan *op.cit.*
7. E. Kedourie and A. Mango, 'Violence in Lebanon', *Encounter*, Vol. LXIII, No. 1 (June 1984) pp.38–42.
8. Victor T. Le Vine, 'The Arab world in the 1980s: have the predicates of politics changed?', *Middle East Review*, Vol. XVI, No. 3 (Spring 1984) pp.3–16.
9. *ibid.*
10. The discussion of the·politics and ideology of Islam which follows, especially in the very early period following the death of Muhammed

in 632, relies very heavily for its detail upon the excellent and clear text by John L. Esposito, *Islam and Politics*, Syracuse, Syracuse University Press (1984).

11. Esposito *op.cit.* p.12.
12. Bernard Lewis, 'The Assassins', *Encounter*, Vol. XXIX, No. 5 (November 1967) pp.34–49.
13. *ibid.* p.42.
14. *ibid.*
15. *See* O'Sullivan *op.cit.*
16. Lewis *op.cit.* p.44.
17. Quoted in 'Why they did it', *Memo* (December 1983).
18. Mohammed E. Ahari, 'Implications of the Iranian political change for the Arab world', *Middle East Review*, Vol. XVI, No. 3 (Spring 1984) pp.17–29.
19. *ibid.*
20. P. J. Vatikiotis, paper delivered at the Jonathan Institute's Second Conference on International Terrorism, June 25–6, 1984. Quoted in 'International terrorism and Middle East politics', *Contemporary Mideast Backgrounder*, No. 192 (22 Aug. 1984).
21. Eposito *op.cit.* p.10.
22. *ibid.*
23. *ibid.*

7 The Containment of Terrorism: Violence in Turkish Politics 1965–80

C. H. Dodd

Until recent years there has been comparatively little political violence in the history of the Turkish republic. Even in Ottoman times there was little political violence, if the nationalist struggles of the non-Muslim component peoples of the Ottoman Empire are not taken into the reckoning. Not even the 1908 Young Turk revolution was violent. In 1909 an attempted counter-revolution fomented by fundamentalist members of the Islamic religious institution was firmly put down, but there was no blood bath. After the First World War Mustafa Kemal Atatürk took the momentous steps of abolishing the caliphate, disestablishing Islam, and abolishing what was left of the Şeriat, or holy law. This did produce a substantial degree of political and social disturbance. Indeed, in 1925 and 1926 domestic political opposition was linked with a Kurdish rebellion which strained political moderation to the utmost. The rebellion was firmly put down, yet whilst this provided an opportunity for Atatürk to dispose of some of his political opponents, there was not an extensive amount of violence used and little terror associated with it. Atatürk's regime was never tempted into that most hideous form of state terrorism which constantly shifts the dominant ideology and eliminates those who fall outside the current version, however loyal they might previously have been. In such a situation no-one feels safe—as no-one did at the height of the Terror during the French revolution. Nor did Atatürk's regime single out class enemies for destruction. The main target of his revolutionary regime was religion. Yet religious functionaries were not persecuted; they were pensioned off or turned into state functionaries.

Acting as he did, Atatürk was doing no more than follow

Ottoman traditions. In the nineteenth century, for instance, the Sultan typically sought to buy off his opponents with honoured positions in the bureaucracy. The autocratic Ottoman state was fortunate, however, that it did not have to face the onslaught of anarchist, populist, socialist or any other forms of counter-regime violence to which, for instance, the Russian state was exposed. There was a whiff of it in an attempt by a certain Ali Suavi who, in 1878, tried to depose Sultan Abdul Hamid II in an ill-founded attempt which cost him his life when he was felled by a police truncheon. Ali Suavi was a 'turbanned revolutionary' who showed where the principal potential opposition to the Sultan's rule lay.[1] He was a forerunner of that modern Islamic fundamentalism which has dominated the politics of many Muslim states in recent years and which has given rise to political violence against secularist or Western-inclined regimes, and sometimes, as in the case of Iran, to state terrorism.

In the Arab successor states of the Ottoman Empire nationalism and socialism, in that order, were the doctrines most favoured by the intelligentsia in the earlier part of this century, and sometimes still are. But beginning with the Muslim Brethren in 1928 a fundamentalist Islamic movement with puritanical antecedents was given recognition in a new social and political organization. As was shown in Egypt during the 1950s, and very recently in Syria, the Muslim Brethren are prepared to use extreme violence to overthrow regimes they regard as un-Islamic. The justification lies in the Islamic doctrine that it is a duty to resist impious government. Indeed, in early Islam caliphs were overthrown for this reason, whilst in mediaeval times the Assassins, a heterodox Shi'ite sect, engaged in a regular programme of assassination of Muslim leaders that came close to political terrorism. Unfortunately for Islamic political development neither the precise conditions warranting the removal of a ruler, nor the procedures to be followed were fully laid down. This clearly invited rebellion and the arbitrary use of violence, but abhorrence of rebellion encouraged Muslims later to develop a justification for domestic political quietism which persisted throughout the period of the Ottoman Empire. Even an unjust ruler, it was laid down, was to be obeyed as long as he did not attack Islam. Almost anything was better (for the sake of preserving the Muslim community) than rebellion. Outright violence was reserved for *jihad*, or holy war, against unbelievers.

This political quietism allowed a partnership between religion and state in the Ottoman Empire in which the state was to become dominant. This state dominance permitted a further reduction in the role of Islam in the nineteenth century as the Ottoman state modernized, taking over legal and educational responsibilities from the religious institution as it did so, and developing new ones outside religious control. It was this earlier weakening of the religious institution that helped Atatürk to demolish what was left after the First World War, abolishing outright not just the caliphate, and what remained of Islamic law, but also the religious brotherhoods—which was a great blow to popular religion—and the institutions of religious education.

This dismantling of religious structures has meant that, unlike the rest of the Muslim Middle East, Turkey does not expect political violence to develop from religious claims to authority. Religion has revived in Turkey, as elsewhere, but as yet without able and devoted leadership. Despite some training now for clerics, what leadership there has been has had mainly to be political party leadership. For from 1970 to 1980 Turkey had a religious party, latterly called the National Salvation Party, as one of the competitors at the polls. Religious support has therefore been firmly directed along constitutional lines. And this position, maintained by a vigilant state, must account largely for the fact that, unlike the rest of the Middle East, religious organizations have not participated in violent action against government. However, some very open disrespect was shown in the years just before 1980 to the secularist republic. In 1980 a remarkable religious congress in Konya, an old religious centre, alarmed the military—especially when, allegedly, the Turkish flag was burnt. This constituted one reason for military intervention in September of that year. During the period 1970–80, political violence did reach unheard-of proportions for Turkey, but, untypically for the Middle East, it did not stem from religion.

In fact political violence began in Turkey in the 1960s and

its first practitioners were students. There are a number of reasons why this was so. The first is that even in the later years of the Ottoman Empire students had regarded themselves very highly as the future political and administrative élite. This self-esteem was encouraged by Atatürk who called upon youth to lead his revolution. It was encouraged yet again by the military intervention of 1960. This was not caused by student unrest, but it was triggered off by it—a distinction not always apparent to the student body. Then in the 1960s, with the return to competitive politics, the competing parties in politics made strenuous efforts to recruit student support. It was quite natural for the right-of-centre Justice Party to do this because its predecessor, the Democrat Party (abolished by the military), had clearly been much resented not only by the students, but also by the Atatürkist state bureaucracy whose very ranks the students would mostly fill. Other political parties also began to address themselves directly to the student body. The result was that the Atatürkist élite, broadly sympathetic to the solidarist and statist People's Party, began to be divided politically—starting with the students. Moreover, students were now increasing greatly in numbers. Between 1960 and 1970 there was a threefold increase. Furthermore many more were now being recruited outside the social circles of the Atatürkist élite, who manned the bureaucracy, the state industries, the military and the educational institutions.[2] Finally the students of the decade, and later students too, were grossly dissatisfied with both university facilities and job prospects. Indeed a 1969/70 survey showed only one-fifth of students expecting to find employment after graduating,[3] a considerable decline in expectations as compared with previous decades.

A very significant change occurred in Turkish politics in 1965 when the People's Party established by Atatürk, and under the chairmanship of his lieutenant, İsmet İnönü, decided to go 'left-of-centre'. The party later came under the control of Bülent Ecevit (1972), when its old close connections with the bureaucracy and the military deliberately loosened on the grounds that they inhibited the new socialist appeal of the party to the electorate. The importance of this change was the impetus it gave to radical politicization of the student body. In the process it lost for the party the support of the solidarist element, who now saw the People's Party firmly set on the road to Moscow. A gap now existed for idealistic, Atatürkist youth dedicated to Turkish national unity. The gap was filled by the emergence of idealist organizations, some of which were extremely Left, and others equally Right, or even neo-fascist, in their beliefs. Moreover, the relative moderation of the People's Party gave a fillip to the emergence of a much more socialist Workers' Party which also attracted more student support. This party was parliamentary when it was formed, but it soon despaired of achieving social and political change by parliamentary means, and passed into more radical hands in 1969, after the party's failure in the elections of that year. In 1971 it was abolished by the military, when they intervened again in Turkish politics. The effect of these developments on the student body was dramatic. Impelled also by vigorous left-wing journalism, some very leftist student sectarian radical groups began to emerge. One new and important theme to appear in the new journalism was a critique of the thesis that the bureaucracy constituted an Atatürkist bulwark against imperialism. It was argued that the bureaucracy 'far from being the social group which offered the strongest resistance to foreign penetration, were in fact its instigators'.[4] There was some truth in the claim. The Atatürkist establishment was dedicated to making Turkey part of European civilization even if it had shown itself alert to the dangers of foreign economic penetration. However, the new radical political groups came to reject the hallowed notion that the bureaucratic (and military) élite were the guardians of the Atatürkist state, and this was seen to justify the violence they would use in support of *true* Atatürkist ideals.

Activist organizations began in the universities as discussion groups, which initially addressed themselves to student problems. An activist, arrested in 1971, recounted how in these discussion groups 'people would make bold remarks about Turkey's problems. They would say "The ony real patriots are people who think like us and read the books we read". That had a great effect on me. I'd rush out and buy the books they mentioned'.[5]

Marxist-inclined academics would also participate in the discussion groups. These groups then developed into 'ideas clubs' attended by Turkish leftist intellectuals. In 1965 one of these organizations distributed a Workers' Party magazine in a main square in Ankara. This resulted in fights between leftist and rightist students, a development which was to set the pattern for the future. Its immediate effect however was to prompt the emergence of a nationwide Federation of Ideas Clubs. It was reorganized in 1969 as *Dev Genç* (Revolutionary Youth). A Turkish People's Liberation Army followed in 1970, and in the same year the Turkish People's Liberation Front.[6] Both organizations were revolutionary and engaged in violence of various types. These leftist revolutionary groups immediately met with violent opposition in the universities from newly-formed rightist groups, and this violence soon spread outside. NATO and American imperialism were the main targets for the Left. Demonstrations, kidnapping, and bank robberies, were the most usual instances of this activity. The whole movement towards leftist activism and violence was also given an impetus by the student riots in France in 1968, but most important was the incapacity of the right-of-centre Justice Party government to put down the violence. The government had a good majority in the Assembly, but attempts to introduce legislation to curb leftist activity in 1967 were not successful. Fearing the military and distrusting the bureaucracy, the Justice Party was anxious to avoid direct confrontation. Instead it stood back and adopted the tactic of allowing rightist groups to attack the Left.[7] It was to set the pattern for the future.

The military intervention of 1971 at first showed socialist inclinations, but later turned powerfully against leftist groups as the generals mastered the junior officers who, it seems, pushed the military command to intervene. Over 2000 persons were eventually arrested, tried, and imprisoned as a result of a vigorous anti-terrorist campaign mounted by the military, and three were hanged. Some of the sentences were clearly deserved, but the prosecution of authors or translators of books and articles expounding leftist doctrines led to much criticism abroad. Professor Mümtaz Soysal was imprisoned for alleged communist propaganda in an introductory textbook on government. But the effect of the arrest of *bona fide* terrorists or would-be terrorists, was ruined by an amnesty granted in 1974 after the return to an elected government, much to the chagrin of the military.

Not unnaturally then, in 1976 violence began to reappear. Terrorists of the 1960s who had either been killed in clashes, or had been executed, now became martyrs for a variety of new or resurrected groups (it is always a great boost to have martyrs in a pantheon of heroes). Four basic currents or, even schools, of terrorists emerged. One grew out of the Turkish People's Liberation Party and Front led by Mahir Cayan in the late 1960s (they espoused a Marxist–Maoist doctrine). One notorious band within this school was the Marxist–Leninist Armed Propaganda Unit—responsible for thirty-five murders, some of them American servicemen. This was a near-terrorist group, properly speaking, with an assassination policy. Other groups within the school, like Revolutionary Youth or *Kurtuluş* (Liberation), seem to have had less precise aims.

Also deriving from the 1960s were a number of groups recognizing the supremacy of the Turkish People's Liberation Army led by Deniz Gezmiş, also a martyr, a Turkish Che Guevara hanged in 1972. People's Liberation was another more diffuse group, which also followed this line, but it also contained at least one terrorist squad. A third school was Maoist. It was led originally by a Dŏgu Perincek. This group formed itself into a political party, the Turkish Worker Peasant Party, which was tolerated largely on account of its anti-Russian character. A number of clandestine groups operated under a Maoist label. Finally, in Eastern Turkey the Apoists, named after Abdullah Apo Ocalan, appear to have been the main group seeking Kurdish national autonomy. On the whole it seems that these groups cooperated with one another from 1975 to 1980 faced as they were with determined rightist groups perhaps fewer in number, but more coherently organized. These rightist groups were often said to be supported by the small, but effective Nationalist Action Party, whose doctrine was nationalist, anti-communist and not at all supportive of the bourgeosie either, which it rather despised.

The character of political violence after 1975 was not markedly different from the 1960s save that it now moved much more outside the universities, which after 1971 were under much closer police control. Attacks by groups on one another were frequent. Sometimes they resulted only in a few casualties, but on other occasions these sectarian disputes would escalate into major incidents. This could occur if local terrorists could incite sympathetic social groups into violent action against potentially hostile groups. This occurred in Kahramanmaraş in December 1978, where heterodox Shi'ite Muslims (Alevis) were incited into conflict with the orthodox Sunnis. As a result one hundred persons were killed, mostly Alevis.[8] A similar event occurred in Çorum in June, 1980, a town to the north-east of Ankara. There were thirty deaths— again extremists seem to have been instigators of the disturbances. Clearly much of the violence in many towns and villages resulted from heightened tension between antagonistic groups or families. Since feuding does not lie far below the surface in Turkish villages, hostility can easily break out in violence. In this respect the presence of small armed groups was clearly a catalyst.

The activities of these groups also extended to the creation of so-called liberated areas. Leftist groups were most prominent in this development, but rightist groups also declared liberated zones. In some cases these were small areas of cities, but in a few instances whole villages or towns would be declared free, as in the case of Fatsa on the Black Sea coast (ominously near the Russian frontier) where it occurred with the connivance of the left-wing mayor.

These developments were disturbing enough and made everyday life hazardous for those not involved and not least for uncommitted university students. This sort of inter-group violence was accompanied, however, and increasingly, by the assassination of mostly minor, but also some major political personalities. There was no assassination, or attempted assassination, of members of government, whichever party was in power, but victims included a former prime minister, Nihat Erim,[9] the Deputy Chairman of the Nationalist Action

Party, a People's Party deputy, a left-wing trade union leader, the editor of a right-wing Istanbul newspaper, the Chairman of the People's party in Kayseri province, and two Nationalist Action Party provincial chairmen. Moreover, in the course of their duties some soldiers, including senior officers, fell victim to terrorist bullets. On the whole the violence which occurred, much of it in the provinces, partook of the nature of civil war between activists none of which had the slightest chance of seizing power. These battles must partly have derived from, and in turn fomented, existing social antagonisms—and much of the killing of persons of note was probably inspired by a desire for revenge. Clearly peripheral elements in the political system were involved, though the role of the Nationalist Action Party is less than clear in this regard.

The principal danger of the violence was that it might have spread to engulf more and more of Turkish life. In this regard it was highly significant that important areas of Turkish life were becoming quite deeply politicized and that violence and counter-violence were helping in this development. This politicization had come about in various ways, however. In the first place, the far Left had no hope of achieving their aims through the political system and sought to develop their influence in unions and professional associations. In some, like TOBDER, the teachers' association, this was not difficult. The far Right responded in similar fashion. More important, the prevalence of political coalitions and frequent changes of government provided opportunities for the removal of public officials and their replacement by political appointees. This affected *inter alia* the police (already divided into rival professional associations with opposed political views) and the Ministry of Education. The politicization of state and other institutions was also important because they provided a backing for terrorist organizations which they did not receive from the general population—save where a terrorist group could create a sense of identification with some dissatisfied section of society. This was only substantially possible for the Kurds, and occasionally for left-wing groups who intermittently obtained support from the Alevi's who, as a religious minority, always voted for the more secularist People's Party.

The actual damage to the state and society achieved by this violence was not all that great by 1980, but clearly if it continued there was a fair potential for disruption. The major political parties were too evenly divided in the Assembly for firm government to occur. Moreover, they had become too polarized, mainly on personal, but also on policy, grounds to form a coalition government, which would certainly have cut down the violence. And the two minor parties were too anti-systemic to be anything but disruptive. In August 1980 deaths from violence had risen to 350, as compared with 100 in the previous January. Turkey was reckoned at that time to be the sixth most violent country and was fast approaching the level of violence of Northern Ireland in the ratio of deaths to population.[10] The statistics of terrorism are notoriously difficult to interpret, however, especially in a country like Turkey where reported casualties may have more to do with feuding than with terrorism. It seems that during the year preceding military intervention between one and a half and two and a half thousand persons died in incidents connected with terrorist activities.[11] Four times as many leftist as rightist activists were arrested in the year before military intervention.[12] Of the terrorists captured, about 40 per cent were either students or unemployed (which will include those at school), the next largest groups being workers and self-employed. Well over a half were of ages between sixteen and twenty-five.[13] During the period December 1978 to September 1982 some 26,000 persons were convicted by martial law tribunals, of whom 18,000 received one-year sentences of imprisonment. There were 143 death sentences and 92 of life imprisonment.[14] As of 1 September 1982 there were some 15,700 persons—former members of parliament, lawyers, members of the press, unionists and members of associations—who were either under detention, on remand, or convicted;[15] members of various leftist and secessionist associations formed the vast majority, 86 per cent. Of these the majority were leftists. To judge by other figures, secessionists played a much smaller part in the violence than leftists. Again, as of 1 September 1982 leftist activists in illegal organizations on trial numbered 17,570, as compared with

4,522 members of secessionist and 1,228 members of rightist organizations.[16]

Clearly, either military intervention has cracked down harder on the Left than on others, or, if justice has been as even-handed as is claimed, there were very many more leftist activists involved in violence than others. Clearly, too, it was youth who engaged in violence for the most part. This came about partly because, as has been noted, academics, journalists and politicians gave a firm lead in politicizing youth in the universities. In particular leadership was provided by those who had despaired of any achievement of a left-wing regime through parliamentary means. Secondly, the strong Atatürkist tradition—nationalist, solidarist and reformist—could not easily find expression in what to youth appear to be sordid party political struggles. A large section of the young found an outlet in leftism, initially divisive but promising a heady unity in the long run. Another section could not accept a Marxist solution, even less a socialist one, whether on grounds of the social disruption that would be entailed, or out of fear of Turkey's traditional national enemy, Russia. In the conditions of modern Turkey the Atatürkist tradition, which forms an important part of early education, had to be reinterpreted. The spirit, if not the letter, of Kemalism has been important to them.

But there are reasons beyond the political and ideological which must to some degree explain the development of violence.[17] Some, which are universal in character, have been alluded to already, namely the student movement in 1968 in France, the general decline in respect for political authority in recent years, the generation gap induced in part by rapid technological change, the general levelling up (or down) and the decline in the individuality of certain occupational groups, which have created problems of identity. In addition, the growing complexity of society and the increasing roles played by the state and large economic concerns have produced a more impersonal and bureaucratic society. These and other general factors have doubtless played their part, but it is in the peculiar conditions of a changing Turkish society that clues to the violence may also be sought.

To begin with the question of identity, in the Ottoman

Empire everyone had his or her status as a member of a group and this was shown by dress, speech, style and other identity-forming mechanisms. These particularistic forms of identification were hateful to the Kemalist republic which sought (very effectively) to replace them by uniformity of appearance and behaviour. Turkish nationalism and solidarism were the ideas most stressed. They served to help alter the seat of loyalties—the flag and the national anthem were the successful symbols of this transformation. Other particularistic loyalties were suspect to the new republic, but under the surface these maintained their hold outside the Westernized towns. It is not therefore surprising to find that ideological divisions among youthful recruits to the national political system were soon expressed in sartorial and other differences. Hence the distinctive clothing of different groups—the Parka being a favourite sign of leftist identification.[18] Hence, too, the sideburns of the nationalist Right, the Latin American moustaches of some factions of the far Left, the pointed beards of other leftist intelligentsia and the total beards of Muslim groups. These symbols invaded the bureaucracy—so at least one knew whom not to approach for help. Among violent youth these were vital identity-conferring traditionalist symbols that accentuated differences.

It also does not help that recruits over recent years have increasingly been recruited to the institutions of higher education from the countryside, or from the shanty town areas of the large cities, where the country often still lives on. It has often been observed that internal immigrants to the town have not become urbanized: rather they have peasantized the towns. The older traditions are not therefore broken down but rather released in new and less restricted environments where parts of them can grow enormously misshapen. Moreover, it has also been pointed out that the Westernizing Kemalist republic actually removed a great deal of responsibility from village elders to arbitrate and conciliate in the feuds which were always prevalent in Turkish village life. With the relative incapacity of the state to solve these problems from afar, though imposing legal redress, violence actually increased in the villages and has been transmitted to society generally through the processes of economic and social development. Moreover, and more pessimistically, it has been observed by Paul Stirling:

'The village lineage exists to defend its members . . . But at the same time the existence of the lineage depends on its having enemies against which to defend its members, since it has no other occasion for corporate action. A lineage at peace with its neighbours would lose the main point of its existence.[19]

Another factor in the upbringing in villages has been discerned, namely, the role of epic heroes as persons to be imitated. This tradition, originally appearing in folk poetry and folklore, has, it appears, found a modern form of expression. Whilst the founding fathers of the Turkish republic are now among the gallery of heroes, both the Turkish Left and Right have their own. For the Left the most prominent is the Communist poet Nazım Hikmet, who suffered long terms of imprisonment rather than recant. As noted earlier, notorious terrorists of the 1960s have now entered into the pantheon of heroes.

Then, again, and to take more developmental considerations into account, it must be observed that some very substantial changes have occurred in Turkey over the past half-century—all of which have revived in some ways the rural culture of the Ottoman Empire. Quite apart from the general influx of villagers as shanty-town dwellers, the Western culture so carefully fostered by the Kemalist republic has been affected in other ways. Very important is the fact that since Kemalist times Turkey has developed her own native bourgeoisie. The (much less developed and largely commercial) bougeoisie was previously composed of Greeks, Jews and Armenians. The new commercial and industrial bourgeoisie has arisen from land-owning and artisan backgrounds, and the education it has sought has been scientific and technological rather than cultural. Indeed the high European cultural ideals held by the Kemalist élite have everywhere declined. Teachers are not as well trained in them, and the schools have been swamped by the large numbers from rural backgrounds. It has been observed that 'Impersonality, boredom and surrender to ambient influences' characterize the school education system.[20]

These considerations strongly suggest that it is a revived or liberated traditionalism which is a major cause of contemporary violence, even though it has also been noted that the Kemalist republic played a large role in breaking down the capacity of village institutions to exert traditional modes of social control over the inhabitants. In one study of terrorism in Turkey it is suggested that the upheavals of modernization, including large-scale migration to cities, have seriously weakened old traditions, producing in persons who have been displaced feelings of estrangement and, subsequently, anomie, when they find that their own patterns of values do not fit the new environment in which they find themselves. Violence then becomes a means of political participation, the only means open to those estranged from the values of their environment, and unable therefore to express themselves through the appropriate forms of behaviour.[21]

These views preface a study of 287 captured terrorists made by Dŏgu Ergil in 1980. This study lends some support to these views. In the first place it may be noted that the study shows that only a small percentage of terrorists were university graduates (3 to 4 per cent of this sample), and the latter as a whole might therefore be said to have made a successful transition to a more urban, more modern style of life. Over a quarter were partially integrated into their new environment, having studied for a while at university or other institutions of higher education. About 40 per cent were either *lycée* graduates or had spent a number of years in *lycées*, which suggests that *lycées* rather than universities were the educational institutions where extremist politics developed. In this study half of those arrested were students of one sort or another,[22] a rather higher figure than the national statistics quoted above, but this study was undertaken in Ankara where there is a larger student population. In fact some 60 to 70 per cent of those questioned had spent most of their life in large cities, though about half of them had been born in villages or small towns.[23] Interestingly, over one-fifth of the sample had fathers who were government officials; 36 per cent of the leftists had fathers who were manual workers, but then 28 per cent of the rightists also came from this background.[24] The leftists came from slightly poorer family backgrounds, but the differences were not very remarkable.[25] On the whole the left wing terrorists were slightly more working class, but there is no evidence from this research to suggest that the violence between left wing and right wing groups was between, say, the deprived children of the working class and those from a *petit bourgeois* background. The rightists, it may be noted, paid more attention to the ideas of their family elders and to the leaders of their organizations than did the leftists, who were more influenced by the views of their comrades. But overall the conclusion has to be that the conflict between warring elements in Turkish society derived from the ideological adherence by sociologically similar groups of youth to two opposed interpretations of the Kemalist tradition, neither of which found much favour with the major political parties. Yet the intensity of the violence owed much to the fact that it provided a means for the expression of social antagonisms often quite local. It is clear that the social norms of rural society are now more dominant than before, and that feelings of alienation and anomie are widespread in members of a part-educated generation who have little prospect for the future beyond working for a pittance in some administrative backwater.

CONCLUSION

This recent Turkish experience of political violence cannot on any strict definition of the word be said to amount to political terrorism. 'The primary aim of terrorism, after all, is to induce terror in intended subjects who may be entire populations, specific sectors of society or isolated individuals.'[26] Where political terrorism is adopted it may have a variety of aims. One may be the creation of general political instability or even chaos; another may be to overthrow a government which is pursuing or failing to pursue, certain courses of action. A third major aim may be to provide publicity for the cause. The main forms of action consist of threatening the assassination of political leaders and creating major disturbances designed to terrify those who support, and can influence, political leaders.

Political terrorism has been used by many social groups: by minorities, by nationalist or anti-colonial movements in order better to attain their ends, and of course by those in power to control unruly subjects. Undoubtedly the most fearful and effective terrorism is that of a highly organized and dedicated group with its own vision of a new future, equipped with some justifying ideology, and operating with complete ruthlessness and efficiency in a disturbed and disaffected society among whom it has supporters able to sustain it materially.

On this understanding of political terrorism, Turkey has experienced only its beginnings. In the 1960s the left wing groups showed signs of using terrorism to force the government into less Western-oriented policies, but with the hostility of right wing groups their attempted use of violence to affect the determination of governmental policy had to give way to the waging of war on their opponents. Something similar frequently shows signs of occurring in Northern Ireland, but counter-attacks by Protestant groups are restrained by a government whom they generally support. Had the government of Demirel followed this line in the 1960s then left wing violence would undoubtedly have been directed at government and could have become more truly terroristic. However, social and political conditions clearly prevented any development along these lines. The result was therefore a minor civil war between mainly youthful elements drawn from diametrically opposed political groups. The military intervened to suppress this disturbance, and blamed the politicians of all parties, and the nature of the political system, for allowing it to occur. The two major political parties could have suppressed some of the violence by entering into the coalition the military constantly demanded. They would not have found it very easy, however, to depoliticize the police, the educational system and other parts of the public realm. That would have depended on a very close accord in the coalition, which would probably not have been forthcoming, and would have meant tight control by each major party of its more extreme supporters. Moreover, to have attempted to depoliticize the unions and professional associations would have been an immensely difficult task. This is an area to which the military regime devoted much effort. As of 1 September some 18,000 persons belonging to unions or associations were either under detention, under arrest, on remand, or convicted. In the upshot the leaders of the major political parties apparently thought the rigorous suppression of violence was not worth the political sacrifice they would have to make, but, misjudging the military mood, they paid a larger price in the end by seeing their parties abolished and themselves banned from politics for ten years, which effectively means for life.

NOTES

1. An account of his thought is in Şerif Mardin, *The Genesis of Young Ottoman Thought* (Princeton, Princeton University Press, 1962).
2. *See* D. Barchard's very perceptive 'The intellectual background to radical protest in Turkey in the 1960s' in William Hale, ed., *Aspects of Modern Turkey* (London and New York, Bowker, 1976).
3. Reported in the author's *Democracy and Development in Turkey* (Beverley, The Eothen Press, 1979) p. 169.
4. Barchard *op. cit.* p. 30.
5. *ibid.* p. 31. He reports that George Politier's *Les Principes Elémentaires de la Philosophie* played a key part in the lives of many young radicals.
6. *See* G.S. Harris, 'The Left in Turkey', *Problems of Communism*, Vol. xxix (July–Aug. 1980) pp. 26–41.
7. Barchard *op. cit.* p. 31.
8. They constitute about one-fifth of the population and are mainly to be found in Central Anatolia. They have traditionally supported the People's Party on the gounds that it was less supportive of religion and therefore less likely to favour the Sunni majority.
9. Assassinated by leftists.
10. *Briefing* (Ankara) (8 Sept. 1980).
11. Figures contained in *State of Anarchy and Terror in Turkey*. In what appears to be an official publication (no date) this shows 2677 civilian deaths and 135 deaths among security forces. These dropped to 227 and 55, respectively, in the year following military intervention.
12. *ibid.* p. 62.
13. *ibid.* pp. 64 and 65. Only 15 per cent were university graduates. It is not clear how many at university are included among secondary school graduates.

14. *ibid.* p. 73.
15. *ibid.* p. 76.
16. *ibid.* p. 72.
17. A perspective account on which I much rely is by Şerif Malrdin, 'Youth and violence in Turkey', *Arch. Europ. Sociol.*, Vol. xix (1978) pp. 229–254.
18. Mardin 'Youth and violence in Turkey' p. 238.
19. Quoted in Mardin 'Youth and violence' from P. Stirling, 'A death and a youth club: feuding in a Turkish village', *Anthropological Quarterly* (Washington, 1960) pp. 172–3.
20. Mardin, 'Youth and violence' p. 251.
21. Doğu Ergil, *Türkiyede Terör ve Şiddet* (Ankara, 1980).
22. *ibid.* p. 121. Over a quarter of the leftists were, however, manual workers.
23. *ibid.* pp. 114–14, 115.
24. *ibid.* pp. 129–30. Of the rightists' fathers, 18 per cent were farmers or peasants as against 12 per cent of the leftists.
25. *ibid.* p. 136.
26. Paul Furlong, 'Political terrorism in Italy' in *Terrorism: A Challenge to the State*, ed. Juliet Lodge (Oxford, Martin Robertson, 1981) p. 59.

8 The Urban Guerrilla in Latin America

Richard Gillespie

To the outside world, Latin American politics have long conjured up images of political violence, instability and military intervention.[1] Of course the external view is coloured by distance and constrasting cultures, and often shaped by a Western Liberal tendency to regard authoritarian regimes as unstable. Nonetheless the use of political violence clearly has enjoyed greater legitimacy in Latin America than in the metropolitan countries. Much of that violence has emanated from inter-élite or intra-élite disputes and its relevance to the study of insurrectional violence has been mainly that it has bred widespread scepticism with respect to constitutional processes. For models of insurrectionary violence and direct sources of inspiration, the modern urban guerrilla has a limited bank of regional examples to draw upon. While sentimentally he or she will identify with Latin America's long tradition of rural guerrilla warfare and the various revolutionary upheavals of the past, the continent's history provides few cases of violent struggle which offer direct guidance to the urban guerrilla.

At a symbolic level, some Latin American urban guerrillas have identified with violent nationalist images drawn from or imposed on the past. It was only half in jest that the Montoneros in Argentina, through their chanting on demonstrations, revived the spectre of the *mazorqueros*, the henchmen of the nineteenth century dictator Rosas, and announced to the 'oligarchy' the advent of a 'Third Tyranny' (the governments of Rosas and Perón having been labelled the first and second 'tyrannies' by Argentine Liberals).[2] Also relevant is the anarchist tradition of the River Plate basin: it seems hardly accidental that urban guerrilla movements in the late 1960s and early 1970s became strongest in Argentina

150

and Uruguay, countries which received many persecuted libertarians among the immigrants who arrived from Italy and Spain around 1900. At that time, several attempts were made at 'propaganda by the deed', emulating assassination bids abroad. That which became legendary was Simón Radowitzky's slaying in 1909 of Argentine police chief Ramón Falcón, a killer of Indians and repressor of syndicalists who had directed an infamous massacre of protesting workers just a few months earlier.[3]

The Montoneros superseded Radowitzky's example by killing three federal police chiefs in the space of two years in the mid–1970s. However, one should not exaggerate the extent to which the events of distant decades encouraged later political violence. While certainly marked by vengeance killings and attacks on deemed symbols of oppression, the activity of the Montoneros and similar forces went beyond individual *ad hoc* deeds of violence. For the first time, sustained campaigns of violence were informed by coherent (if at times ignored) strategies which were designed to lead to an eventual insurrectional seizure of power. Behind this new form of political violence, the most direct influences were neither temporally nor geographically distant. The fundamental point of departure for the urban guerrillas was the Cuban revolutionary success of 1959, qualified by the many defeats suffered on the mainland over the next eight years by radicals seeking to repeat the rural guerrilla success. Clearly Castro's struggle itself formed part of a historical tradition: the Cuban rebels had studied Sandino's campaign in the Segovias as well as their country's own independence struggle; guerrilla tactics had been employed too in the Mexican revolution and much earlier by Indians resisting Iberian conquistadores. But it was only with the Cuban revolution that important sectors of the Latin American Left really began to consider armed struggle as a viable means of pursuing their political objectives.

The magnetism of revolutionary warfare tended to attract younger people, unimpressed by the seemingly unproductive reformist routines of traditional parties of the Left. Though the 'lessons' which combative radicals drew from the Cuban experience were dubious, armed struggle in one form or another was adopted in many parts of Latin America, and is still present a quarter of a century after the fall of Batista. In 1979 the Sandinista victory in Nicaragua provided fresh impetus to the combative approach. The urban guerrilla strategy itself became fashionable in the late 1960s following the death of Guevara in Bolivia in 1967, an event which marked the end of a phase in which rural guerrillas adhered most closely to Cuban–inspired theories. Very quickly the urban guerrillas had an impact on political life that was out of all proportion to the numbers enrolled in their ranks. By 1975 in Argentina, peak individual guerrilla actions were characterized by the extortion of multi-million pound kidnap ransoms, the mobilization of hundreds of fighters, the wearing of uniforms for assaults on army garrisons, and scores of casualties. But in no country did urban guerrilla strategies achieve their aims and their failure in the 1970s has provoked some recent rethinking on the part of the Latin American Left.

'Urban guerrilla warfare' should not be confused with 'terrorism', especially when the latter term serves as a pejorative. It may be defined as 'a form of unconventional war waged in urban or suburban areas for political objectives' and differs from political terrorism through being more discriminate and predictable in its use of violence.[4] Its frequent equation with terrorism is encouraged by the fact that urban guerrillas seldom reject terrorism as one of several forms of action, and indeed tend to use it extensively when they are politically weak and isolated. The countries selected as examples with which to illustrate this critique—Argentina, Uruguay and Brazil—are those in which the strategy had its greatest impact, though the Brazilian guerrilla performance ranks lower than those of Argentina and Uruguay in terms of both duration and significance.[5] Prior to outlining reasons for urban guerrilla failure, brief mention will be made of common factors present in the emergence of urban guerrilla warfare in the three countries examined, of urban guerrilla theory, and of the general course of armed struggle in each country. In explaining the failure, more attention will be paid to defects in the strategy than to adverse external conditions such as the strength of the guerrillas' military opponents.

THE BACKGROUND

Urban guerrilla warfare in Argentina, Uruguay and Brazil had national peculiarities but the principal factors involved in its emergence were remarkably uniform from country to country. In each case, the personnel of the urban guerrilla was drawn largely from the lower middle classes: the core was university based but white collar employees and members of the liberal professions also featured prominently. Working class participation was not always negligible, especially in the case of the Argentine Montoneros, yet nowhere did it exceed around 30 per cent.[6] All three countries have large lower middle classes, Uruguay leading with a 50 per cent component. Political, social, economic and ideological factors intervened in the radicalization and 'militarization' of thousands of youths during the 1960s, the main ones being:

First, legal forms of free political expression had been suppressed by military rulers in Brazil (after the 1964 coup) and Argentina (following the 1966 Onganía coup), while in Uruguay civil liberties were curbed progressively by civilian governments from 1965. Popular parties and movements were proscribed in the stratocracies, and even in the 'Switzerland of Latin America' (Uruguay) constitutional left-wing progress was hampered by a power duopoly exercised by the Colorado and Blanco parties and by aspects of the electoral system (in 1971, most voters opted for reform candidates, yet the right-wing Bordaberry became President). Moreover, from 1968 political power in Uruguay was highly concentrated in the executive, with President Pacheco fully exploiting new special security powers and suspending constitutional rights by means of an almost continuous state of siege. By 1970 the Tupamaros were calling the Pacheco government 'the dictatorship',[7] and executive powers were strengthened further when Bordaberry declared a 'state of internal war' in 1972. In each place, the closure of avenues of political expression and the readiness of power holders to resort to violence to frustrate radical aspirations and weaken opposition forces led many to conclude that, in the words of Perón, 'against brute force, only intelligently-applied force can be effective'.[8]

Second, in all three countries, members of the lower middle classes were affected adversely by serious national economic problems. Previously relatively privileged, many found themselves victims of rising inflation and-or declining career prospects. Some shifted simultaneously in a nationalist and socialist direction, for the major beneficiaries of the economic policies under which they suffered were often not only big, but also foreign, capitalists. Radicalism motivated by socio-economic decline not only contributed to the rise of the urban guerrilla but also to the development of white collar unionism, especially among public and bank employees.

Third, given that students and former students predominated in urban guerrilla organizations, one must appreciate the importance of governmental attacks on the universities, in which an unprecedented degree of violence was used. During the late 1960s, students in each country were shaken by police invasions of their campuses (the violation of university autonomy in Uruguay in 1968 being the country's first), by purges of liberal academics, declining job opportunities in several areas, and by their acquaintance with police truncheons during attempts at peaceful protest. Student demonstrators killed by the police provided martyrs and widespread middle and working class indignation was expressed by huge crowds at their funerals and in protest strikes.

Fourth, the impact of ideas emanating from or inspired by the Cuban revolution was enhanced by the weakness and historical failures of the traditional Left in these countries. Revolutionary nationalists such as the Tupamaros and Montoneros attributed past defeats above all to Communist and Socialist neglect of the 'National Question'. More generally, the proto-guerrillas mistook instances of economistic mass militancy for revolutionary fervour and concluded that it was only the bureaucratic *methods* of the traditional Left (and of Peronist leaders in Argentina) that were an obstacle to radical solutions to national crises. 'Objective revolutionary conditions' were considered present or maturing and urban guerrilla warfare, by demonstrating the possibility of revolutionary success, was deemed capable of luring the masses away from traditional reformist leaderships.

Fifth, in terms of the strategic debate taking place within the revolutionary Left, urban guerrilla warfare was seen by many as the next 'logical' step following the collapse of rural guerrilla campaigns. Most of the social forces to which the guerrillas looked for support resided in urban areas (80 per cent of Uruguayans and Argentines and 54 per cent of Brazilians were urbanites); levels of mass political awareness and organization were highest there and arms, money and other resources far more accessible than in the countryside.

Lastly, in Argentina and Uruguay especially, the diffusion of radical Catholic ideas helped to create an intellectual and moral climate conducive to the resort to arms. Radical Catholic theses rarely advocated the initiation of urban guerrilla warfare but did go some way towards legitimizing it by differentiating between 'the just violence of the oppressed, who find themselves forced to use it to gain their liberation' and 'the unjust violence of the oppressors'.[9] Liberation theology facilitated the moral leap from pacifism to armed struggle for the many Catholics who joined the Montoneros and Tupamaros; it urged Christians to participate in social and national liberation struggles and commended the self-sacrifice of those who dedicated their lives to popular causes.

URBAN GUERRILLA THEORY

The importance of urban guerrilla theories is often exaggerated. Spanish Civil War veteran Abraham Guillén was certainly a mentor of the Tupamaros, yet as they admitted of themselves, 'action, practice, came first, and then theory'.[10] Debray's heresy of programming guerrilla warfare ahead of the building of a revolutionary party ('The guerrilla force is the party in embryo')[11] did find adherents, but in its origins at least, the appeal of urban guerrilla warfare was eminently anti-intellectual. A cult of action emerged in the course of a revolt against the bureaucratic practices and empty rhetoric of the traditional Left. Guerrilla impatience at the pace of developments was evident, particularly in the case of Argentina's Revolutionary Armed Forces (FAR), which explicitly stated that it was pursuing the 'short cuts' which

would make the conquest of power 'nearest and shortest'.[12]
The emphasis was upon action, in Uruguay as a means of
uniting the Left and in Argentina as a way of overcoming a
stalemate in the post-war conflict between Peronist and anti-
Peronist forces. In Brazil, Marighela at times seemed to
advocate action for action's sake: 'Take the initiative, assume
the responsibility, do something. It is better to make mistakes
doing something, even if it results in death'.[13]

Some practitioners of the new variant of armed struggle
claimed that 'objective' revolutionary conditions already
existed, and presented themselves as 'a subjective fuse to
trigger the explosion'.[14] However, the maturity of conditions
was not deemed crucial; echoing Debray, the Tupamaros
asserted that 'the very act of taking up arms, preparing for and
engaging in actions which are against the basis of bourgeois
law, creates a revolutionary consciousness, organization, and
conditions'.[15] Urban guerrilla warfare, it was argued, would
act as a catalyst to accelerate social and political processes
leading to revolution; it would expose the corrupt and
oppressive nature of the regimes being challenged, while
winning mass support through demonstrating the
vulnerability of state forces. Under no circumstances did the
theory envisage the guerrillas themselves inflicting a military
defeat on their enemy; rather, success depended on the
guerrilla nuclei developing into people's armies.

Strategic thinking differed from country to country and
from organization to organization. In Brazil, urban guerrilla
warfare was initially considered by most pioneers as a means
of providing logistical support for a rural guerrilla movement
and people's war in the countryside. But militants who set out
in the mid-1960s to survey hundreds of kilometres of rural
terrain, looking for an ideal 'strategic zone', soon discovered
that suitable land for rural warfare (mountains and jungle)
was remote from population centres, while geographical
conditions were adverse where a politicized peasantry was
indeed to be found (the north-east). In the end, strategic
planning was adapted to social and political realities: what
support there was for armed struggle lay in the major cities,
chiefly among students, not among rural workers cowed by
the repression of the Peasant Leagues.

The Uruguayan guerrillas also looked originally to a rural campaign, but by the mid-1960s national realities had overshadowed Cuban influence and an urban strategy was implemented. Tupamaro strategists foresaw the possibility of direct or vicarious intervention by the USA against their movement, yet felt this would only strengthen their social base, enabling them to lead a resistance struggle against an occupying army. Finally, in Argentina, Peronists and Guevarists disagreed over strategy. While the urban guerrillas of the Peronist Left saw themselves as the 'special formations' of a movement based on mass activity, the Guevarists presented themselves as the embryos of a future revolutionary army which would operate over both urban and rural terrain.

THE COURSE OF URBAN GUERRILLA WARFARE

Brazil

The Brazilian urban guerrilla movement was the weakest of the three and never posed a serious threat to the post-1964 military regime. Its relative debility must be seen in the light of widespread middle class support for the new rulers, regarded initially as rescuing the nation from a communist threat, supposedly constituted by the deposed Goulart government, and as crusaders against spiralling inflation. Launched in 1968, a year after the disintegration of a rural *foco* in the Serra do Caparão, the Brazilian armed campaign lasted only four years. It was waged by groups which broke with the Brazilian Communist Party (PCB) and Workers' Politics (POLOP), the latter being a Left Marxist tendency formed in the early 1960s. Various combat organizations were created, the most notable being National Liberation Action (ALN), the Popular Revolutionary Vanguard (VPR), and the Armed Revolutionary Vanguard (VAR-Palmares).

It is doubtful whether any guerrilla movement could have established itself successfully in Brazil in 1968, the year which saw the introduction of Institutional Act V. This strengthened presidential power, sounded the death-knell of rearguard attempts at redemocratization, and removed the final constitutional obstacles to ruthless anti-subversion measures. However, the mainly student guerrillas had deficiencies of their own which condemned them too: organizational ineptitude, particularly in the case of the ALN; and, related to it, a poorly controlled, though discriminate, use of violence. ALN leader Carlos Marighela, after thirty years in the PCB, rebelled against the party's bureaucratism only to adopt a position close to reliance upon spontaneity. He promoted the creation of tiny 'firing groups' of four to five fighters, in such a way as to almost invite infiltration and guarantee anarchy: 'Small autonomous organizations and individual revolutionary militants and free-shooters join our organization with absolute freedom of action provided they accept, defend and fulfil without reservation all our strategic and tactical principles'. Even at the top, no premium was placed upon security, for leaders, in order to merit the confidence of fighters, were expected to participate in the 'most dangerous' activities.[16] Paradoxically, the fragmentation of the Brazilian guerrilla movement, the frustration of unitary efforts, and the inorganic nature of the ALN all favoured early guerrilla survival by making the task of the enemy security services more difficult; but these questionable advantages were outweighed quickly by the insurgents' inability to coordinate and control their activities for precisely the same reasons.

The year 1968 was one of preparation, during which the guerrillas trained and equipped themselves through a number of bomb attacks and 'expropriations'. A new phase opened with the assassination of US Army Captain Charles Chandler in October 1968, the following year witnessing a series of diplomatic kidnappings. Dozens of detainees recovered their freedom following the abductions of the US, German and Swiss ambassadors, and a Japanese consul. However, each of these 'triumphs' gave rise to waves of arrests which more than made up for the number of liberated guerrillas, and unrestrained torture subsequently led to further military successes, including the death of Marighela in an ambush in November 1969. By late 1971 repression had destroyed the armed organizations and had claimed the lives of the remaining guerrilla commanders, Carlos Lamarca, Joaquim

Câmara Ferreira, and Mario Alves.

Brazil's urban guerrillas foundered so rapidly because they embarked upon a high-casualty strategy at a time when mass movements had been subdued (and thus provided guerrillas with no protection and meager assistance) and when the military regime was at its strongest and most confident. Given that their following was small, it was certainly rash for them to escalate the armed struggle so quickly, though one can see why they did it: the release of dozens of prisoners, achieved through kidnappings, provided the guerrillas with an illusion of success, as did the world headlines which they attracted. But only student activists were impressed; the labour movement, reeling from repression, generally regarded the armed actions as irrelevant to its needs. For their part, Marighela's followers isolated themselves from workers by engaging in activity which required very few participants and by rejecting mass work. Only 'mass front' work was countenanced by the ALN, and this was to involve armed actions oriented towards the mass movement rather than actual involvement in mass forms of opposition to the regime.

Marighela's strategy and the Brazilian guerrilla campaign were thus highly militaristic and aggressive at a time when the needs of the Left were defensive. To his credit, the ALN leader recognized that 'we cannot defend ourselves against an offensive or a concentrated attack by the *gorilas*. And that is the reason why our urban technique can never be permanent, can never defend a fixed base nor remain in any one spot waiting to repel the circle of reaction'.[17] But given such an admission, it was surely foolhardy to embark upon an urban campaign in the first place. The lack of rural potential obliged the insurgents to initiate their struggle in the cities, but in turn rendered the latter suicidal; once urban repression became overpowering, the rebels lacked the option of a secure retreat into the countryside.

Uruguay

Urban guerrilla warfare in Uruguay was dominated by a single organization, the National Liberation Movement (MLN Tupamaros), though a handful of smaller groups (OPR-33, FARO, PCR/MIR, and December 22nd Groups) mounted occasional attacks. The core of the Tupamaros was constituted by Socialist Party dissidents influenced by revolutionary nationalist ideas, who soon united with anarchists, Maoists, Trotskyists, and other nationalists on the basis of a common method. Their watchword was: 'words divide us, action unites us'.[18] Operations began in 1963, but the MLN was structured only in 1965 and regular actions began only in 1968. Originally Cuban influenced, their subsequent expertise in urban guerrilla warfare owed more to collaboration with Argentine Peronist guerrillas (the Tacuara Revolutionary Nationalist Movement), the strategic thinking of Arbraham Guillén,[19] and study of the Algerian guerrilla.

The Tupamaros attracted considerable popular sympathy and acquired moral authority through a series of 'armed propaganda' actions aimed at highlighting social injustices and the corrupt dealings of prominent government and business figures. Food and other goods were seized and handed over to the poor; journalists drew parallels with Robin Hood and his outlaws. By July 1972 opinion polls were suggesting that 20 per cent of Uruguayans were sympathizers.[20] However, following the repressive sequel to the guerrilla occupation of the town of Pando in October 1969 (three rebels were killed after surrendering, sixteen were captured and tortured), the Tupamaros were drawn into a war of vengeance against the security forces. Guerrilla operations were suspended briefly during the November 1971 elections, but were stepped up after the Tupamaro-backed Broad Front won 18 per cent of the votes. Having obtained intelligence on the state-sponsored death squad by abducting one of its organizers in February 1972, the Tupamaros assassinated three of its leaders in April and thereby lost all control over the level of political violence. The Uruguayan army, which had been gathering information about the MLN since 1969, now became fully involved in counter-insurgency and the guerrillas could not withstand the onslaught. Partly as a result of treachery, the next three months witnessed over 100 Tupamaro deaths, 600 to 700 arrests, and the loss of seventy 'safe' houses.[21] By the end of 1972, the organization was no longer a viable fighting force, despite a final attempt to retreat to rural earthen dugouts (*tatuceras*), similar to those used by Grivas's EOKA Cypriots, for operations in rural and suburban areas on a temporary basis.

It had been hoped that the creation of Tupamaro Support Committees (CATs) would enable the guerrillas to *organize* a mass following; however, the Tupamaro belief that 'the supreme effort would be the armed fight, and this would unite and coordinate behind it all other forms of struggle'[22] doomed the CATs to remain mere recruitment agencies of the military apparatus as the campaign developed. Nor did the Tupamaros gain the opportunity to lead national resistance to an army of occupation. They correctly estimated that the government would appeal for external assistance to counter insurgency, but misjudged the form it would take. Rather than grant the Tupamaros the boon of having Brazilian soldiers patrolling the streets of Montevideo, their international opponents used more covert but deadly effective means of intervention: the supply of FBI and DOPS (Brazilian political police) officers to organize and assist the death squad; aid to the official security forces; and finally, after the Tupamaro decline, a Brazilian loan of 30 million dollars to help defeat a two-week general strike against the military coup of July 1973.

Argentina
Armed struggle became a regular feature of Argentine political life in 1969 and it lasted throughout the 1970s.[23] During the early years, Argentina shared the fragmented urban guerrilla pattern of Brazil, but by the end of 1974 most of the organizations had either coalesced around one of two poles, pro-Peronist revolutionary nationalism (Montoneros) and Guevarism (People's Revolutionary Army—ERP), or they had collapsed. The Montoneros had absorbed the FAR, ENR, Descamisados and FAP-17, and the ERP the FAP National Command, leaving Argentine urban guerrillas divided over their attitudes to Peronism and the revolutionary process. While the Montoneros considered that Argentina had to pass initially through a distinct 'national liberation' stage of revolution prior to setting out on a road to 'national' socialism, and thus fully supported the 1973–4 Peronist governments of Cámpora and Perón, the Guevarist ERP

condemned these administrations as representing a 'national bourgeoisie' which had become so tied to foreign capital that it could no longer perform a progressive role.

Before 1974, the Montoneros were less militarily active than the ERP, yet far greater recruitment success was achieved due to their positive orientation towards the mass movement of Peronism and greater tactical flexibility. While fighting during 1970–3, the Montoneros kept offensive violence to a minimum, selected their targets well with popular traditions and sentiments in mind, and devoted much attention to the promotion of a sympathetic Peronist Youth movement. Above all, by subordinating guerrilla warfare to mass political work in late 1972 and early 1973, to play a leading part in campaigns for the return of Perón from exile and to elect Cámpora as President, and then by suspending regular armed actions in favour of sixteen months of mass activity from May 1973 to September 1974, the Montoneros were able to win a mobilizable following of over 100,000 people. The ERP might well have derived benefits from the post-1973 popular disillusionment with the rightward-moving Peronist administrations had they not committed the blunder of prolonging their guerrilla attacks after Peronism had netted over seven million votes at the polls. Whereas the Montoneros made use of the legal opening to build mass organizations, the ERP ignored public opinion and, ironically, Guevara's own warning against armed opposition to elected governments.[24]

Both organizations made what, with the advantage of hindsight, must be regarded as grave strategical errors. The ERP attempted to make up for their political weakness by moving to the rural province of Tucumán, hoping to establish a firmer base among local sugar workers and dominate 'liberated zones'. In fact, this only increased their isolation. The big cities of Buenos Aires, Rosario, and Córdoba remained the principal venues of labour struggles, and though the workers in the declining provincial sugar industry lent them limited support, it was undermined quickly by right-wing terror when the army moved into Tucumán in 1975. Hundreds of ERP combatants lost their lives in the skirmishes of that year, and a desperate return to the cities in December proved catastrophic. About 140 ERP members were killed after attacking an important army garrison at Monte Chingolo in Buenos Aires province; the military had foreknowledge of the assault and made no attempt to take prisoners alive.

The Montonero mistake was to resume warfare in September 1974, following the death of Perón and his replacement as President by his wife Isabel. Certainly, they had suffered badly at the hands of fascist commandos and the Triple A death squad while operating legally, but their resort to arms denied them the chance to capitalize upon growing labour opposition to the government, seen especially in the general strike of mid-1975. In military and financial terms, they became the strongest urban guerrilla force yet seen in Latin America: their peak military action in the northern city of Formosa involved the mobilization of some 500 members, and their famous kidnapping of business magnates Juan and Jorge Born earned them a record ransom of over 60 million dollars. However, while their operations represented a spectacular military advance, all lacked popular participation and the political constituency of the Montoneros ceased to expand. They outlasted the ERP, a force already in ruins by the time of the deaths of Santucho and other leaders in July 1976, but were weakened severely by the repressive measures introduced after the military takeover of March 1976. Though dozens of security policemen were killed by powerful Montonero bombs in that year, the conflict became increasingly one between unevenly matched military apparata. Between March 1976 and July 1978 some 4,500 Montoneros perished,[25] and by the end of the decade the urban guerrillas had been obliterated.

OVERVIEW OF THE URBAN GUERRILLA FAILURE

1. The Political Context

While it is true that the political context in which a guerrilla organization attempts to develop is an important determinant of its degree of success, general principles as to the optimal conditions for the launching of urban guerrillas are elusive. Clearly, when possibilities exist for legal mass activity, the initiation or continuation of warfare is likely to engender extreme guerrilla isolation; yet on the other hand, urban guerrillas have yet to prosper against well-equipped authoritarian regimes prepared and able to use draconian methods against them, their periphery, and those beyond it. Faced with an unfettered military regime which was still on the offensive after stifling student and worker opposition in 1968, the Brazilian guerrilla movement never really got off the ground.

As for durability, experience suggests that the most propitious conditions for the implementation of urban guerrilla strategies are either: against a quasi-democratic regime, inhibited by legal restrictions and electoral considerations from all-out repression, but sufficiently intolerant of democratic opposition for guerrillas to be able to pose credibly as the only viable popular alternative; or under an authoritarian military regime lacking political legitimacy, already weakened by mass opposition or crises of some kind, and preparing to return authority to politicians. The greater vitality of the Montoneros is an indication of the benefits to be gained from participation in mass movements and from exploiting opportunities to operate legally. Because of their role in encouraging the military step-down of 1973 and helping bring back Peronism, plus their winning of substantial, visible social support, the last Peronist government was unable to move against them decisively until late in 1975, when they were outlawed.

A final point here is that political conditions can and do change during the course of urban guerrilla campaigns. When their enemy is on the defensive, guerrillas can be flexible and modify tactics and strategies to meet new political circumstances; but they cannot retreat when their enemy is on the offensive—unless, of course, they pull out altogether and abandon their countries until conditions at home change.

2. Organizational Factors

Organizational strength undoubtedly contributed to the superior durability of the MLN over the loose, penetrable structure of the Brazilian ALN. Indeed, the molecular architecture of the Uruguayan guerrillas came as near as possible to perfection: Tupamaro forces were divided into self-sufficient columns, each possessing its own recruitment, intelligence, military and technical apparata, as well as their own fronts of work among the people, students, trade unions and army. 'Compartmentalization' was designed to ensure that no member knew more about the organization than was necessary for personal effectiveness, and members were kept ignorant of the real names of militants. The boast of Tupamaro 'indestructability' rested upon the belief that, even if several columns were wiped out completely, the others would be unimpaired and therefore able to go on operating and multiplying.

Yet some centralization and coordination was vital if the anarchic dissipation of ALN forces was to be avoided in Uruguay, and this ensured that there would be leaders who could occasion irreparable losses if persuaded to cooperate by the enemy. Losses through treachery, infiltration and the information extracted during the torture of captured guerrillas were much greater than casualties attributable to military inferiority. The defection of Héctor Amodio Pérez from the MLN, motivated by his removal from the leadership of the key Column 15 of Montevideo at the organization's Congress in March 1972, played a central part in the Tupamaro demise. Captured in May, he revealed the location of thirty 'safe houses' and bases, including a 'people's prison', an important field hospital, and several arsenals and documentation centres, before being spirited out of Uruguay.[26] Mario Piriz also left Uruguay a free man after betraying around 300 of his former comrades. In Argentina, the ERP only detected the treason of Juan Ranier, and shot him, several weeks after his tip-off had led to over 100 guerrilla losses at Monte Chingolo. Cooperation secured by use of torture and drugs also produced 'results', but so too, in Argentina, did appeals to captured guerrillas' sense of military realism once the security forces had gained the upper hand.

Of course, treason and infiltration worked both ways and brought occasional benefits to the insurgents. The most mighty garrisons have gates which sympathetic conscripts can open to guerrilla attackers, as happened several times in

Argentina. On the whole though, in this war of interpenetration, of infiltration and counter-infiltration, those forces drawing upon state resources had an overwhelming advantage and there was little that their opponents could do to overturn it. By 1971 the Tupamaros had come to realize that urban guerrilla warfare was a 'high-loss' business, and inevitably so since combatants were operating right in the heartland of enemy territory. Faced with this reality, survival depended upon rapid and efficient recruitment, yet here new problems arose: as a Tupamaro leader stated, 'When an organization like ours grows . . . security mechanisms are strained. There is insufficient time to recruit new cadres'; also, 'the same men who catch our eye because we consider them potential militants have also caught the eye of the police for the same reasons'.[27] Moreover, the enemy's use of 'overkill' when responding to guerrilla challenges did much to discourage likely recruits at the time when they were most needed. It was those who were on the fringes of the guerrilla organization, upon whom recruitment depended, who were the most vulnerable, being identified with subversion but lacking the protection of being underground. Not only did the risks of personal loss increase, but also the danger to family, friends and associates. Thirty members of the Santucho family were killed, imprisoned, tortured or forced to leave Argentina during the 1970s.

3. Isolation
Urban guerrillas can be effective through time only if they establish a significant mass base as a source of recruits, auxiliaries, resources and intelligence data. Yet a high degree of social isolation is guaranteed by their adopted strategy, for a number of reasons. Firstly, urban guerrilla warfare is, at least in its origins, a highly élitist form of struggle, embarked upon by would-be vanguards of the masses. At worst, it can reflect contempt for the collective struggles of labour: the miniscule National Revolutionary Army (ENR) of Argentina, for instance, before affiliating to the Montoneros, declared that its killing of union leader José Alonso in August 1970 had been designed to 'show the whole Peronist working class that it had a superior weapon to all those employed during those

eighteen years (of resistance)' and to indicate that the 'main mission of revolutionaries' was 'crushing traitors'.[28] Labour's response was a general strike in protest. At best, it reflected impatience with the reformism of most workers, and sought to catalyse their radicalization through exemplary actions which, as it turned out, catalysed reaction rather than revolution.

Isolation was, secondly, very much a question of class. While most of those who took up arms belonged to the lower middle classes, the mass of workers exhibited a clear preference for collective means of action—strikes, demonstrations, rallies, occupations. In a majority of cases, worker antipathy to the urban guerrilla was an expression of strong economistic sentiment and a reformist rather than revolutionary political stance (even in the case of the CP-led Uruguayan labour movement); but even radical labour groupings, such as the late 1960s CGT of the Argentines, looked to collective methods. This preference rested upon memories of collective triumphs, recognition that labour was strongest when acting in a united fashion, and upon the collective nature of the productive process. Moreover, the urban guerrilla option was less open to the working class activist, often the sole provider of a family's sustenance, for economic reasons.

Thirdly, leaving aside the question of whether or not social support is available, urban guerrilla warfare is a physically isolated form of struggle. Since the urban guerrilla operates right in the centre of enemy territory, he cannot like his rural counterpart establish 'liberated zones'. There is thus no possibility of organizing a substantial social–economic–political support base while fighting a guerrilla war in the cities, and this was precisely the reason why the Brazilian insurgents envisaged their urban campaign as a mere preparation for a 'people's war' in the countryside.

Finally, regarding guerrilla actions themselves, there was everywhere a marked tendency for military operations which were in some way related to popular demands to constitute a declining aspect of urban guerrilla repertoires as campaigns developed. 'Armed propaganda' actions, specifically designed to awaken popular sympathies, were the most successful in terms of public relations, but were restricted to the early phases of warfare. As far as the Tupamaros were concerned, after an early stage of publicizing the existence of their organization, continued armed propaganda would have led only to a loss of popular prestige through 'giving the false impression of seeking publicity more than the defeat of the enemy'.[29] When the urban guerrillas reached levels of development where open confrontations with the armed forces became technically feasible, their operations became totally divorced from popular activity. Attacks on military bases, multi-million-dollar kidnappings, and assassinations of army and police chiefs demanded nothing of the workers except applause. In Debray's words, urban guerrilla warfare everywhere degenerated into 'a technological battle between specialists in clandestine violence, with the masses in the role of spectators around the ring where the professionals were fighting it out'.[30]

4. Militarism

Though many urban guerrillas started out as political activists who regarded armed struggle as an extension of politics by other means, those guerrilla organizations which grew soon became dominated by military rather than political criteria. As the urban guerrillas developed militarily, as they moved on to higher planes of warfare through a series of *saltos* (leaps), the political wisdom of specific guerrilla actions tended to take second place to considerations of what was technically feasible. The foremost military operation of the Montoneros, their October 1975 spectacular in Formosa, which included an aeroplane hijacking, the occupation of an airport, and an assault on the garrison of one of Argentina's strongest regiments, brought them no political kudos: it was intended to undermine military morale, provoke divisions in the armed forces, and demonstrate Montonero military prowess; its political contribution to popular struggles was nil and the press highlighted the fact that most victims of the attack were 'nine workers who by force of circumstance found themselves in the armed forces as conscripts'.[31]

Given the isolated nature of urban guerrilla warfare, military *saltos* tend to 'intensify a situation militarily to a point far beyond what can be sustained politically',[32] leaving insurgents vulnerable in the face of the inevitable backlash. Increasingly, guerrilla behaviour came to be dictated by what the Montoneros called 'the dialectic of confrontation'; the guerrillas were drawn into an escalating spiral of violence in which they found themselves more and more *responding* to enemy moves rather than determining the rules of the game. They felt obliged to reply blow for blow to state counter-measures in order to demonstrate their own continuing vitality and the vulnerability of their foe. Trapped by this dialectic, the guerrillas channelled most of their resources into the military front, to the detriment of mass political work, and did little to contribute to campaigns for more militant labour leaderships. The military struggle acquired a dynamic of its own and the task of winning over the masses was reduced to that of incorporating activists into the military apparatus.

Some guerrillas mistook their military might for social influence and, like Bonet of the Argentine ERP, deluded themselves into considering that they were 'the proletariat in arms'.[33] Others recognized that their mass support was limited, lost confidence in the revolutionary potential of workers, and adopted a 'we won all that we could' attitude, prior to concentrating solely on military action. In Argentina the ERP on three occasions—following the assassination of leader Luis Pujals in 1971, the Trelew massacre of captive guerrillas in 1972, and the 1974 Catamarca massacre of ERP insurgents who had surrendered to the army—dissipated their energies in vengeance campaigns.

Perhaps the urban guerrillas would have been more circumspect over promoting armed confrontation had they appraised the strength and capacities of their opponents more accurately. References to the collapse of the weak Batista regime in Cuba were inappropriate. What the guerrillas failed to see was that the armies of Argentina, Brazil, and Uruguay also had a potential for *saltos* and could surprise them with well-timed escalations of their own. The Tupamaros in particular underestimated the state's ability to strengthen its repressive *apparata* rapidly: they confidently began a sustained campaign in 1968, when the armed forces possessed only 12,000 poorly equipped and ill-trained troops and the 22,000-strong police had only 1,000 men trained to combat guerrillas; but subsequently they could not match the military expansion of the state forces, assisted by US, Argentine and Brazilian specialists, and were caught off-balance when the enemy launched its counter-offensive in 1972.

Militarism, in part a product of the weakness of revolutionary parties in the countries concerned, was inherent in the logic of urban guerrilla strategy. Yet opportunities to extend left-wing influence, squandered by the militaristic Left, did exist in Uruguay, where there were six general strikes in 1971–3, and Argentina, which witnessed the biggest strike in its history in 1975. By stepping up guerrilla campaigns during these years, the insurgents placed themselves in political quarantine and offered no effective challenge to established labour leaders. In fact, their activities made it easier for governments to curb the activities of industrial militants, on the pretext that the latter were 'industrial guerrillas'. Nevertheless, military escalation continued relentlessly, pursued by guerrillas who feared that repetitious actions would lead to public apathy. As the Tupamaros commented in 1971: 'the Organization and its activity have had something of the effect of a vaccine injected into the social body. At first, it caused convulsions, but the organism came gradually to secrete its own antibodies, and it can now absorb it without danger. The time may come when it has been once and for all desensitized'.[34] Faced with this prospect, the standard guerrilla response was to attempt increasingly audacious and spectacular military operations.

5. Ideological and Theoretical Weakness
Urban guerrilla theory was a defective guide to action, for it failed to explain really how guerrilla action would impel the masses to revolutionary deeds. It merely assumed that efficient military operations would galvanize them, yet one might more reasonably expect the reverse to be true. If, for example, the kidnapping of a manager by guerrillas succeeds in securing better working conditions at his factory, the need for workers themselves to struggle is greatly diminished; and labour passivity may result too from repressive governmental

measures introduced to counter the guerrillas.

Most of the urban guerrilla formations were weak on revolutionary theory and ideologically vague. The method of the urban guerrilla was not the only cement holding the groups together—otherwise one could not account for the multiplicity of organizations in Brazil and Argentina—but it was considered the most decisive factor in defining who was a revolutionary. Quite typically, an Argentine FAR leader admitted in 1971, 'we put things into practice before making up theories about them'.[35] In the short run, this was a decided advantage for the fighters: the vague revolutionary nationalism of the Montoneros and Tupamaros found an echo among all but the most powerful social classes. However, in the long term, theoretical and ideological guerrilla poverty proved damaging, facilitating as it did the growing predominance of military over political considerations in guerrilla decision making.

URBAN GUERRILLA WARFARE REASSESSED

Urban guerrilla warfare in Latin America has been undeniably effective but its effects have been other than those sought by the insurgents. It contributed to the destabilization of governments in Uruguay and Argentina but never managed to go beyond that negative achievement to the establishment or exploitation of 'revolutionary situations'. Social isolation plagued the urban guerrillas and those successful in organizing mass support only achieved that objective by coming 'above ground' and ceasing, temporarily, to be urban guerrillas. Experience suggests also that urban guerrilla strategies can prosper only (and then just in a limited way) when political circumstances constrain either the will or ability of established powers to be ruthless in combating them.

The defeats of urban guerrillas in Uruguay, Argentina and Brazil, and the experience of repressive military rule which followed, eventually led the Latin American Left to reassess its strategic options. In recent years Southern Cone revolutionaries have learnt to dismiss the seductive idea of the

1960s which held that the worse things got, the better they were.[36] The crisis of Peronism in Argentina, the election of an imaginative, conciliatory president in Colombia, and the implosion of the New Jewel Revolution in Grenada have led various Latin American and Caribbean personalities to re-examine the value and possibilities of political democracy.[37] The old Leninist differentiation between bourgeois and proletarian democracy remains highly influential, but it is now tempered by an appreciation that at least bourgeois democracy is preferable to bourgeois dictatorship, and by a reminder of what can happen where 'proletarian democracy' is just a theoretical cover for Stalinism.[38]Long years of military rule or political exile have led some activists to moderate their demands, in the hope that they may live their remaining years without terror[39] in their home countries. At the same time, the Right's readiness to resort to arms itself so regularly in recent years, and its choice of authoritarian rather than placatory responses to movements for change, have given the Left a renewed opportunity to appear as the standard bearer of democracy in the region.

Nicaragua's revolutionary success, characterized by a combination of rural guerrilla warfare and urban insurrectionism, immediately gave an impetus to people's war practitioners in El Salvador and Guatemala.[40] In South America, however, the existence of more formidable states and more complex social structures has counselled against an uncritical importation of Central American schemas by the Left. There, in the countries where the urban guerrillas foundered, a new emphasis upon mass activities fills the Left's discourse on strategy. If Chile's urban insurgency of the early 1980s constitutes an exception to the norm, it is because of the Pinochet regime's determination to remain in power even after the loss of its erstwhile Christian Democratic backers, and because of the Christian Democrats' exclusion of the Communist Party from the moderate opposition alliance, the *Alianza Democrática*.[41] Since 1980 the Chilean Communist Party has accompanied the Movement of the Revolutionary Left (MIR) in asserting a right to armed rebellion, though even here guerrilla actions are conceived of as just tactical supports for strategic mass challenges to the regime. Urban guerrilla warfare as a strategy has lost its following throughout the continent.

NOTES

1. This study is a substantially revised and updated version of an article which appeared in *Conflict Quarterly* (Canada) (Fall 1980).
2. Montonero chants around 1973 included the following: 'Y llora, llora / la puta oligarquía / porque se viene / la tercera tiranía' (So weep, weep, you whore of an oligarchy! The Third Tyranny is coming!); and 'Si por la calle / ves un mazorquero / déjale el paso / y sácate el sombrero' (If you should come across a mazorquero in the street, take off your hat and let him pass). While an exile in 1955–73, Perón had encouraged his more militant supporters to use violence against non-Peronist governments: 'The more violent we are, the better: terror can only be defeated by superior terror', he wrote. 'Violence in the hands of the people is not violence; it is justice.' *See* Perón's letter to John William Cooke, 3 November 1956, in the *Correspondencia Perón-Cooke*, 2 Vols. (Buenos Aires: Granica, 1973), Vol. 1, p. 35; and Jorge Pinedo, *Consignas y lucha popular en el proceso revolucionario argentino, 1955-1973* (Buenos Aires: Freeland, 1974), pp. 41, 92 and 101.
3. *See* David Viñas, *Rebeliones populares argentinas*, 2 Vols. (Buenos Aires: Carlos Pérez Editor, 1971), Vol. 1, pp. 151–271; and *idem* (ed.), *Anarquistas en América Latina* (Mexico: Katún, 1983).
4. Paul Wilkinson, *Terrorism and the Liberal State* (London: Macmillan, 1977) p. 60. The grey zone between urban guerrilla warfare and terrorism could be seen on two occasions in 1984 when Salvadoran rebels raided a bank and a supermarket in San Salvador to obtain finance for a rural campaign, yet when things went wrong and they were cornered by the security forces, they took civilian hostages in order to facilitate their escape [*El País* (Madrid), 13 May 1984 and 4 Aug 1984]. The only important insurgent movement in Latin America which indisputably practices terrorism is the neo-Maoist Sendero Luminoso in Peru. *See Qué Hacer* (Lima) (August 1984).
5. In Venezuela, the activities of the Tactical Combat Units (UTCs) in Caracas were short-lived, almost entirely terrorist in character (especially the 'kill a cop a day' campaign), and subordinate to the rural guerrilla strategy of the Armed Forces of National Liberation (FALN). Urban guerrilla warfare in Colombia (M-19) soon gave way to an exclusively rural struggle and then the ceasefire agreement signed with the Betancur government in August 1984. In Central America urban guerrilla warfare has been subordinated to rural warfare, though the Guatemalan FAR had an urban phase in the mid-1970s and the Sandinistas used urban guerrilla tactics, though not the strategy, during the insurrection of July 1979.

6. On social composition, *see* my *The Peronist Left* (University of Liverpool: unpublished PhD thesis, 1979); James Kohl and John Litt, *Urban Guerrilla Warfare in Latin America* (Cambridge, Mass.: MIT Press, 1974), pp. 143–4 and 191; João Quartim, *Dictatorship and Armed Struggle in Brazil* (London: NLB, 1971) p. 131; and Alain Labrousse, *The Tupamaros* (Harmondsworth, Middx., Penguin, 1973) pp. 115–16.
7. *See* Leopoldo Madruga's 'Interview with Urbano', in Kohl and Litt *op.cit.* p. 275.
8. Juan Domingo Perón, quoted in *Militancia* (Buenos Aires) (19 July 1973) pp. 35–8.
9. Document quoted in John Gerassi, ed., *Revolutionary Priest* (Harmondsworth, Middx., Penguin, 1973) p. 49.
10. MLN Tupamaros, *Actas tupamaras* (Buenos Aires: Schapire, 1971) p. 36.
11. Régis Debray, *Revolution in the Revolution?* (Harmondsworth, Middx., Penguin, 1968) p. 105.
12. '13 Preguntas a las Fuerzas Armadas Revolucionarias', *Nuevo Hombre* (Buenos Aires) (10–16 Nov. 1971) pp. 2–3.
13. Carlos Marighela, quoted in Kohl and Litt *op.cit.* p. 29.
14. 'Interview with Urbano', p. 284.
15. 'Thirty Questions to a Tupamaro', in Labrousse *op.cit.* p. 133.
16. Marighela, *For the Liberation of Brazil* (Harmondsworth, Middx., Penguin, 1971) pp. 57–8.
17. *Idem*, 'Minimanual of the Urban Guerrilla', in Kohl and Litt *op.cit.* p. 101.
18. Quoted in *Tupamaros and Generals* (London and Leeds: Latin America Review of Book and Books of Leeds, 1974) preface.
19. For Guillén's writings, *see* Donald C. Hodges, ed., *Philosophy of the Urban Guerrilla* (New York: Morrow, 1973).
20. Tupamaro interview, Kohl and Litt *op.cit.* p. 302.
21. *Ibid.* p. 193.
22. 'An interview with a Tupamaro' (MLN leader Julio Marenales), in María Ester Gilio, *The Tupamaros* (London, 1972) p. 132.
23. *See* my *Soldiers of Perón; Argentina's Montoneros* (Oxford: Clarendon, 1983) and 'Armed Struggle in Argentina', *New Scholar* (California), Vol. 8, 1982.
24. Che Guevara, *Guerrilla Warfare* (Harmondsworth, Middx., Penguin, 1969), p. 14. Subsequently, in response to Latin American governmental support for the US boycott of revolutionary Cuba, Guevara relaxed his conditions for the initiation of warfare. All governments on the mainland then became legitimate targets, but he still insisted that all peaceful possibilities of struggle should be exhausted before violence was used.
25. Interview with Montonero Manuel Pedreira, Havana, 1978.
26. He went on to work for Uruguayan military intelligence and was suspected of responsibility for the attempt to assassinate Edén Pastora in May 1984 [*El País*, international edn., 18 June 1984].

27. Julio Marenales interview, p. 135.
28. ENR communiqué, republished in *La Causa Peronista* (Buenos Aires) (27 Aug. 1974).
29. *Actas tupamaras op.cit.* p. 19.
30. Debray, *The Revolution on Trial*, Vol. 2 of *A Critique of Arms* (Harmondsworth, Middx., Penguin, 1978) p. 164. Debray was not entirely blameless for this state of affairs. He was the anonymous author of the first part of the Tupamaro manual, *Actas tupamaras*.
31. Socialist Workers Party (PST) communiqué, quoted in *La Opinión* (Buenos Aires) (8 Oct. 1975).
32. Kohl and Litt *op. cit.* p. 25.
33. Rubén Pedro Bonet, in Francisco Urondo, *La patria fusilada* (Buenos Aires: Crisis, 1973) p. 132.
34. Quoted in Debray, *The Revolution on Trial op. cit.* p. 154.
35. FAR interview, Kohn and Litt *op. cit.* pp. 380–1.
36. Mario Benedetti, 'País desde lejos', *El País*, international edn. (27 Aug. 1984).
37. *See* the interview with former Peronist Left ideologue José Pablo Feinmann in *Clarín* (Buenos Aires), international edn. (24–30 Sept. 1984); the statements by M-19 leader Álvaro Fayad prior to signing a ceasefire agreement with the Colombian government, in *El País*, international edn. (27 Aug. 1984)) and the autopsy report on the Grenadian revolution by Clive Thomas, *Caribbean Contact* (Barbados) (September 1984). More recently the Salvadoran rebels have recognized that they cannot win power by an armed struggle alone; and that, if they did, a revolutionary state created by such means would be a target for US interventionism. *See* the interview with Rubén Zamora, *The Sunday Times* (London) (4 Nov. 1984).
38. Thomas *op. cit.*
39. On state terrorism, *see* Eduardo Luis Duhalde, *El estado terrorista argentino* (Barcelona: Argos Vergara, 1983).
40. For guides to the guerrilla movements of these countries, *see* my 'From Farabundo Marti to FMLN' and 'Anatomy of the Guatemalan Guerrilla', *Communist Affairs* (London) (January 1982 and October 1983).
41. Carmelo Furci, 'The Communist Party and the Anti-Pinochet Opposition' *ibid.* (April 1984) pp. 192–4.

ABBREVIATIONS

ALN	*Acão Libertadora Nacional* (National Liberation Action) Brazil
CATs	*Comités de Apoyo Tupamaro* (Tupamaro Support Committees) Uruguay
CGTA	*Confederación General del Trabajo de los Argentinos* (General Labour Confederation of the Argentines)
CP	Communist Party
DOPS	*Departamento de Ordem Política e Social* (Department of Political and Social Order) Brazil
ENR	*Ejército Nacional Revolucionario* (National Revolutionary Army) Argentina
EOKA	*Ethniki Organosis Kypriakou Agoniston* (National Organization of Cypriot Fighters) Cyprus
ERP	*Ejército Revolucionario del Pueblo* (People's Revolutionary Army) Argentina
FALN	*Fuerzas Armadas de Liberación Nacional* (Armed Forces of National Liberation) Venezuela
FAP	*Fuerzas Armadas Peronistas* (Peronist Armed Forces) Argentina
FAR	*Fuerzas Armadas Revolucionarias* (Revolutionary Armed Forces) Argentina
FAR	*Fuerzas Armadas Rebeldes* (Rebel Armed Forces) Guatemala
FARO	*Fuerzas Armadas Revolucionarias Orientales* (Eastern Revolutionary Armed Forces) Uruguay
FMLN	*Frente Farabundo Martí para la Liberación Nacional* (Farabundo Martí National Liberation Front) El Salvador
M-19	*Movimiento 19 de Abril* (19 April Movement) Colombia
MIR	*Movimiento de Izquierda Revolucionaria* (Revolutionary Left Movement) Chile
MLN-T	*Movimiento de Liberación Nacional-Tupamaros* (Tupamaros National Liberation Movement) Uruguay
OPR-33	*Organizaciones Populares Revolucionarias del 33* (Popular Revolutionary Organizations of the 33) Uruguay

PCB | *Partido Communista Brasileiro* (Brazilian Communist Party)
PCR/MIR | *Partido Comunista Revolucionario/Movimiento de la Izquierda Revolucionaria* (Revolutionary Communist Party/Movement of the Revolutionary Left) Uruguay
POLOP | *Política Operária* (Workers Politics) Brazil
PST | *Partido Socialista de los Trabajadores* (Socialist Workers Party) Argentina
Triple A | *Alianza Anticomunista Argentina* (Argentina Anti-Communist Alliance)
UTCs | *Unidades Tácticas de Combate* (Tactical Combat Units) Venezuela
VAR-Palmares | *Vanguarda Armada Revolucionaria-Palmares* (Armed Revolutionary Vanguard-Palmares) Brazil
VPR | *Vanguarda Popular Revolucionaria* (Popular Revolutionary Vanguard) Brazil

9 Gandhi's Theory of Non-violence: His Reply to the Terrorists
Bhikhu Parekh

Almost right from the beginning the Indian attitude to violence has been characterized by a deep and healthy ambiguity. The ambiguity arose from its attempt to come to terms with what it took to be the two fundamental but contradictory features of the world. First, living beings are qualitatively different from the non-living. They represent the divine, and feel pain. As such 'all life is one' and is sacred. *Himsa* or violence is therefore evil and must be avoided. Second, *Jivo Jivasya Jivanam*. Every living being lives on or forms the livelihood of some other living being. To live is to kill and destroy. Violence is thus inherent in existence and inescapable.

While appreciating the sacredness of all life, most Hindu writers accepted violence as an inevitable feature of human existence. Both individual and collective existence required men to do violence to nature and each other. Since it is inevitable, it is not regrettable. It is simply a fact, a brute fact, which men must accept and live with. Accordingly most Hindu writers argued that men need to kill non–human beings in order to live, as also that they sometimes need to do violence to one another in order to preserve the social order. The two Hindu epics freely acknowledged not only the necessity but also the desirability of political and military violence, and their heroes, who are both incarnations of God, engage in and justify massive acts of violence. In the *Gita*, which is a part of *Mahabharata*, the Lord himself makes out a formidable philosophical case for the use of violence to combat injustice.

A small body of Hindu opinion, however, was uneasy with

this view, and condemned violence in almost all its forms. It not only disapproved of war and political violence, but was also uneasy about the human need to destroy non–human life. From its ranks grew two powerful dissident movements, namely Buddhism and Jainism which attempted to provide an alternative view of violence. They condemned war, and some of their followers even condemned all forms of physical punishment, including imprisonment and proposed a wholly non-violent state. The Jains went even further and advocated an intensely ascetic way of life from which even the minimally necessary violence to non–human life was eliminated. They advocated strict vegetarianism that excluded the use of certain types of vegetable; disapproved of agriculture on the ground that it involved systematic and massive destruction of non–human organisms; urged their followers to walk barefoot and with great care lest they should trample upon living organisms; and so on. Buddhism and Jainism included *karuna* (compassion) and *ahimsa* (non-violence) among the cardinal virtues and sought to organize personal and political life on their basis.

The Indian tradition of moral and political thought thus contained two different strands of opinion. Most Hindus regarded violence as an inescapable fact of life and approved of its use in certain situations. Some Hindu and most Buddhist and Jain writers disapproved of violence in principle, and thought that it was possible and desirable considerably to minimise and even eliminate it altogether. The conflict between the two strands of thought came to a head during India's struggle for independence. After 1857 when Britain ruthlessly put down the rebellion and acquired direct control over India, many Indians began to feel that their freedom could only be attained by means of violence and that such violence was fully justified. Many of them drew their inspiration from the two epics, especially the *Gita* which, after several centuries of relative neglect, suddenly became the most popular religious text. It is striking that almost every major advocate of terrorism either wrote a commentary on or extensively quoted from it. Some of them also drew inspiration from the European nationalist movement. However although they sometimes spoke in Western idioms, their basic arguments and categories were largely Hindu. When Gandhi later appeared on the scene, he too invoked the Hindu tradition and especially the *Gita* to *attack* terrorism and justify his uncompromising insistence on non-violence. Unlike the terrorists, Gandhi had to engage in tortuous reinterpretations of both, so much so that some Hindus thought he was really a Christian, and others that he was really a Jain masquerading as a Hindu. It is a measure of Gandhi's moral authority over the Hindus and his political skill that he was able to persuade the bulk of them to accept non-violence as an integral part of their tradition and the only proper way to fight for independence.

I

Although India's struggle for independence was largely non-violent, it was shadowed and periodically vitalized by a small but vocal terrorist movement. The movement began in the 1870s, reached its peak during the period surrounding the Partition of Bengal in 1905, went into decline, re-emerged in the 1920s and enjoyed a chequered existence until India's independence in 1947.[1]

The terrorist movement was not confined to India and enjoyed support among overseas Indians, especially in Britain, Canada, the USA and South-East Asia. Many of its overseas supporters were concentrated in London from where they published a weekly called the *Indian Sociologist*, collected money and arms, and recruited young revolutionaries. Some young Indians went to Paris to learn from Russian revolutionaries how to manufacture bombs. One of them acquired a 'bomb manual' and sent off its cyclostyled copies to his eager colleagues in Bengal. The Indian terrorists were fascinated by the bomb and saw 'this Russian method' as the only effective means of deliverance from the British rule. For many of them, as the presiding judge at Tilak's trial observed, 'the advent of the bomb in India', was a 'great historical event', and the only source of hope. Not surprisingly one of the most interesting books to come out of the terrorist movement was entitled the *Philosophy of the Bomb*.[2]

By international standards the Indian terrorist movement was fairly sober and restrained. It was never attracted by the doctrines that glorified violence as a law of nature, or a 'blood bath' that cleansed away the psychological 'muck of the ages', or as the highest expression of human energy and freedom. It saw violence primarily as a means to achieve India's independence, and justified it on three grounds. First, as their behaviour especially before and during the Partition of Bengal in 1905 showed, the British were contemptuous of Indian public opinion. Popular petitions and appeals had proved futile, and hence violence was the only course of action left to Indians. Second, the British rule was based on terror and ruthless suppression of dissent, and terror could only be met with counter-terror. Third, under the British rule the Indians had become 'lifeless', 'cowardly' and 'passive', and incapable of organized action. They had lost all confidence in themselves, were overawed by the British might and even frightened at the sight of an English face. Their paralysing sense of inferiority and impotence could only be broken by demonstrating to them that they had the power to strike back if only they had the will, and that the British were not as powerful as they looked. Violence was the only way to do this.

Gandhi was familiar with the terrorist movement. He even met many of its prominent members in London and had long discussions with them. He was wholly unpersuaded by their arguments. He was, however, convinced that they had a great appeal for his countrymen, and were likely to receive wider support unless their advocacy of violence was effectively countered. Accordingly he decided to write *Hind Swaraj*, his first and most important book cast in the form of a dialogue. As he says in the Preface:[3]

It was written in 1908 during my return voyage from London to South Africa in answer to the Indian school of violence and its prototype in South Africa. I came in contact with every known Indian anarchist in London. Their zeal was misguided. I felt that violence was no remedy for India's ills, and that her civilization required the use of a different and higher weapon for self-protection.

Unconvinced by Gandhi's arguments the terrorist movement

continued in one form or another until 1947 and enjoyed
some popular support. Almost every terrorist act triggered
off a public debate between the advocates of violence and
non-violence, and Gandhi was a prominent participant in it.
In this paper I intend to examine his reasons for rejecting
terrorism and his proposed alternative to it.

II

Gandhi agreed with the 'school of violence' that the liberal
methods of rational discussion, parliamentary opposition and
electoral pressure were either not available or ineffective in
India. He was, however, convinced that violence was not the
answer. His objections were at two levels. First, violence was
in principle unacceptable. And second, it was inappropriate
and undesirable in the specific context of India's struggle for
independence.[4]

Gandhi disapproved of violence on four grounds, namely
the ontological, the epistemological, the moral and the
prudential.

Gandhi's ontology is rather confused. He seems to think
that the universe is grounded in and sustained by a Supreme
Principle, which he generally calls Reality or Truth and, as a
concession to convention, God. The Supreme Principle
regulates the movement of the natural world, and is
manifested in living beings in the form of a soul. Both animals
and human beings have souls, with the all important
difference that the soul in an animal is dormant and
unselfconscious. All living organisms thus embody the divine,
and are sacred. As Gandhi puts it, 'I subscribe to the belief or
the philosophy that all life is in its essence one'.[5] Sometimes
Gandhi takes the view that the animal has the same worth as
man.[6] His well-considered view, however, seems to be that
man is higher, largely on the ground that he is self-conscious
spirit and capable of leading a moral and spiritual life.[7]

For Gandhi then all men are 'sons of the same God', are
'kith and kin', 'ourselves in a different form' and 'ultimately
one'.[8] The fact that men occupy different bodies blurs their
consciousness of this 'fundamental truth' and encourages the

belief that they are all different and unrelated. It generates *ahamkar* or ego-consciousness and the consequent ideas of 'mine and thine'. For Gandhi the body is ultimately nothing more than a particular configuration of material elements, and thus no different from other material objects. It cannot therefore constitute man's distinctive essence. Man is distinguished from the rest of the universe by the fact that he is a spiritual being. Not the body but the spirit constitutes his essence.[9] Since all men share a common spiritual essence, they are one. Individuality or particularity is an 'illusion'[10].

Gandhi contends that since all men are one, their relations can only be based on love and good-will, not hatred and ill-will. Love springs from and sustains human unity, whereas hatred and ill-will are divisive. Love therefore is the 'law of our species', of 'our being'.[11] Now love implies care and concern for others, an active desire to help them grow and flourish, and thus rules out violence. The use of violence is incongruous with man's spiritual nature and detracts from his dignity as a human or spiritual being. For Gandhi violence ultimately rests on the assumption that some men are so fallen that they can never be won over by love and must be humbled or destroyed by force. In his view this amounts to denying the fundamental ontological fact about men, namely that each of them embodies a spirit or a divine spark which, however deeply buried under the thick crust of prejudices, can eventually be awakened.[12]

Unlike many other critics of violence, Gandhi advances a novel epistemological argument against it.[13] In his view the use of violence implies a belief in absolute and infallible knowledge. In order to be justified in taking the extreme step of harming or killing someone, one must assume that one's objectives are *absolutely* right, violence will *definitely* achieve them and that one's opponent is *totally* mistaken. The consequences of violence are irreversible in the sense that a life once terminated or damaged can never be revived or easily put together. And irreversible deeds require infallible knowledge to justify them. For Gandhi such infallible moral and empirical knowledge is denied to man. As he puts it, 'we see truth in fragment and from different angles of vision. Conscience is not the same thing for all men'.[14] And again,

'People's conceptions of true interests and just laws differ', so that 'what appears to be Truth to the one may appear false to the other'.[15]

Gandhi appreciates that, taken to its logical extreme, his theory of 'relative truth' undermines the very basis of action, for a man can never act if he constantly entertains the nagging doubt that his objectives might be wholly wrong. Gandhi rejoins that we must at least acknowledge our fallibility and leave room for reflection and reconsideration. In his view violence does not allow this. It generates bitterness which 'blurs our vision' and prevents us from appreciating the opponent's point of view. It produces strong feelings, and is not psychologically conducive to calm retrospection. It creates a sense of physical insecurity in the parties involved, and does not allow a reasoned dialogue either. And since violence requires investment of enormous emotional energy and commitment, it makes acknowledgement of mistakes and graceful retracing of steps exceedingly difficult. In other words, for Gandhi violence is doubly flawed; it assumes infallibility and rules out corrigibility.

Gandhi also rejects violence on the moral ground. For him morality consists not merely in doing what is right, but doing so *because* one believes it to be right. A man who helps another by accident, or for fear of blackmail, or to curry favour with him is not moral, although his action is, for it does not spring from his belief or character but ulterior considerations. For Gandhi morality requires the unity of character and conduct, harmony between belief and behaviour. In his view violence disrupts the unity. It requires a man to behave in manner contrary to his beliefs; it forces him to change his conduct, but does nothing to change his beliefs or improve his character. By creating a split between his belief or character on the one hand and his conduct on the other, violence undermines his moral integrity and diminishes his status as a moral being.[16]

Finally, Gandhi rejects violence on the ground that it can never achieve lasting results. When we describe a particular act of violence as successful, we mean that it has achieved a specific objective. Judged within the narrow framework of the specific objective, the act of violence has no doubt been successful. Gandhi contends that if we were to view it in terms of its long-term consequences and the kind of society it creates, our judgement would be very different. Its 'apparent' success encourages the beliefs that violence succeeds and it alone succeeds, and develops the habit of using it every time one runs into resistance. Further with every such apparent success, the 'illusion' of individuality gains strength and men begin to lose awareness of their spiritual nature and ultimate unity. Since such awareness is the ultimate basis of every moral community for Gandhi, he contends that its diminution represents a deeper loss of the community's moral capital. Again, Gandhi goes on, violence has a habit of generating an inflationary spiral. With every apparently successful act of violence, the community concerned comes to accept it as inevitable and becomes insensitive to it. Its tolerance of violence increases, and over time an increasingly larger amount of it becomes necessary to achieve the same objective. Initially throwing a stone might be enough to draw attention to a grievance; soon one must assassinate a man and a little later a large number of them to achieve the same result. However insignificant it may seem, Gandhi argues, each act of violence adds to an escalating spiral and contributes to the eventual disintegration of the community from which no one benefits. Its initial apparent success conceals its ultimate failure.

III

As we observed earlier, Gandhi not only objects to the use of violence in general, but also in the specific context of India's struggle for independence. His arguments here were perceptive, if uneven, and have not received the attention they deserve.

For Gandhi independence means absence of foreign rule. It is essentially a negative concept and cannot be an end in itself.[17] It if involves nothing more than replacing the foreign with indigenous masters and exploiters, it does not mark a significant improvement and is hardly worth dying for. In Gandhi's view India's independence is desirable only because it is a necessary condition for achieving certain larger and far more important goals, of which two are of greatest importance to him. First, like the terrorists he argues that under foreign rule Indians have become 'unmanly', 'spiritless', timid, cowardly, lacking initiative, energy and pride, dependent upon the government for almost everything, given to sycophancy and 'simulation', content to be treated as sub-human, frightened of those in power, and so on. In Gandhi's view, the utter moral degradation and dehumanization of his countrymen has to be arrested and reversed.

Second, according to Gandhi India has been 'hypnotised', brainwashed and even forced into accepting an alien civilization which is not only incompatible with its history and genius but positively inferior to its own.[18] The Indian civilization, which is rich, spiritual and ancient, has grown up with its people, sustained them in times of crises, and is ideally suited to their temperament, character and surroundings. The foreign rule has introduced alien Gods, turned Indians into cultural schizophrenics, destroyed their pride in their past and confidence in themselves and forced them to adopt a way of life wholly incongruous with their character and deepest aspirations. Gandhi insists that India must put an end to this nightmare by evolving its own pattern of life and thereby making a distinctive contribution to the world. To be sure, he did not suggest that India had nothing to learn from the British, rather that learning from them was quite different from copying them and that India also had something to teach them.

For Gandhi then independence is necessary for the regeneration of the Indian character and civilization. He subsumes both these under the concept of *swaraj*. *Swaraj*, inaccurately translated in the absence of an exact English equivalent as self-rule or self-government, implies a form of polity in which self-disciplined and 'manly' people conduct their personal and collective affairs in a manner consistent with their distinctive *swabhava* or basic dispositions. For Gandhi independence is a 'merely' legal and political, whereas *swaraj* is a moral concept referring to the quality of the character and civilization of a community. Independence can be given, *swaraj* can only be won; independence can be a gift, *swaraj* is an achievement; independence is essentially negative, *swaraj* is positive.

For Gandhi then the struggle for independence cannot be dissociated from the far more important struggle for *swaraj*. Since independence is only desirable as a condition of *swaraj*, the struggle for it must be so organized that it facilitates the achievement of *swaraj*, for otherwise independence would only lead to the rule by an arrogant indigenous minority just as keen as their colonial predecessors to keep their subjects 'unmanly' and just as out of sympathy with the indigenous civilization.

Gandhi argues that the terrorists are obsessed with independence and fail to ask why it is desirable and what India should do with it. They say that the British should be driven out because they are exploiting India, but fail to appreciate that the indigenous rulers might be no better and that the British rule would be unacceptable even if they were to stop exploiting the country. Gandhi argues, further, that the terrorists want to drive out the British rulers but not the British civilization. For him the preoccupation with material wants, large-scale industrialization, centralization of the economy, individualism and the modern state are all part of British civilization. He argues that if independent India committed itself to all these as the terrorists want it to, it would remain economically, morally and culturally dependent on Britain, and thus British economic, moral and cultural rule over it would continue. The British may physically leave India, but their capital and spirit would remain. Gandhi cannot see how this amounts to independence from Britain. Indeed he contends that if the Indians wanted to retain the British civilization, they might be better off under the British rule for, after all, the British were bound to be better at administering their civilization than the 'half-Anglicized' Indians.

Gandhi goes on to argue that even as the terrorist violence does nothing to end Britain's economic, moral and cultural hold over India, it perpetuates the unmanly condition of its people. In his view violence is by its very nature cofined to a few and does not actively involve the vast masses of men. It is

thus élitist in orientation, encouragers the cult of leadership
and likely to do little more than replace the British with a
small minority of indigenous rulers. Further, since the masses
are not actively involved, the violent struggle for idependence
cannot arrest their moral degradation, let alone develop
manly qualities in them. Nor can it generate a sense of
community based on the solidarity of suffering, and the
consequent sense of political power. As Gandhi puts it,
'Violence may destroy one or more bad rulers, but . . . others
will pop up in their places for the root lies in us'. He goes
further and challenges the terrorist equation of violence with
courage. In his view it is easy to shoot or throw a bomb at a
man in the dark, but far more difficult to stand up to him in
broad daylight and challenge him to do his worst. One may be
prepared secretly to use violence against a man in power, and
yet shrivel in his presence. Violence thus calls for physical
bravery, but not necessarily moral courage. And it implies
that one is not afraid of *death*, not that one is not afraid of
one's *opponent*. For Gandhi non-violence 'requires far
greater bravery than swordmanship'. He agrees that violence
is 'more manly' than cowardice, but insists that it is 'less
manly' than non-violence.

IV

For Gandhi then violence was not a proper method of struggle
against the British. It was morally undesirable, incapable of
achieving *swaraj* and, given the enormous disparity in the
instruments of violence at the disposal of the government and
the people, unlikely to achieve independence either. He went
on to propose an alternative method which, he claimed, was
in accord with man's spiritual nature and sure to achieve both
swaraj and independence. His method of *satyagraha* was
based on the three principles of *satya* (truth), *ahimsa* (love or
non-violence) and *tapas* (suffering). It required that the goals
of struggle should be just or truthful, and those engaged in it
guided by love for and a desire to 'convert' their opponents by
patiently suffering whatever punishment was meted out to
them. Gandhi developed several forms of action, which

collectively constitute his method of *satyagraha*. Of these non-cooperation, civil disobedience and fast were the most important.

No government can last a day, Gandhi argues, without the cooperation of its subjects. Indeed its power and authority have no other basis than their support. Now to support a government is to cooperate with it, and to cooperate with it is to be morally responsible for its actions.[19] If a citizen is convinced that this government is unjust, he has therefore a moral duty not to cooperate with it. In Gandhi's view non-cooperation can take many forms, and may be mild or severe. Following the Jallianwalla Bagh tragedy of 1921 in which hundreds of innocent people were brutally killed, Gandhi launched his first major non-cooperation movement. His followers refused to serve in the British army, civil service and the courts of law, boycotted British schools and universities, surrendered the honours and titles conferred by the government, refused to subscribe to government loans and attend government functions, and so on. Non-cooperation was later extended to cover the boycott of British cloth and other manufactured products. Later, in a diferent context, Gandhi asked his followers to refuse to pay taxes. In short, the method of non-cooperation in its acute form involved severing all ties with the government and denying it all help and support.

Obeying the laws of the government is also a form of cooperation with it, and therefore to non-cooperation Gandhi later added the powerful weapon of civil disobedience. 'Imagine a whole people,' Gandhi said, 'unwilling to conform to the laws of the legislature, and prepared to suffer the consequences of non-compliance. They will bring the whole legislative and executive machinery to a standstill.'[20] As he understood it, civil disobedience was an open, peaceful, principled and courteous violation of laws believed to be unjust. When the Government passed the Salt Act of 1930 Gandhi, after giving enough advance notice, urged his followers to join him in violating the law by illegally manufacturing salt. When resisters were beaten, and they were beaten a lot, they did not fight back. An observer described a scene thus: 'When those in front fell down wounded by the shots those behind came forward with their breasts bared and exposed themselves to the fire, so much so that some people got as many as twenty-one bullet wounds in their bodies, and all the people stood their ground'. The resisters even cooperated with the police by duly leaving behind their names and addresses. They did not resist arrest, and nor did they complain against the punishment inflicted upon them. They event ensured that their tormentors were in no way harmed, and gave the police advance copies of their programme of action. Throughout the crisis the honesty of the government was never questioned, attitudes on either side were not allowed to harden, channels of communication with the government were kept open, attempts at reconciliation by third parties were encouraged, and in general the atmosphere of good-will was assiduously cultivated. Violence was frowned upon, and almost every time it was used, those involved were chastised and disowned by Gandhi. When a compromise was finally reached, Gandhi attributed it as usual to the moral power of his own and his followers' suffering.

In addition to the two methods of non-cooperation and civil disobedience, Gandhi adopted the third highly dubious method of fasting. He fasted over a dozen times in his life, the duration of his fasts varying from the sacrifice of one meal a day to the famous 'fast unto death'. Gandhi knew that his fasts made his followers and opponents extremely uneasy, and went to considerable length to justify them. Ignoring for the present many inconsistencies in his justification of them, and ignoring also the differences between his various kinds of fast such as the purificatory, the penitential and the political, Gandhi's general case for 'fast unto death' was twofold.[21] First, it was an expression of his sense of outrage at an evil practice and his consequent refusal to live in a world where this kind of evil was being practised. Second, it was a last desperate attempt to stir the 'sluggish conscience' of his opponent. In his view his fast was not a cowardly suicide, nor a quasi-Romantic gesture of self-immolation, but an act of martyrdom for a cause. He felt that when the 'heart' of the opponent had become so hardened that the usual methods of non-cooperation and civil disobedience proved futile, the only course of action available to a devotee of non-violence was to make the supreme sacrifice of his own life in the hope that such an extreme action would shake his opponent into a radical reappraisal of his position. In his view his 'fast unto death' was not designed to make the government yield to his demands, only to 'compel' it to discuss them in a spirit of good-will and compromise.

V

We outlined above Gandhi's critique of violence and his alternative theory of *satyagraha*. They obviously raise many large and important issues. Since we cannot here discuss them all, nor even some of them in the detail they deserve, a few general remarks should suffice.

Gandhi's critique of violence makes important and valid points. Violence does have a tendency to generate an inflationary spiral and to get out of control. It also raises deep moral questions and cannot be viewed merely as one means among several, the choice between which can be made on exclusively pragmatic or utilitarian grounds. Violence might deliver results in the short term but become counter-productive in the long run, and therefore several different considerations need to enter into our judgement of it. Further, as Gandhi insists, violence raises not only moral but also epistemological questions, and a theory of it is suspect unless grounded in a well-considered moral and political epistemology. At a different level Gandhi is right to wonder whether the enormous increase in the quantity and intensity of violence during the last two centuries may not owe its origin to the modern bourgeois–industrial civilization itself, especially its ruthless exploitation of nature, endless multiplication of wants, search for instant gratification, individualism, greed, the centralized economy and the decline of moral and spiritual depth. Gandhi is also right to question the widespread view that persuasion and violence are the only available methods for securing social change. Since pesuasion has its obvious limits, this view has been invoked either to justify all forms of violence or, for those who find violence unacceptable, acquiescence in the status quo. With all its limitations Gandhi's method offers a new arena of action and opens up the possibility of fighting against injustice while avoiding the evils of violence.

Although Gandhi's critique of violence in the colonial context is much less persuasive, it does make important points. His attempt to link *swaraj* with the rejection of industrial civilization is anachonistic and rightly rejected by his countrymen. He is wrong to suggest that violence is essentially Western and that the Indian civilization is basically non-violent. He fails to appreciate that the struggles for independence and *swaraj* are rather different in nature, cannot be easily integrated and that his attempts to combine them led to confusion and lack of direction. His beliefs that violence somehow remains confined to a few terrorists and does not require the more or less active support of the community at large, and that non-violent struggle avoids élitism, are also mistaken. In spite of these and other limitations, Gandhi's theory of the colonial struggle for independence contained insights unmatched by any other. His distinction between independence and *swaraj* was perceptive and original. It allowed him to locate the struggle for independence within a wider framework and avoid the kind of narrow and romantic nationalism that has disfigured many an Asian and African country. Further his *satyagraha* required a measure of commitment from large masses of men and gave them an emotional stake in their country's independence. Above all, his method had the unique consequence of removing the pall of fear that had paralysed his countrymen for centuries and instilling in them a spirit of fearlessness and organized action they had long lacked. Even his worst critics have acknowledged his and his method's great contribution in raising ordinary men and women in India to great heights of moral courage, self-confidence and sacrifice.

While Gandhi's critique of violence thus makes important points to only some of which we have referred, his own alternative theory of non-violence or *satyagraha* suffers from severe limitations. First, he was wrong to regard violence as carnal and non-violence as spiritual in nature. Second, he exaggerated the difference between non-violence and violence. Third, he failed fully to appreciate the nature and role of violence in human affairs and, when he did, did not quite know how to come to terms with it. Fourth, he was wrong to argue that *satyagraha* only exercised moral pressure. And finally, although he did not intend it, his theory of *satyagraha* tended to glorify suffering.

On the basis of his dualist ontology Gandhi goes on to classify human activities as either entirely physical or entirely spiritual. For him sex, violence and so on belong to the first category, and religion, art, love and so on to the second. Although the dualist ontology is unconvincing and Gandhi's version of it is especially so, his mistake lies not so much in subscribing to it as in what he does with it. One may accept the dualist ontology, and conclude that the body and the spirit are not mutually indifferent and exclusive substances but complementary principles involved in all human activities. Rather than classify human activities as *exclusively* one or the other, we can now see them as *predominantly* or *essentially* one or the other depending upon which of the two elements inspires and informs them. Take, for example, the sexual activity. Raping a girl and making love to a woman one adores are both sexual activities; yet they are vastly different. In one case, the sexual act is almost entirely physical, although it may not be so if the rape is motivated by say, an unreciprocated love, a political desire to humiliate a capitalist's daughter or a racial desire to violate a white or black girl. In the other case, the sexual act is born out of and intended to express and nurture love. The individuals involved deeply feel and care for each other and express their mutual love and affection in various ways, of which the sexual act is but one. Indeed the bodies here are only the vehicles for expressing deep spiritual feelings. The sexual act here is not primarily or 'essentially' physical; rather it is a spiritual act in which two mutually committed spirits affirm and confirm their affection and love through physical means. Not lust but love is its inspiring principle. Not to appreciate the qualitative difference between a rape and genuine love and to condemn them both as carnal is wholly to misunderstand their nature. As Gandhi himself said, love is a spiritual emotion. There is no obvious reason why the love between friends or parents and children should be considered spiritual, but not that between a man and a woman.

What is true of sexuality is true also of violence. Violence is not necessarily physical. It does, of course, involve physical harm. However, causing harm may not be the basic objective. Like the sexual act, an act of violence might be born out of love of one's fellow men, a profound sense of outrage at a blatant injustice, or moral indignation against the hypocrisy and chicanery of a cruel social order. In each case an individual is activated by the highest moral principle, and violence is only an incidental and much-regretted means sadly made necessary by the opponent's intransigence. Even as the crudely interpreted body–spirit distinction prevented Gandhi from distinguishing between a rape and a tender love that spontaneously spills over into 'making love', it prevented him from appreciating the morally crucial distinction between a mad, selfish or irresponsible act of violence on the one hand and a principled, publicly motivated and morally responsible act of violence on the other.

Let us now turn to the conceptual distinction between violence and non-violence. Violence harms, injures and may even destroy life, but so can non-violence. A boycott of a product may rob a section of the community of its livelihood and, when prolonged, led to starvation and death. Or a strike by the workers in an electrical power station may cause a black-out in a hospital operation theatre, leading to a loss of life. To say that in one case harm is intended and in the other it is not is hardly satisfactory for, if the workers continue the strike in the full knowledge that people are dying or suffering as a direct result of it, they clearly intend these consequences. Gandhi once remarked that this was not violence, as the strikers had no duty to preserve the lives of men dying as a result of their action. 'There is no violence when there is no infraction of duty'.[22] This is strange both because considerations of duty are irrelevant to deciding whether or not an action is violent, and a human being, especially for Gandhi, has a prima facie duty to preserve life.

This is not to say that there is no difference between violence and non-violence. By definition violence always harms people or destroys property. Non-violence, on the other hand, does not *always* harm, and is at any rate not intended to cause harm. There is obviously all the difference in the world between shooting someone and standing one's ground unarmed, between Hitler and Jesus. The point, however, is that non-violence covers a large spectrum at one end of which no harm is done to anyone, whereas at the other recognizable harm is done intentionally and knowingly as, for example, in the case of a prolonged strike in a hospital, so that at this point non-violence borders on violence. As long as Gandhi defined non-violence narrowly to mean no more than moral appeal to another's conscience on the basis of innocent and uncomplaining suffering, it made sense to draw a rigid distinction between non-violence and violence. However in that case his non-violence was largely ineffective, as Gandhi soon realized. In order to make it effective he had to broaden its meaning and include such non-moral types of pressure as strike, boycott, non-cooperation and civil disobedience. As we shall see, they contained elements of violence, and therefore non-violence and violence could no longer be neatly separated.

As Gandhi acquired greater political experience and came to appreciate the complexity and intractability of political life, he moved realistically, though reluctantly, from the restrictive to the wider view of non-violence. He was a political leader concerned to attain specific goals, and knew that he had to reconcile his commitment to non-violence with his equally strong commitment to India's independence and social and economic justice. He knew too that while a private individual might be able to afford the moral luxury of a puristic attitude to non-violence, a political leader could not. He also realized that his colleagues and followers did not share his attitude to non-violence and that he had to come to terms with them if he was to secure their support.

Gandhi therefore began to modify his view of violence. Having called off his *satyagrahas* in 1919 and 1922 when some of the people involved had resorted to violence, he did not do so from 1930 onwards. He announced in 1930 that 'civil disobedience will continue even though violence may break out'. And again, 'my attitude has now undergone a change. I feel that I cannot afford to wait till people learn never to resort to violence'. He even thought that if most members of his community did not believe in violence, it was his 'duty' as a leader and a good citizen 'to vote for the military training'. In his view non-violence of a society was 'necessarily different' from that of the individual; an individual 'may defy all precaution, not so society'.

Gandhi realized too that sometimes non-violence may be ineffective in eradicating an injustice and required a painful choice between perpetuating it and resorting to violence. He had no doubt what he would choose. He observed:[23]

God would not excuse me if, on the Judgement Day, I were told to plead before him that I could not prevent these terrible things from happening because I was held back by my creed of nonviolence.

Indeed, he thought that he 'would be promoting violence' and guilty of an 'immoral' act if he were to let go a good cause undefended simply because this could not be done non-violently.[24] Given a choice between truth and non-violence, he preferred the former. For him its pursuit could under certain circumstances justify or at least condone violence.

Consider, for example, the following interview with Louis Fischer in which Gandhi was prepared to justify violence in the course of a likely economic struggle in independent India:[25]

Gandhi: Peasants will stop paying salt tax. This will give them the courage to think that they are capable of independent action. Their next step will be to seize the land.

Fischer: With violence?

G: There may be violence. But then again the landlords may co-operate.

F.: You are an optimist.

G.: They may cooperate by fleeing.

F.: Or they might organize violent resistance.

G. There may be fifteen days of chaos, but, I think, we could soon bring that under control.

Gandhi realized too that sometimes violence might be the only way a desperate and helpless people can express their pride and dignity, or that it might be an unfortunate but wholly understandable response to an unbearable pressure. Thus he was sympathetic to the violence used by the Czechs to fight their German invaders during the Second World War. He approved also of the Polish resistance, and called their violence 'almost non-violence'.[26] He did not object to the violence that broke out in India during the 'Quit India' movement on the ground that it was born 'out of sheer desperation', and thought that history will pronounce it 'comparatively nonviolence'. He even came to appreciate that 'defensive' violence was different from the 'offensive'.[27] 'It is true that in the long run the difference is obliterated, but the initial merit persists'. He allowed independent India to maintain a standing army on the ground that non-violence 'dictates a recognition of the vital necessity', and sanctioned its use of force to counter Pakistan's invasion of Kashmir.

Gandhi even claimed to hit upon a 'new aspect' of non-violence that 'has enmeshed me in no end of problems'.[28] He began to wonder if killing must necessarily be equated with violence, and non-killing with non-violence. 'I have come to see what I did not see so clearly before, that there is non-violence in violence'. In his view to kill a mad dog, a cow in great pain, or mercy-kill a man acutely suffering from an incurable disease is *not* an act of violence.[29] In each case one is guided by love and wishes to alleviate rather than cause pain. Since Gandhi equated violence with harm and hatred, he could not see how these might be considered acts of violence.

Gandhi then was gradually inching his way towards a better appreciation of the role of violence in human affairs, and groping towards a more satisfactory theory of political action than the one he had initially developed. He modified his earlier views in response to specific situations, but the modifications were haphazard, *ad hoc* and not integrated into his general framework. Not surprisingly he landed himself into contradictions and conceptual tangles. He continued to insist that violence was motivated by hatred, even though he knew that it could be born out of love. He continued to say that it was never justified, although he himself justified it in several cases. He continued to insist that violence and non-violence were polar opposites, although he admitted that some forms of non-violence bordered on violence and some types of violence were really non-violent, and consequently found himself forced to introduce such confusing expressions as 'non-violent violence', 'almost' or 'comparatively' non-violent and 'not really violent'.

As we saw, Gandhi's *satyagraha* involved non-cooperation, civil disobedience and fast. Despite his claims to the contrary, none of these was wholly or even substantially non-coercive and moral. Non-cooperation involved social ostracism of the British and exerted social pressure on them; it involved boycott of the British cloth and exerted considerable economic pressure; and it also put enormous political and administrative pressure on them by denying the civil service, the judiciary, the police and the universities the required manpower. Britain increasingly found it difficult to rule over a country whose prisons were never empty. As was only to be expected, Gandhi's *satyagraha* exercised various kinds of pressure, of which moral pressure was but one. Professor R.C. Majmudar was hardly exaggerating when he observed that there was 'no real *satyagraha* campaign in India, in the sense that there was no campaign in which moral pressure was the only pressure relied upon'.[30]

Since his method exerted non-moral pressure as well, Gandhi's claim that it genuinely *converted* his opponents was untenable. In some cases, such as Judge Broomfield's remarks at Gandhi's trial in 1922, it did 'convert' them in the sense that they came to realise that they were unjust and insensitive. In some other cases, however, the government gave in largely because it realized that its policies had run into such fierce opposition that it was far more prudent to accept a compromise than provoke a rebellion. In yet other cases the fear of violence played on important part. When Gandhi threatened a 'fast unto death', both he and the government knew, though neither wished, that there would be large-scale violence in the event of his death. The government generally gave in out of fear of consequences and not because it was persuaded of the justice of his demands.

As we saw Gandhi set great store by the moral power of suffering. His claim is not so much wrong as exaggerated. When the police beat up the unarmed resisters, the impact of their suffering was rather complex and varied. In some cases, it had the desired moral outcome. A white sergeant, having to hit a tall, undefending Sikh, suddenly held back his arm in horror, saying, 'It is no use, you can't hit a bugger when he stands up to you like that'. He 'gave the Sikh a mock salute and walked off'.[31] Again, the 'crack troops' of the Indian army, posted in the North-West Frontier provinces to suppress non-violent agitation, chose to be court-martialled rather than open fire on an unarmed mass meeting.[32] There were many similar occasions when the police felt morally degraded by their use of force. There were also, however, other cases where their reaction was more complex. The police simply felt disgusted, exasperated and revulsed at having to beat people up. It was not the suffering of their victims that 'touched their heart', but rather that not being used to this kind of brutaility, they simply gave up.

Consider, for example, the following incident. Following the Salt Act of 1930, the Congress decided to raid the government-owned saltworks in Dharasana. About 2,500 people participated. The police lashed out, hitting the unprotected heads of the 'raiders' with steel-spiked clubs. The raiders, however, continued to march undaunted. The police hit them yet more until most of them fell to the ground. They then squeezed the testicles of the wounded, thrust sticks up their anuses and kicked them in the abdomen. Webb Miller, an American journalist who saw and reported the event, remarked, 'In eighteen years of reporting in twenty-two countries, during which I have witnessed innumerable civil disturbances, riots, street fights and rebellions, I have never witnessed such harrowing scenes as at Dharasana'.[33] The pain and agony of the raiders had virtually no impact on the police. The Viceroy in his letter to George V found the whole thing rather 'amusing', and expressed his perverse happiness at the fact that his policemen had 'obliged' the resisters with a few 'honourable' bruises they had begged for![34] The point of this example is that the suffering of Gandhi and his followers did not always have the desired effect on the government. Sometimes it had the opposite effect to that intended in the sense that instead of converting and uplifting them, it brutalized the police and provoked them into savage acts of fury; and at other times the agitation produced disgust and exasperation rather than genuine moral conversion. Gandhi's assertion that his and his followers' suffering penetrated the defences of the government and awakened their sense of common humanity was a gross exaggeration.

At a more general level Gandhi's emphasis on suffering as a means of political change contains a grave danger. Like violence, suffering too can easily generate an inflationary spiral. This is clearly noticeable in India where suffering has become so much a part of life that death and misery no longer arouse the response they should. One could literally watch people starve to death and yet do nothing about it, as was clear during several famines in recent years and is seen in the apparent case with which abject poverty and human degradation are tolerated. Further it is not difficult to imagine a community turning suffering into a ritual, a cult. This was evident in Gandhi and some of his followers who sometimes almost idealized suffering as a test of their spiritual strength. As Nehru put it, it then became 'morbid, and even a little degrading'.[35] When suffering is glorified and made an integral part of a society's moral culture, it may even produce the opposite results to those intended. The amount of suffering a *satyagrahi* might be required to undergo in order to eradicate or even draw attention to an injustice could be so great and incompatible with elementary human pride and limits of tolerance that the community might come to reject non-violence as a realistic or desirable method of social change, and an otherwise non-violent people might become the most violent. There has been a powerful trend in this direction in post-independent India. It should not surprise us if Gandhi's legacy turns out to be the opposite to what he intended.

NOTES

1. For a good discussion, *see* Rajat K. Ray, *Social Conflict & Political Unrest in Bengal* (Delhi, 1984).
2. Ram Gopal, *How India Struggled for Freedom*, (Bombay, Book Centre, 1967) pp. 111 ff., 179 ff. and 208ff. *See also* Bipan Chandra, *Nationalism and Colonialism in Modern India* (Orient Longman, 1979) pp. 223 ff.
3. M.K. Gandhi, *Hind Swaraj or Indian Home Rule* (Navajivan, 1939) p.16.

4. For Gandhi's views on violence, *see* his *Satyagraha in South Africa* (Madras, 1928) and *Non-Violent Resistance* (New York, Shocken Book, 1967). For good discussions of Gandhi's theory of *satyagraha*, *see* Joan Bondurant, *Conquest of Violence: The Gandhian Philosophy of Conflict* (Univ. of California, 1965) and Raghavan N. Iyer, *The Moral and Political Thought of Mahatma Gandhi* (New York, Oxford Univ. Press, 1973) chs. 8, 9, 10 and 11.

5. N.K. Bose, ed., *Selections from Gandhi* (Navajivan, 1970) Nos. 78–80.

6. *The Collected Works of Mahatma Gandhi* (Ministry of Information and Broadcasting, Govn. of India, Navajivan, 1958 onwards) Vol. 23, p. 108.

7. *Non-violent Resistance op.cit.* p. 41. Also *Collected Works*, Vol. 30, pp. 363 and 572 f., and *Young India* (14th Apr. 1927).

8. *Young India* (18 Dec. 1924).

9. *Young India* (24 June 1926) cf. Dietrich Bonhoeffer, *The Cost of Discipleship* (Macmillan, 1959) p. 132, where he says that only by 'stricktest daily discipline . . . can the flesh learn the painful lesson that it has no rights of its own'.

10. *Harijan* (7 Sept. 1934). Also *Collected Works*, Vol. 24, p. 117.

11. *Young India* (11 Aug. 1920).

12. *Young India* (3 Nov. 1927); *Harijan* (24 Dec. 1938, 27 May 1939 and 13 Apr. 1940).

13. *Collected Works*, Vol. 19, p. 466; *Young India* (23 Mar. 1931).

14. *Young India* (23 Sept. 1926).

15. *Young India* (1919–2) p. 18.

16. *Collected Works*, Vol. 23, p. 27, and Vol. 58, p. 230; *Harijan* (8 Mar. 1939).

17. *Hind Swaraj op.cit.* pp. 28 f.

18. *ibid.* p. 101

19. *Young India* (1 June 1921 and 18 Aug. 1920).

20. M.K. Gandhi *Constructive Programme* (Navajivan, 1948) p. 8.

21. *Young India* (30 Sept. 1926 and 17 Apr. 1930); *Harokam* (11 Feb. 1933, 18 Feb. 1933, 15 Apr. 1933, 8 Jul. 1933 and 13 Oct. 1940).

22. For a detailed discussion, *see Young India* (10 Apr. 1924).

23. *Harijan* (9 Mar. 1940).

24. *Young India* (1 June 1921).

25. D.G. Tendulkar, *Life of M.K. Gandhi* (Bombay, 1951–4) Vol. 6, pp. 98 f.

26. C. Shukla, *Conversations of Gandhiji* (Vora, Bombay, 1949) p. 80.

27. *ibid.*

28. *Young India* (18 Dec. 1924) and *Harijan* (21 Oct. 1939, 19 May 1946 and 9 June 1946).

29. *See Harijan* (8 Sept. 1930) and *Young India* (8 Nov. 1926).

30. M.D. Lewis, ed., *Gandhi* (D.C. Heath & Company, 1966) p. 64.

31. Negley Farson, a correspondent of Chicago Daily News, in Eugene Lyons, *We Cover the World* (New York, 1937) pp. 141 f.

32. *See* Dr Pattabhi Sitaramayya, *Mahasabhano Itihas* (Ahmedabad,

1935) p. 523 f. *See* the interesting example mentioned by Dave Dellinger in a sensitive and sympathetic short study of non-violence in *Studies on the Left*, Vol. 5, No. 1, p. 93. Consider also the following. Seeing himself on the TV kicking a demonstrator and smashing an egg on another, a restaurant owner in Cambridge, Maryland, shouted, 'It was disgusting. I was wrong. Yes, I was. I am ashamed. I'll never forget it. It makes me feel very little, less than a man'. *Los Angeles Times* (14 July 1963) p.A.

33. Quoted in Robert Payne, *The Life and Death of Mahatma Gandhi*, (London, Bodley Head, 1969) p. 397.

34. *ibid*. p. 398.

35. *Autobiography*, (London, Bodley Head, 1958) p. 546.

Part IV
Terrorism and the International Order

10 Fighting the Hydra: international terrorism and the rule of law*
Paul Wilkinson

Throughout the bloody history of modern international terrorism between 1968 and 1980, US citizens and facilities were always major targets.[1] But it was the abduction of the entire US diplomatic mission by Khomeini's students in Tehran in 1979 that really brought home to the American people and government that international terrorism was potentially far more than a peripheral law and order problem.[2] It had become a major national security issue. Slogan-chanting Iranian students were able to inflict untold psychological damage to America's morale and its international credibility—particularly in the Middle East—by maintaining their brazen defiance of international law for months on end. As it became evident that the Carter administration was powerless to secure the release of the hostages, and especially after the failure of the military rescue mission, the hostage crisis became a millstone around President Carter's neck. Combined with other factors it created an image of weakness which undoubtedly played a major part in enabling Ronald Reagan to defeat Jimmy Carter in the November 1980 election. The public were heartily sick of seeing America 'pushed around' by a third-rate power, and longed for a strong and assertive foreign policy.

However harshly historians judge the Carter administration's overall handling of the hostage crisis they will at least give it some credit for successfully concluding the complex diplomatic negotiations which brought the hostages' release in 1981.[3] But in the shadow of this traumatic experience, and in view of Ronald Reagan's profound commitment to opposing communist expansion in all its forms, it was hardly surprising that the new administration started out by declaring that combatting international terrorism was one of its major priorities. The urgency with which President Reagan and the new Secretary of State, Alexander Haig, pursued this aim, was greatly increased by two other factors: (i) their belief that the Soviet Union is the author of the major international conspiracy to use terrorism to undermine the free world, and (ii) their determination to defeat what they saw as the direct threat to US security from the subversion and terrorism exported by the revolutionary regimes in Cuba and Nicaragua in their own hemisphere. With apparently perfect timing an American journalist published a book which dramatically suggested that the Soviet Union and its allies were behind *The Terror Network*,[4] while the State Department produced a whole dossier of evidence to establish substantial involvement by Cuba and Nicaragua in assistance to Marxist guerrilla forces attempting a take-over in El Salvador.

This conjunction of events certainly served to place the problem of combatting international terrorism much higher up the policy agenda. It also helped to increase greater public awareness and concern. Unfortunately it also had the effect of vastly oversimplifying the debate. International terrorism became a fashionable 'boo' word for any movement or foreign intervention seen as inimical to American interests, often a mere synonym for communist revolutionism. Concentration on the alleged Soviet role, though a useful corrective to widespread ignorance of Moscow's use of this weapon, tended to blind many observers to the hydra-headed and complex nature of terrorist violence worldwide. The picture was distorted by obscuring the deep indigenous roots of many violent groups and the complex variety of ideologies, political aims and diverse state sponsors involved.

While the debate on terrorism in the first Reagan administration was marked by increasing confusion about definition and causes, since October 1983 attention has increasingly centred on the so-called military options for dealing with international terrorist attacks against Americans and to hit back at the alleged state sponsors of such attacks.[5]

This policy debate, still very much alive in Washington, was a natural reaction to the massacre of US marines and French troops on 23 October 1983 by Shiite terrorists using truck bombs. This attack was the most lethal in the history of modern international terrorism: America lost more lives in Lebanon in 1983 than in the previous fifteen years of international terrorist incidents.[6] But what caused the intense policy debate in Washington was not simply the scale of the attack and the weaknesses in security that it exposed (though these were inevitably major issues), but the realization that the terrorists had succeeded in forcing the US government to plan the withdrawal of the US marines from Lebanon, and in thus significantly limiting US policy options in the Middle East.[7] In brutal terms it demonstrated that terrorism was a potent weapon even against the military and economic might of a superpower. The propaganda of atrocity reached its target in the US media, public and congress, and created pressures for policy changes which the President and his advisers were quite unable to withstand. Clearly the full danger of such a demonstration was that other factions, and the pro-terrorist states which Washington suspected were sponsors of the attacks on Americans in Beirut, would seek to emulate the Shiite attacks. Hence the urgency with which President Reagan, nearing the end of his first term, signed a new National Security Directive ordering the government to explore and develop the military options to deal with international terrorism. The Secretary of State, George Shultz, made a speech on 3 April 1984, the same day that the President signed the new Directive, stating that if the nation was to successfully combat state-sponsored international terrorism America must be prepared to use force. Since that date there has been growing evidence of a difference of view within the administration concerning the circumstances when the use of force would be appropriate and the ways in which such force should be used.[8]

We shall be dealing with the debate on policy options later. But it is important to clarify at the outset the political origins and context of the current debate.

Before proceeding to a discussion of the problems of

international response to terrorism, including the use of international law, it is important to define the scope of the subject. It is wrong to equate terrorism with violence and insurgency in general. Some journalists and politicians have tried to use it as a synonym for guerrilla war, but terrorism is a special mode of violence which, since the late 1960s, has more often than not been used entirely alone, in a pre-insurgency situation. And it is this type of attack—spasmodic bombings, shootings, kidnappings—which has been the characteristic modern pattern in Western democracies. Terrorism can be briefly defined as *the systematic use of murder, injury and destruction, or threat of same, to create a climate of terror, to publicize a cause, and to intimidate a wider target into conceding to the terrorists' aims.*[9]

Historically it is also true that most major insurgencies and civil wars have involved a mixture of rural guerrilla, conventional war, economic sabotage, foreign intervention and terrorism as an auxiliary weapon. But it is important to note that many rural guerrilla leaders have, as a matter of policy, sought to wage their struggles according to the rules and conventions of war. They have often consciously sought to avoid the use of indiscriminate terror against innocent civilian targets, either on moral grounds, or because they feared losing public support or provoking a massive repressive crackdown by the authorities which would endanger their own movement.

Yet although terrorism is only one among many methods of struggle it is still a broad enough concept to encompass a wide variety of different types[10] and applications. One fundamental distinction made in the academic literature and the data bases is between international and domestic terrorism. The former is the export of this form of violence across international frontiers or against foreign targets in the terrorists' state of origin. Domestic terrorism is confined to one specific locality or country within the frontiers of a single state. In practice it is of course extremely difficult to find examples of purely domestic terrorism. In almost every case some cross-border movement of terrorists, or terrorist weapons and explosives, is involved. And in almost every terrorist campaign the perpetrators of violence seek to reach the international media and influence foreign opinion and governments.

Another key categorization is in terms of the perpetrators. *State regimes of terror* are as old as the history of permanent human settlement. They do not necessarily require advanced technologies or control and repression, though modern totalitarian states have been able to exploit the new techniques of surveillance and control of information to strengthen their grip on vast populations. *State-sponsored international terrorism*[11] is used almost instinctively as a tool of foreign policy by regimes which routinely use regimes of state terror to suppress dissent at home. The recent activities of the regimes of Colonel Gaddafi and Ayatollah Khomeini provide ample examples of the use of this weapon for three major purposes: to intimidate and destroy exiled opponents and dissidents, to weaken adversary states, and to export revolution.

Factional terrorism is that which is waged by a whole range of sub-state actors for a wide variety of aims and motives. The major types are: (i) *the extreme nationalists*, autonomists, and separatists who claim that their main aim is self-determination or autonomy (e.g. the IRA, ETA, the FLNC in Corsica, the Tamil terrorists in Sri Lanka); (ii) *ideological terrorists* who want to change the whole nature of the existing political social and economic system (e.g. on the extreme Left the Red Brigades, Direct Action, the RAF and on the extreme Right the Black Order and other neo-fascist terrorist groups in Europe); (iii) *exile group terrorists*, forced normally by police or governmental action in their home countries to operate exclusively abroad (e.g. the Armenian Secret Army for the Liberation of Armenia (ASALA) and the Croatian terrorists); (iv) *issue group terrorism* employed by those who seek to block or change specific policies rather than to revolutionize the entire political system (e.g. Animal Liberation Front—a UK 'animal rights' group—and the anti-abortion bombers in the USA); (v) *religious extremist groups*[12] seeking to impose their own fanatical belief system and religious order (e.g. the Shiite fundamentalists' Islamic jihad).

In any worthwhile analysis of a specific terrorist campaign it is of course essential to take account of the unique political, historical and cultural context and the ideology and aims of the groups involved. One needs to interpret the role and effectiveness of terrorism in the overall development of each conflict in which it appears. Is it being used as an auxiliary weapon in a wider strategy of revolutionary warfare? Or is it being used in isolation in a pre-insurgency mode? What degree of popular support, if any, do the perpetrators of terrorism enjoy? How severe and prolonged is the violence? Is it merely spasmodic and small in scale and destruction caused? Or is it growing in intensity, frequency and lethality to the point where it threatens to trigger off a full-scale civil war?[13]

Context is all in the analysis of political violence. In view of the enormous diversity of groups and aims involved, generalizations and evaluations covering the whole field of modern terrorism should be treated with considerable reserve. Over-simplified analysis of the phenomena tends to induce simplistic and dangerous proposals for panaceas. It is a snare and a delusion for any democratic government to assume that there is some quick-fix solution to the whole problem of modern terrorism. For what we are really contending with is a hydra. As soon as the authorities believe they have cut off the head of the movement, another arises in its place. Terrorism is one of the ugliest manifestations of the intractability of human conflict. It is inextricably interwoven with the whole complex of interactions in the international system and the reactive behaviour of all actors in the system. One cannot envisage a world without the pervasive element of terror violence unless one assumes a change in the whole nature of international organization and human behaviour. Even a world under the hegemony of a totalitarian superpower such as the Soviet Union would not be a place without terror: violence would simply become the global monopoly of the Party dictatorships. The essence of the dilemma for open and pluralist democracies is that the measures they would need to take in order to totally eradicate the threat of terrorism would mean the extinction of the basic freedoms guaranteed by the democratic rule of law and their replacement by a Big Brother state of Orwell's nightmare.

Anyone who claims to have a total solution to terro
democracy is either a fool or a knave. This does not m
there is nothing democracies can do about reducing
violence. There are measures of proven effectivenes
they can undertake while remaining true to their basic values.
But such measures are bound to be limited not only by the
fundamental requirement that they must be consistent with
the maintenance of basic civil rights and democracy, but also
by the inherent complexities in the causation and
development of political violence.

Let us examine more closely some of the aspects of these
complexities which help to explain the manifest weaknesses
of international law and organization for dealing with the
problem of international terrorism on both a global and a
regional basis.

One of these aspects is the existence of a number of regimes
in the international system which systematically resort to
coercive intimidation in order to control their populations, to
suppress dissent, and maintain themselves in power. It is
sometimes assumed that although the large-scale violations in
human rights can or should provoke international
condemnation and pressure on the regime on the part of
democracies, there is nothing inherently conducive to
international conflict in this situation. But does a state such as
the Soviet Union only become a threat to peace when it
decides to embark on a military crusade of ideological
expansionism? Not so. A regime's persistent use of state
terror against its own citizens in itself has profoundly
disruptive implications for foreign relations. Other states—
especially those which are military weaker and contiguous
with the violator state—will feel a sense of threat and danger
in such behaviour. They will be naturally frightened and
suspicious of a state that treats its own population so
ruthlessly. Those states which feel insecure will tend to band
together in defensive alliances. Bipolarization and the
formation of alliance blocs, on both global and regional
levels, is likely to ensue. The populations and governments of
foreign states are likely to find themselves appealed to by
victims of oppression. Fugitives from persecution will seek
refuge behind the safety of their frontiers. Support

organizations for the oppressed populations of terroristic regimes will form. Diplomatic and political interventions to secure improvements in human rights are likely to be mounted. When they are attempted they almost inevitably lead to a deeper polarization between the violator state and the part of the international community which respects human rights. Severe violations of domestic human rights by states are therefore also to be seen as substantial obstacles to improved international relations, the relaxation of tension and the development of trust and cooperation.[14]

Regimes of state terror also tend inevitably to provoke movements of resistance and opposition at home and abroad. If they cannot mount a successful campaign in their original homeland as a result of the severity of the state repression, they will try to do so from abroad. In response the regime of terror instinctively reaches for the weapon of state-sponsored international terrorism to silence and destroy its exiled opponents. In a notorious example, Stalin sent one of his assassins to murder Trotsky in Mexico. The Bulgarians sent an agent to London to murder the dissident writer Georgi Markov, using a poison-tipped umbrella. Gaddafi sends his hit-squads to hunt down leaders of opposition movements living as refugees in Western Europe and the United States.

Moreover, terroristic states are quite ready to use international terrorism as a weapon to undermine rival states in a form of undeclared covert warfare. They find terrorism a low-cost, low-risk method, for which they can always plausibly deny any responsibility. This has been the characteristic style, for example, of Ayatollah Khomeini's international terrorist ventures against neighbouring Arab states in the course of the Iran–Iraq war.

These and many other examples show how the very existence of terroristic states in the international system is conducive to the escalation of state-sponsored international terrorism. But they are also conducive to terrorism in two other crucial respects. First, by attempting, if only with limited success, to export ideologies of revolution and to establish client movements and regimes dedicated to coercion for revolutionary ends they constantly multiply the number of groups and states capable of employing terrorism. They significantly increase the number of sanctuaries, training areas and sources of arms, cash and diplomatic and propaganda support for international violence. Each newly established revolutionary regime thus becomes an additional launching-base and conduit for the promotion of further international terrorism. A vivid example of this process at work can be seen in the role of Cuba. In addition to its revolutionary efforts in the Caribbean and Latin America, the Castro regime has been employed as a proxy for Soviet strategic goals throughout Africa and even as far away as the Middle East.

Secondly, in an international system, which is inherently anarchic, due to the lack of a single supranational legal sovereign, the terror states are able to block any effective global action against international terrorism. Asking the Soviet Union to join in such a system would be rather like inviting a Mafia chief to take control of the police force. The Soviets and their communist allies regard what we regard as sponsorship of international terrorism as being an ideologically necessary and entirely justified assistance to 'national liberation' and 'fraternal revolutionary movements', that is, a vital tool of their foreign policy.[15]

Far from being able to act effectively on this issue, the member states of the UN have not even been able to agree on a definition of international terrorism. The discussion in the Ad Hoc Committee set up in 1973 in the wake of the Munich Olympics massacre in 1972 was vitiated by a fundamental split between those states who wanted to concentrate all the attention on the terror of colonial and racist regimes and assistance to national liberation struggles and those Western states which were primarily seeking UN action to prevent factional terrorism against the innocent.[16]

These fundamental differences of values and ideologies rule out for the foreseeable future any general international legislation designed to deal with the broad range of terrorist crime in general. But limited progress has been made in international legislation to deal with very specific offences such as aircraft hijacking and the protection of diplomats. States of almost all ideological hues have gradually come to recognize that *their* civil airliners and airports cannot gain immunity from aircraft hijacking simply by pretending that it does not happen. The Tokyo Convention on Offences and Certain Other Acts Commited on Board Aircraft (1963) set out for the first time the jurisdictional guiding principles which require all contracting states to make every effort to restore control of the aircraft to its lawful commander and to ensure the prompt onward passage or return of the hijacked aircraft together with its passengers, crew and cargo. The Hague Convention (1970) requires all parties to extradite apprehended hijackers to their country of origin or to prosecute them under the judicial code of the recipient state. And the Montreal Convention (1971) extended the scope of international law to cover sabotage and attacks on airports and grounded aircraft, and laid down the principle that all such offences be subject to severe penalties.

Likewise, even the more radical states came to recognize that *their* diplomats and embassy premises are as much at risk as everyone else's from the growing plague of attacks on diplomatic targets. Castro's Cuban representatives in the USA, for example, have been the targets of attacks by anti-Castro exile groups such as Omega 7. And the Soviet Union ranks as one of the most victimized states in the league of those states subject to attacks on their diplomats abroad. Hence there is very little serious opposition in principle to the idea of international legal measures aimed at helping deter, prevent and punish the assassination and kidnapping of diplomats. After the spate of diplomatic kidnappings in their region between 1968 and 1971 the Organization of American States formulated a Convention to Prevent and Punish Acts of Terrorism Taking the Form of Crimes Against Persons and Related Extortion that are of International Significance. And there is a UN Convention on the Prevention and Punishment of Crimes Against Internationally Protected persons, including Diplomatic Agents, adopted by the General Assembly in 1973. The OAS Convention sought to define attacks against internationally protected persons as common crimes, regardless of motive, thus making it possible to apply the *aut dedere aut punire* (extradite or prosecute) formula which has been used in most efforts at international legislation on terrorism.

But are these worthy Conventions of much practical use?[17] The case of diplomatic terrorism appears to demonstrate their virtual irrelevance. Implementation has inevitably to be left to the contracting state's authorities. If the receiving state is weak and ineffective in providing for the security of diplomatic missions, all the sending state can do to help protect its representatives is to protest and to do what it can to improve the physical security of the embassy buildings and diplomatic residences. The result is obvious from the statistics on international terrorism: attacks on diplomats have continued unabated and the profession is still the favourite target of international terrorists worldwide.[18]

In the struggle to suppress aircraft hijacking[19] the value of the Tokyo, Hague and Montreal Conventions also appears to have been only marginal. What really helped to reverse dramatically the rising curve of hijackings was a combination of the system of comprehensive personnel and baggage searches at aircraft boarding gates and the dramatic successes of hostage rescue missions such as Entebbe and Mogadishu, which vividly demonstrated to the terrorists that the authorities could hit back and inflict crushing defeats on the hijackers. There is only one specific contribution from international law which can be said to have played a key role in this battle. Bilateral agreements between states of completely opposed ideological colour *have* been effective. For example, the Anti-Hijack Pact between the USA and Cuba (1973) was an arrangement of mutual convenience. Castro had become as weary of receiving the criminals and psychopaths who hijacked US flights as the US government had of losing aircraft and passengers to Havana. The Anti-Hijack Pact helped to ensure the return of aircraft, crew, passengers and hijackers. In effect it bolted the door to the favourite refuge of US aircraft hijackers. Another striking example of bilateral agreement between unlikely partners was the agreement by the Marxist government of Somalia to allow the West German G-SG9 in to rescue the passengers and crew of a hijacked Lufthansa in 1977.

In sum, while there is always scope for trying to strengthen these global international conventions and to pressure more states into ratifying and implementing them, these alone are almost useless. They are a classic illustration of the inadequacy and weakness of international legal measures in dealing with violence and intimidation. There is simply no machinery for sanctions against offending or defaulting states which alone could ensure enforcement. Small wonder that the state sponsors of international terrorists feel free to treat the international law with derision and contempt. Look at the recent example of the Iranian regime which stood by while Shiite fundamentalist hijackers tortured and killed passengers in a Kuwaiti airliner hijacked to Tehran. And by Fall 1985 the Iranian authorities had still failed to bring the hijackers to justice. The suspicion that the Iranian regime condoned and even encouraged the hijacking, voiced by the American officials and by some of the released passengers, is given added substance by this behaviour. When are the international community going to consider invoking similar sanctions against Iranian civil aviation to those taken previously against the Kabul regime?

But if the prospects for global cooperation against international terrorism are so poor, surely the chances of effective regional cooperation among the NATO democracies should be far better? After all the Western democracies in theory share similar basic values, including the belief in the sanctity of individual human life, the rejection of violence as a method of resolving internal political differences, and a commitment to democratic government and the rule of law. They also have a considerable post-war experience of close cooperation in both defence and economic organizations (NATO and the EEC).

Certainly it can be said that the West Europeans have achieved the most ambitious and comprehensive arrangements for regional cooperation against terrorism.[20] The Council of Europe Convention on the Suppression of Terrorism (1977) is not an extradition treaty, but it takes a valuable step towards facilitating the extradition of suspected terrorists between the European democracies.[21] In effect it removes the whole range of serious terrorist crimes from the political offence exception. In other words those who commit serious terrorist crimes cannot simply evade justice by slipping across frontiers and claiming that their crime was committed for political motives. Another major advantage of the Convention is that it binds parties to affording the mutual assistance necessary in criminal investigation if the terrorist is to be brought to justice. The major weakness of the measure is that certain European states have not yet ratified the Convention. France, despite its considerable terrorist problem and many land frontiers with European neighbours, has still failed to ratify even though it signed the Convention in 1977. Recently, however, the French government has significantly altered its policy on the extradition of terrorist suspects. For example, in Summer 1984 it agreed, for the first time, to extradite three Basques suspected to terrorism to Madrid. By Spring 1985 it seemed likely that the French authorities would begin to take a firmer line against Italians living in France who are wanted by the Italian authorities on charges connected with the Red Brigades terrorist campaign in Italy.

Other aspects of Western European cooperation against terrorism include closer intelligence and police cooperation through the TREVI system, improved cross-border and bilateral collaboration in many areas, and a common stance on aircraft hijacking and the use of diplomatic cover for terrorism, as enunciated at the Bonn and London Summits.

Despite the disappointing record of Western political and judicial cooperation against terrorism the prospects for improvement are still much better among this group of states than they are in the international system generally. The 1984–5 wave of attacks by a loose alliance of extreme left-wing terrorists against NATO targets seems likely to stimulate closer intergovernmental cooperation. And in any case there is a powerful trend towards greater European political cooperation in response to a whole range of pressing issues.

Yet ironically the greatest danger to democratic societies from terrorism in the long term does not stem from internal violence, but from growing instability in the Third World. Established liberal democracies have proved remarkably resilient in resisting prolonged and fanatical terrorist campaigns. There is no historical example of a West European democracy being destroyed by the weapon of terrorism. Hence, although the very openness of Western societies and the abundance of prestigious targets they afford are likely to continue to attract the attention of both domestic and international terrorists, all the evidence suggests that these socieities have adequate political, moral and economic resources to cope successfully with such outbreaks.

Since 1980 there has been accelerating growth in the incidence and lethality of terrorism in the Third World.[22] Countries in Africa and Asia which negotiated their independence peacefully and relatively smoothly are now increasingly afflicted by the disease of bombings, assassinations and kidnappings which were formerly more characteristic of Latin America and Western Europe. The cases of Uganda, Sudan, India and Sri Lanka are tragic illustrations.

What makes these developments so dangerous is that these are the very states least able to cope with prolonged terrorist campaigns and other forms of severe internal conflict. Most of these newly independent countries are suffering from profound religious and ethnic divisions. Many have unstable and ineffective political systems and lack the economic resources and specialist security personnel and skills to tackle this type of problem. And there is no international agency capable of filling the gap with some temporary task force, even supposing that such assistance would be acceptable to the government concerned.

It is, moreover, precisely in this high risk conflict-ridden area that terrorism is most likely to be used as one part of a wider insurgency. And since 1945 revolutionary take-overs in Asia, Latin America and Africa have tended to bring to power Marxist-style regimes which are typically anti-Western in their foreign and economic policies, and which become launching pads for further revolutionary seizures of power.

Last but by no means least of the dangers is the effect of terrorism in exacerbating Third World conflicts and acting as a catalyst for civil war, foreign intervention and full-scale international war. The history of the crisis in Lebanon provides an ominous illustration of this process of escalation.

It is as dangerous to seek simple solutions to the problems of terrorism in the context of Third World conflicts as it is within the democratic states' own borders. For example, it is sometimes suggested that the answer is to provide the balm of effective conflict resolution.[23] Of course, it is true that some international terrorism is linked directly to struggles for 'national liberation' or 'autonomy', and where the political leadership of a nationalist movement is sufficiently pragmatic and moderate its aims will sometimes be susceptible of negotiation. But it is obviously quite foolish to imagine that all so-called 'national liberation' movements have a valid claim to legitimacy in terms of attested popular support, or that all such movements are led by pragmatic moderates. Even if some broad conflict resolution is possible at the political and diplomatic levels—and this is an extremely unlikely prospect in such polarized situations as Southern Africa or the Arab–Israel conflict—this will not automatically bring an end to terrorism. Does anyone really believe that the militant Syrian and Libyan-backed factions of the PLO would abandon terrorism against Israel even if King Hussein and Arafat were able to deliver a Palestinian mini-state on the West Bank? In almost every terrorist conflict there is a hard core of irreconcilables who stubbornly refuse to abandon the struggle until their maximum aims are realized. Even in a world which made dramatic progress in the resolution of conflict by diplomacy, there is going to be a continuing need for the security and juridicial measures to deal with high levels of terrorist violence. If these measures are beyond the capabilities of impoverished and fragile developing states, it is sadly extremely unlikely that any international organization will acquire the authority and resources to do the job for them.

Western governments and public opinion may, not unnaturally, respond to the upsurge of terrorist violence in the Third World in a different way. When they see their diplomats and embassies hit, their soldiers and civilians victimized and seriously endangered, some will advocate withdrawing altogether from the high-risk zones. Others demand immediate use of military force to pre-empt or to retaliate against terrorist organizations and their state sponsors. The first of these options is not really a practicable policy for America. A great power with vital economic and political interests, alliances and strategic commitments in every part of the world cannot retreat into the isolation of a fortress America. Nor would it be in the interests of America's West European and Pacific allies. Western Europe and Japan are far more dependent than the USA, for example, on Middle East oil supplies. All the industrial countries desperately need access to the raw materials, energy supplies and markets of the Third World. These countries cannot afford to withdraw their presence and influence. On the contrary the logic of their international situation and the whole trend of their recent foreign policies has been to work in association with their American allies to promote greater stability, peace, and prosperity in the Third World and to prevent the take-over of these areas by pro-Soviet and other anti-Western movements and regimes.[24]

As regards the use of military options, of course Western military units stationed abroad must defend themselves if they are attacked. Our armed services should be better trained and prepared for the problems of operating in terrorist situations abroad. Nor should we underestimate the value of special élite military units for such tasks as hostage rescue.[25] The democracies have every right to use these special skills by enlisting military aid to the civil power when the lives of their innocent citizens are threatened by terrorists at home and abroad. And outstandingly successful rescue operations, such as Entebbe and the London Iranian Embassy siege,[26] undoubtedly have a deterrent and demoralizing effect on the terrorists.[27]

But it is one thing for military units to aid the civil power, to exercise the right of self-defence and to rescue hostages. It is quite another for them to carry out military raids on foreign soil with the aim of pre-empting, destroying or punishing terrorists.[28] Such raids will inevitably be seen internationally as acts of war against sovereign states. Almost inevitably innocent civilians will be killed or injured. This is unavoidable even when raids are restricted to terrorist bases, because almost invariably terrorists base their HQs in areas of civilian population. There is a grave danger of losing the suport of both domestic and international opinion when such raids cause the loss of innocent lives. A great power like the US cannot afford to disregard international opinion or to undermine its moral credibility. In any case it is notoriously difficult to identify and locate the perpetrators of the terrorism one is trying to punish. It is even more difficult to prove beyond reasonable doubt the links between the terrorists and an alleged state sponsor. Most dangerous of all, any military offensive of this kind is almost bound to provoke retailiation and escalation. A military action which starts with raids on selected targets may well end up launching lateral attacks indiscriminately on the population of the host state, or even in a full-scale war.

Terrorism is certainly an evil, but it is by no means the worst evil. It pales into insignificance when one compares it with the lethality and destructiveness of a major civil or international war. Those who have the responsibility for determining the response of Western governments to international terrorism must be aware of these pitfalls and risks. They should always ensure that they have tried to use all the available non-military methods of bringing strong pressure to bear against pro-terrorist states. There is a whole range of non-military options available. States guilty of promoting and instigating terrorist attacks can be arraigned and condemned in the court of world opinion, by concerted Western action at the UN and in other international fora. Individual diplomats from terrorist states who abuse their role can be declared *persona non grata*. Whole diplomatic missions from rogue states can be drastically reduced or expelled. Formal diplomatic relations can be broken. A concerted Western embargo against the export of high technology goods, weapons, and services, can be organized. Products from the rogue states can be boycotted. Against medium-sized and small terrorist states such actions are likely to be extremely effective if they are backed by sufficient industrial countries.

A cool and considered response to terrorism drawing on a judicious mixture of all these types of pressures and inducements is much more likely to be successful in bringing a reduction in terrorism without taking the real risks of substituting far more dangerous levels of conflict in the place of the evil one is attempting to combat. The true Grotian response by Western states to terrorism must combine firmness with a commitment to act within the framework of the rule of law. Heaven knows this rule of law internationally is pathetically weak. But it is all we have got. If powerful Western states disregard the inhibitions of international law and use means against terrorism which are totally disproportionate to the threat, they will risk increasing the very anarchy in which terrorists flourish.

NOTES

*   Also appearing in *Harvard International Review*, 1985, Vol. 7, No. 6.

1.   According to US Department of State figures, almost 40 per cent of the victims of international terrorist attacks, world-wide, between 1968–80, were Americans.

2.   For a discussion of the wider implications of the hostage crisis, *see* Paul Wilkinson, 'After Tehran', *Conflict Quarterly*, Vol. 1, No. 4 (Spring 1981) pp. 5–14.

3.   Roy Assersohn, *The Biggest Deal: Bankers, Politics, and the Hostages of Iran* (Methuen, 1982) provides a well-researched and fascinating analysis of these negotiations.

4.   Clare Sterling, *The Terror Network* (Weidenfeld and Nicolson, 1981).

5.   *See* for example the contrasting views of Mr Shultz and Mr Weinberger voiced in a number of speeches, 1984–5, and recent press debate, such as Philip Geyelin, 'Mr Shultz's impractical doctrine', *International Herald Tribune* (7 Nov., 1984).

6.   Two hundred and sixty-seven US lives were lost by terrorism in Lebanon in 1983 according to *Patterns of Global Terrorism: 1983*, US Dept of State (September 1984).

7.   *See* the Report of the Department of Defense Commission on the Beirut International Airport Terrorist Attack of October 23, 1983, chaired by Admiral Robert L.J. Long; and Brian Jenkins, *Combatting Terrorism Becomes A War* (Rand publications) (May 1984), and *The Lessons of Beirut: Testimony Before the Long Commission* (Rand publications) (February 1984).

8.   Compare, for example, Secretary of State Shultz's speech to the Jonathan Institute Conference, Washington, 1984, with Mr Caspar Weinberger's 'doctrine' on the use of US military force abroad.

9.   For an analysis of the concept of terrorism and definitional problems *see* Paul Wilkinson, *Political Terrorism* (Macmillan Press, 1974) and Alex P. Schmid, *Political Terrorism: A Research Guide to Concepts, Theories, Data Bases and Literature* (North-Holland Publishing Company, 1983) pp. 5–159.

10. A preliminary typology was outlined in the author's *Political Terrorism* (Macmillan, 1974) and considerably refined in *Terrorism and the Liberal State* (Macmillan, 1977) Ch. XII.

11. *See* Paul Wilkinson, 'State-sponsored international terrorism: the problems of response', *The World Today*, Vol. 40, No. 7 (July 1984) pp. 292–8.

12. For an intriguing comparison of earlier religious terrorist movements *see* David Rapoport and Yonah Alexander, eds., *The Morality of Terrorism, Religious and Secular Justifications* (Pergammon Press, 1982) Part 1, 'Religious terror', pp. 3–126.

13. *See* Paul Wilkinson, *Terrorism and the Liberal State* (Macmillan, 1977) pp. 139–70.

14. *See* discussion by Richard Falk, 'Responding to severe violations' in Jorge I. Dominguez *et al.*, *Enhancing Global Human Rights* McGraw-Hill, 1979) pp. 207–57.

15. Soviet involvement in aid to Middle Eastern movements is documented in Yonah Alexander and Ray Cline, *Terrorism: the Soviet Connection* (Crane Russak, 1984). Roberta Goren, *The Societ Union and Terrorism*, (1984) gives a more comprehensive historical review of Soviet policy and practice.

16. L.C. Green, 'Double standards in the United Nations: the legislation of terrorism' (1979) *Archiv der Voelkerechts* 18:2, and Alona Evans and John Murphy, eds., *Legal Aspects of International Terrorism* (Heath, 1978).

17. For a valuable collection of the relevant treaties, agreements, and other measures, and an expert introductory commentary, *see* Robert Friedlander, *Terrorism: Documents of International and Local Control* (3 vols.) (Oceana Publications, 1979).

18. According to the US Department of State's publication *Terrorist Attacks Against Diplomats* (Dec. 1981), in 1975 '30% of all terrorist attacks were directed against diplomats'. By 1980 the number increased to 54 per cent of the total.

19. *See* Richard Clutterbuck, *Living with Terrorism* (Faber and Faber, 1975) and Paul Wilkinson, *Terrorism and the Liberal State*, Ch. XXXIV.

20. *See* Council of Europe, *European on Convention on the Suppression of Terrorism* (10 Nov. 1976) and Council of Europe, *Compendium of Documents of November 1980 Conference on the Defence of Democracy Against Terrorism in Europe: Tasks and Problems* (Strasbourg, 1981).

21. For a much less favourable view *see* A.V. Lowe and J.R. Young, 'Suppressing terrorism under the European Convention', *Netherlands International Law*, Vol. XXV, No. 3 (1978) pp. 305–33.

22. *See Patterns of Global Terrorism: 1983*, US Dept of State (Sept. 1984).

23. For example in John Burton, *Deviance, Terrorism, and War: The Process of Solving Unsolved Social and Political Problems* (Martin

Robertson, 1979) and Alex P. Schmid and Jenny de Graaf, *Violence and Communication* (Sage, 1982).

24. *See* International Institute for Strategic Studies, *Third World Conflict and International Security* (Papers from the IISS 22nd Annual Conference, 1981), *Adelphi Papers*, 166 and 167.

25. For the work of hostage-rescue squads, *see* Peter Koch and Kai Hermann, *Assault at Mogadishu* (Corgi, 1977) Christopher Dobson and Ronald Payne, *Terror! The West Strikes Back: the Inside Story on the Élite Anti-terror Squads* (Macmillan press, 1982) and *Siege: Six Days at the Iranian Embassy*, written by a team of *Observer* journalists (Macmillan, 1980).

26. *See* Christopher Dobson and Ronald Payne *op. cit.*

27. A dramatic demonstration of this effect was the suicide of the imprisoned RAF terrorists Andras Baader, Gudrun Ensslin and Jan-Carl Raspe, in their cells at Stammheim, following the rescue of the hijacked passengers and crew at Mogadishu.

28. It is not only hard-liners in the US administration who have been considering such policies. For example, Neil C. Livingstone in *The War Against Terrorism* (Heath, 1982) proposes miliary intervention to overthrow the Gaddafi regime in Libya. The more hawkish Washington think tanks have made similar suggestions.

Index